# Women, Royalisms and Exiles 1640–1669

Sonya Cronin

# Women, Royalisms and Exiles 1640–1669

## Towards Writing the Royalist Diaspora

Sonya Cronin
Trinity College Dublin
Dublin, Ireland

ISBN 978-3-030-89608-9 ISBN 978-3-030-89609-6 (eBook)
https://doi.org/10.1007/978-3-030-89609-6



Cover illustration: William Cavendish, 1st Duke of Newcastle-upon-Tyne and his family in Antwerp, 1656. Heritage Image Partnership Ltd / Alamy Stock Photo

This Palgrave Macmillan imprint is published by the registered company Springer Nature Switzerland AG.
The registered company address is: Gewerbestrasse 11, 6330 Cham, Switzerland

# Acknowledgements

I would like to express my sincere gratitude to Dr Crawford Gribben and Dr Ema Vryoubalova for their tireless support, expertise, time and dedication in assisting me with this project throughout the years. I am very grateful to the following for their generosity in discussing the project and sharing information with me: Hero Chalmers, Line Cottegnies, Naomi McAreavey, Philip Major, Marika Keblusek and Sarah Prescott. I would like to thank the staff at Trinity College Dublin Library, especially English Duty Librarian Isolde Harpur, for sourcing obscure and rare books, as well as her kindness throughout what was a very challenging time. My thanks also extend to the Irish Research Council, without whose generous postgraduate funding this book would not exist. Finally, and far from least, more than heartfelt thanks are due to my husband without whose continual support and belief, in both myself and the project, this book would never have been completed.

# Contents

CHAPTER 1

# Introduction

While exiled in Antwerp during the 1650s, Margaret Cavendish wrote by a 'little fire', some 'Feigned Histories' in which she expressed her 'desire To see' her 'Native Countrey' and her 'Native Friends'.[1] She lamented that the opportunity of making this longing a reality was barred by the 'Banishment'[2] of her 'dear Lord' from England's contemporaneously 'dangerous rock'. However, being acutely conscious of the turbulent socio-political unrest raging at home, as well as their now exilic status, Cavendish wrote she was 'content in Antwerp for to stay' and so, she envisioned 'in the Circle of' her 'Brain to raise':

> The Figures of my Friends crowned with Praise:
> These Figures plac'd in company together…
> All setting by a Fire in cold weather[3]

[1] Cavendish, Margaret, *The Preface of Natures Pictures Drawn by Fancies Pencil to the life being several feigned stories, comical, tragical, tragic-comical, poetical, philosophical, historical and moral: some in verse, some in prose, some mixt and some by dialogues*, London, 1656.

[2] In November 1649 William Cavendish, along with twelve others, was excepted from pardon. They were officially 'proscribed and banished as an enemy and traitor and [would] die without mercy, where ever they shall be found within the limits of this nation'. Public Record Office, *Calendar of State Papers, Domestic*, 1649–50, 39.

[3] Cavendish, Margaret, *The Preface of Natures Pictures.*



S. Cronin, *Women, Royalisms and Exiles 1640–1669*,
https://doi.org/10.1007/978-3-030-89609-6_1

Separated from the home she knew and those 'That lov'd' her 'well', Cavendish here draws on numerous literary devices to negotiate her experience of displacement and rupture. The action of sitting by the fire writing 'these Feigned Histories' induced her mind into a state of remembrance. Recalling her homeland—the place from which she used to imagine[4]—she enabled access to her recent past and stirred her 'desire' to reconnect with those from whom she and her husband were separated by their political and geographical exile. Failing the ability to actually return home to see her 'Native Countrey' and her 'Native Friends', she employed her imagination of her homeland as the chief means by which she might 'lend coherence and integrity to a history interrupted, divided' and 'compromised by instances of loss'.[5] Through the creation of 'narrative worlds' which were 'filled with people and objects that represent the very real allegorical principles upon which they were conceived',[6] Cavendish imagined old friends and locales, and gestured towards their gathering together against the figuratively 'cold' experience of exile, thus generating an image set against that of the 'cavalier winter'[7] itself. Through her memory and imagination of her homeland, she invoked a potent scene of reunion in opposition to exile, a scene in which she visualized that 'My Lord and I amongst our Friends was set'. Moreover, by indicating that it is through their common appreciation for 'Tales either in Prose or Rime' that royalist friends might engage in cultural exchange and be bound together during times of displacement, Cavendish comments on the power of literature to reconnect and sustain those royalists affected by enforced dispersion, diaspora and exile throughout the decades of civil war and its aftermath.

Of course, the experience of exile and diaspora has been widely theorized in recent literature. Salman Rushdie describes the identity of emigrants as being:

> at once…plural and partial. Sometimes we feel that we straddle two cultures; at other times, that we fall between two stools. But however ambiguous and shifting this ground may be, it is not infertile territory for a writer to occupy.

[4] Seidel, Michael, *Exile and the Narrative Imagination* (New Haven; London: Yale University Press, 1986), 4.

[5] Seyhan, Azade, *Writing Outside Nation* (Princeton, N.J. Oxford: Princeton University Press, 2001), 4.

[6] Seidel, 15.

[7] Miner, Earl, *The Cavalier Mode from Jonson to Cotton* (Princeton: Princeton University Press, 1971), 64.

> If literature is in the business of finding new angles at which to enter reality, then once again our distance, our long geographical perspective, may provide us which such angles.[8]

Rushdie's comment highlights one of many paradoxes inherent within the experience of exile, as he points to the rich potential of exilic literatures to relay experiences and worlds in new, exciting and dynamic ways. More recently, in the context of the early modern period, Philip Major has noted that much in the modern world has afforded us an insight and understanding of exile, and has argued:

> there is rich potential for marshalling this modern sensibility to the momentous deracination of earlier centuries. In this respect, the mid to late seventeenth century is an abundantly fertile area of enquiry. There are many different ways of looking at the English Revolution and its aftermath, and exile provides a fruitful new lens through which to view this pivotal period in the history of England and the British Isles.[9]

The paradoxical space supplied by the experience of exile and its consequent literary and cultural manifestations is the subject of this book. This study approaches this 'fertile area' through examination of the cultural production of six royalist women who strove to preserve not only their cultural heritage throughout the years of civil war, but also their shared as well as personal identity, as they found themselves 'exiled' in a variety of ways. Examining their contribution through a prism of conventions common to exilic writing, this study argues that Katherine Philips, Margaret Cavendish and the Cavendish sisters were not just writers *in* exile but writers *of* exile and argues their literature, together with the entertainments hosted by Queen Elizabeth of Bohemia and Mary Stuart embody the royalist experience of a critical moment in the history of, not only the writing of the civil war, but of the writing of the much-understudied narrative of the 'royalist diaspora'.

As seen above, through the power of 'Fancy', memory and imagination, Margaret Cavendish conflated scenes past with scenes present in an effort to achieve a type of literary navigation; a re-orientation and

[8] Rushdie, Salman, *Imaginary Homelands* (London: Granta Books, in association with Penguin Books, 1992), 15.

[9] Major, Philip, *Literatures of Exile in the English Revolution and its Aftermath, 1640–1690* (Surrey: Ashgate, 2010), 1.

reconnection with her distant homeland and the friends and family she had been forced to leave behind in the early 1640s. As they seek reconnection, many writers of diaspora and exile find that despite being 'haunted by some sense of loss, some urge to reclaim, to look back', despite the fear that looking back might 'give rise to profound uncertainties' and, despite being incapable 'of reclaiming precisely the thing that was lost', they nevertheless 'create short fictions, not actual cities or villages, but invisible ones, imaginary homelands … of the mind'.[10] This book argues experience of exile from one's homeland, and the attempted reclamation and imaginative reinvention of that place through cultural media led these particular royalist women to create their own types of 'Englands of the mind', that is to say, coherent alternate, or multiple alternatives to a contemporaneous socio-political dystopia they perceived to be run by a 'universall Enemy to all Order, and Government, both in Church and State'.[11]

For centuries, groups of peoples have been displaced by the old orders of monarchy and empire. Deploying the theoretical framework used to understand the experience of diaspora, this book questions what happens as we focus the lens of literary criticism onto those whose cultural output aims to preserve monarchical history and heritage as they themselves became stateless nomads. Drawing connections with and exploring the relationships between the phenomenon of diaspora, literature, history, politics and gender in the seventeenth century, this study insists on a new set of contours by which we may navigate the cultural production of these royalist women, while reaching a necessarily deeper understanding of the variant and dynamic nature of the amorphous phenomenon we come to label as 'royalism', as well as uncovering in more detail what it meant to be a royalist woman during this turbulent period. Including the experience of both those internally exiled at home and those who were externally exiled on the continent, this study shifts preconceptions regarding use of the term 'exile'. Regardless of how or where one came to be 'exiled'—be it geographically or politically—this book works off the premise that the experience of dispersal or dislocation is itself enough to require an investigative study into the cultural manifestations of peripheral life. Thus, it examines the ways in which these royalist women exhibit their sense of allegiance, identity as royalists and, not least, their identity as women

[10] Rushdie, *Imaginary Homelands*, 10.
[11] *The Character of an Agitator*, 1647, 4.

within this newly dispersed conglomerate of communities which spanned the British archipelago and multiple locations across the continent.

Exploring the domains of existence most complicated within the environment of diaspora—one's sense of place, gender and community—this book prises apart traditional ways of reading and understanding royalist women's cultural production during this contentious period. Individual and group connections to *loci* traditionally invested with meaning were disrupted by the subject's experience of displacement, diaspora and dwelling in host countries. Such complications forged new perspectives of the homeland, or place of origin, generating a literature of displacement which is consumed with a sense of place and return to that place. Cavendish, for example, produced episodic transnational narratives which appear to invalidate the homeland in her prose fictions, yet, for Philips the homeland is re-energized and re-imagined in her poetry of retreat. However, paradoxically we find that within both of these imaginative spaces dislocation is itself displaced to make way for relocation and recuperation. Thus, the material text comes to act as substitute *loci* of reunion, succour and represent various empowered forms of personal, cultural and political identities.

The ways in which diaspora impacts upon gender, women's position within the nation state and the fluidity of women's identity as they are 'caught between patriarchies' in the diasporic environment are another important domain which shapes cultural production.[12] Thus, mindful of the implications of this in-between existence, and its potential for autonomy, as we travel across the contrary homelands both in their lives and works, this book reconsiders traditional positioning of the gendered self as it is transformed by the opposing relationships to place and displacement in this particular period and explores the many ways in which the royalist experience of diaspora and exile impacts on the identities of its subjects.

Noting the ways in which diaspora impacts on community, this book specifically examines the concerted effort by royalist supporters to uphold and maintain this community through cultural production. Thinking beyond traditional ideas of women's communities as private and domestic or familial, this book looks to a plurality of broader national and transnational royalist communities and to a reconceptualization of 'community' shaped by dispersal and separation. While on the one hand, intercultural relations enrich and inspired those dispersed to host communities on the

[12] Clifford, James, 'Diasporas' in *Migration, Diasporas and Transnationalism,* Cohen and Vertovec eds. (Northampton: Edward Elgar Publishing, 1999), 314.

continent, on the other hand, I argue that the symbolic cultural community—unified by textual and cultural production and dissemination—also serves as a counter-public sphere worthy of its own investigation. While the literary, cultural, intellectual and ideological counter-public served as both virtual and real forms of community, most crucially these communities further functioned as vital sites of protection of and projection of cultural and political identity at such an incredibly vulnerable time for supporters of the monarchy.

Further to investigating how diaspora impacts on one's sense of place, gender and community, this book illustrates how a reading of its subjects contributions in conjunction with theories of diaspora significantly extends our understanding of the 'waves'[13] of migration previously written about by Geoffrey Smith. While individual investigations focusing on well-known royalist exiles offer invaluable insights,[14] this book broadens our understanding of the phenomenon of royalist dispersion as a group event, while situating well-known royalist women within this royalist diasporic community. In examining these particular royalist women, I include lived experiences, literary productions and performances from a variety of geographical locations such as courts in The Hague, the Rubens townhouse in Antwerp and a rural priory house in Cardigan, for example. By examining royalist women from different locations, the subjects' work can be seen not just operating within its local or national contexts but across the pan-European community and as such interacting and engaging with the broader diasporic group.

Inherent in the concept of diaspora is the notion of dispersal and images of multiple journeys with no two experiences being the same. The women in this book represent these different journeys and experiences, yet they are women who previously shared a common history, nationality and culture. Hence, they are a disparate collective simultaneously bound together by their shared past, at once the same yet different by virtue of their personal experiences. The tension between sameness and difference produces both commonalities which prove a broader group consciousness and

[13] Smith Geoffrey, *Cavaliers in Exile, 1640–1660* (Basingstoke & New York: Palgrave Macmillan, 2003), 4.

[14] See for example: Rees, Emma L.E., *Margaret Cavendish: Gender, Genre, Exile* (Manchester & New York: Manchester University Press, 2003); Battigelli, Anna, *Margaret Cavendish and the Exiles of the Mind* (Lexington: University of Kentucky Press, 1998); Whitaker, Katie, *Mad Madge: The Extraordinary Life of Margaret Cavendish, Duchess of Newcastle, the First Woman to Live by her Pen* (New York: Perseus Books, 2002).

divergences which teach us about specific local, personal and gendered experiences of displacement and dislocation. Sensitive to the variant experiences of exile under consideration, I explore the ways in which these commonalities coalesce to form what we might term a royalist rhetoric of exile, both personal and communal, previously discussed by Philip Major, as well as consider the ways in which gender inflects these rhetorics.[15] If some texts can be seen to uphold and preserve ideals of royalism through the use of comparable royalist metaphors, tropes and genres as is discussed in Chap. 2, in Chap. 4 we find differences and departures which reflect the lived tension between location and dislocation, which complicate unified strategies of exilic writing even further to produce hybridized texts and identities which are continually subject to change and constantly being remade. Cultural continuities and literary similarities notwithstanding, there are differences of note between these women such as class, marital tensions, familial networks, mobility and localities, which lead to variables of cultural, literary, personal and political identity. It is these convergences as well as the differences which demand we think, as Philip Major has written, in terms of 'royalisms' rather than 'royalists',[16] as well as conversely remind ourselves that despite the fact that 'exilic modes of thought, argument and expression vary considerably', there does exist a 'palpable sense of unity to be derived from an overarching and increasingly productive theoretical perspective'.[17]

## Women

While there have been many studies on the women who wrote during the seventeenth century,[18] little scholarship during the 1990s and 2000s was dedicated to early modern female royalist writing. Prior to the 1990s, Sara

[15] Major Philip, *Writings of Exile in the English Revolution and Restoration* (Surrey & Burlington, Ashgate, 2013). Major determines that the 'wide range of exiles and exilic experiences in the period provides a concomitantly rich variety of contemporary writings …each of which plays its part in the displaced persons construction of a rhetoric of exile', 3.

[16] Major, *Literatures*, 3.

[17] Ibid., 9.

[18] For example, see Barash, Carol, *English Women's Poetry:1649–1714* (Oxford: Oxford University Press, 1996); Beilin, Elaine, *Redeeming Eve: Women writers of the English Renaissance* (Princeton, N.J., Guildford: Princeton University Press, 1987); Clarke, Danielle & Elizabeth Clarke, *'This Double Voice': Gendered Writing n Early Modern England* (London & New York: Palgrave Macmillan, 2000); Clark, Danielle, *The Politics of Early Modern Women's Writing 1558–1640* (London & New York: Routledge, 2001); Smith, Hilda,

Mendelson addressed this lacuna in 1987 as she set out not to 'establish a pedigree for modern feminism but to reconstruct [Stuart] women's mental and material world in all its rich complexity'.[19] Over ten years later, Anita Pacheco's edited collection of essays on royalist women provided readings through the lens of feminist criticism. This book shares her aim of rescuing female-authored texts 'from the oblivion to which they have been consigned by a largely male canon of great literature'.[20] However, work on the canon of royalist women writers grows very slowly, and many studies on royalist women writers also choose to include chapters on women writers 'on the other side'.[21] While these valuable studies provide us with a broader view of women's writing in the period, few attend to the literary significance, and impact, which female royalist writers may have had within their own literary and political milieu and what they might be

*Reasons Disciples: Seventeenth-Century English Feminists* (Illinois: University of Illinois Press, 1982); Knoppers, Laura, *The Cambridge Companion to Early Modern Womens' Writing* (Cambridge: Cambridge University Press, 2009); Wilcox, Helen, *Women and Literature in Britain 1500–1700* (Cambridge, Cambridge University Press, 1996). Ross, Sarah C. E., *Women, Poetry and Politics in Seventeenth Century Britain* (Oxford: Oxford University Press, 2015); Baumann, Elizabeth Scott, *Forms of Engagement: Women, Poetry and Culture, 1640–1680* (Oxford: Oxford University Press, 2013); On women's contribution to political tradition in Early Modern England, see Smith, Hilda, *Women Writers and the Early Modern British Tradition* (Cambridge: Cambridge University Press, 1998). On Irish contexts, see: Coolehan, Marie-Louise, *Women, Language and Writing in Early Modern Ireland* (Oxford: Oxford University Press, 2010); Eckerle, Julie., A, and MacAreavey, Naomi, *Women's Life Writing & Early Modern Ireland* (Lincoln: University of Nebraska Press, 2019); Walsh, Ann-Maria, *The Daughters of the First Earl of Cork: Writing, Family, Faith, Politics and Place* (Dublin: Four Courts Press, 2020). For women writing in European contexts, see Akkerman, Nadine, *The Correspondence of Elizabeth Stuart, Queen of Bohemia, Vol II 1632–1642* (Oxford: Oxford University Press, 2011) *Volume III* is forthcoming; Pal, Carol, *The Republic of Women: Rethinking the Republic of Letters in the Seventeenth Century* (Cambridge: Cambridge University Press, 2012).

[19] Mendelson, Sarah, *The Mental Worlds of Three Stuart Women: Three Studies* (Brighton: Harvester, 1987), 6.

[20] Pacheco, Anita, *Early Women Writers: 1600–1720* (New York: Addison Wesley Longman, 1998), 1.

[21] For example, see Barash, *English Women's Poetry*; Salzman, Paul, *English Prose Fiction 1558–1700: A Critical History* (Oxford: Oxford University Press, 1985); Ross, Sarah C. E., *Women, Poetry and Politics*; Seelig, Sharon Cadman, *Autobiography and Gender in Early Modern Literature: Reading Women's Lives 1600–1680* (Cambridge & New York: Cambridge University Press, 2006).

able to teach us about royalism itself. A notable exception includes the recent work by Sarah Ross who situates the practices of Jane Cavendish's occasional verse and Hester Pulter's elegies and emblem poetry within the 'broader engagements and interventions in social, religious and political cultures', offering a 'new critical view of women's relationship to poetry and politics of the period'.[22] Charting the generic precedents for many of Cavendish's poems and the interactive sphere of the 'elite inter-familial coterie', Ross importantly highlights the necessary expansion of our 'understanding of the scope of her literary sources and networks'.[23] This important intervention goes some way to addressing issues concerning our understanding of what it meant to be a royalist woman writer operating and interacting within particular cultural, literary and political circles; however, questions of what happened to their identity as women, as royalists and the effect on their writing as they found themselves displaced, isolated, dislocated from these circles or in exile of one kind or another is a discussion this book aims to initiate.

While there exist numerous chapters in edited collections on royalist female writers, there are very few monographs dedicated to these subjects.[24] Welcome additions came from Anna Battigelli and Emma Rees who both provide full-length treatments of Margaret Cavendish's experiences of exile and the impact on her writing.[25] A watershed monograph discussing multiple royalist women comes from Hero Chalmers's study *Royalist Women Writers* in which she explores how 'patriarchal ideology in royalism can, seemingly paradoxically, enhance female agency by creating opportunities for authorship'.[26] Through the exploitation of courtly tradi-

[22] Ross, *Women, Poetry and Politics*, 4, 5.

[23] Ibid., 111, 112.

[24] For edited collections, see, for example, McElligott, Jason and Smith, David, L., *Royalists and Royalism During the Interregnum* (Manchester & New York: Manchester University Press, 2010) hereafter cited as *RRI*; Major, *Literatures of Exile*; N.H Keeble *The Cambridge Companion to the writing of the English Revolution* (Cambridge: Cambridge University Press, 2001); Cerasano, C.P., and Wynne Davis, Marion, *Readings in Renaissance Women's Drama Criticism, History and Performance, 1594–1998* (London: Routledge, 1998); Grundy, Isobel and Wiseman, Susan, *Women, Writing, History*; Pacheco, *Early Women Writers: 1600–1720*; Smith, Hilda, *Women Writers and the Early Modern British Political Tradition;* Claude, J., & Ted-Larry Pebworth, *The English Civil Wars in the Literary Imagination* (Columbia and London: University of Missouri Press, 1999); Eckerle & McAreavey, *Women's Life Writing*.

[25] Battigelli, *Margaret Cavendish and Exiles of the Mind*; Rees, *Gender, Genre and Exile*.

[26] Chalmers, Hero. *Royalist Women Writers 1650–1689* (Oxford & New York: Oxford University Press, 2004), 7. Hereafter cited as *RWW*.

tions and aristocratic ideals, which placed feminine decorum at the centre of its nostalgic project and 'celebrated royalist women' during the royalist cultural rebellion, Chalmers writes that women writers were positioned as culturally authoritative and as such their writing could be justified over domestic duty thereby defending female authorship. Further, while Chalmers not only shows how women such as Cavendish, Philips and Behn came to be part of the royalist political fabric, she further gestures towards defeat and exile as 'central to the legitimization of Cavendish's and Philips's authorial voices as women writers'.[27] Building on this perspective, this book posits that while shifting patriarchal and socio-political ideologies gave way to a space from within which women might begin to write, and be supported in their endeavours, the added element of the experience of dislocation and exile further expanded this space and allowed a sense of creative autonomy at home, and, that those concurrently situated on the continent benefited from exposure to local forms, or traditions, within host countries. This book, then, not only documents how politically conscious women responded to and engaged with the royalist cultural cause but how they articulated their experience of localized, national or transnational 'exiles' to produce both contrasting and continuous forms of cultural, political and personal identities that speak of the royalist rupture and clarifies their position as writers that are at once *in* exile yet also writers *of* exile.

## Royalisms

A great deal of critical work has been undertaken by scholars in the area of Republicanism and the Protectorate since the years of the civil war itself with far less attention given over to royalists and royalism. As Philip Major asserts, '[u]nquestionably, the contours of our understanding of the mid-seventeenth-century have been dramatically reshaped by the plethora of monographs and articles on its panoply of radicals, republicans and revolutionaries'.[28] This imbalance of scholarship focused on the narratives of the 'other side' has understandably led to a secondary disparity in our perception of royalism itself and the occlusion of important questions of identification and difference such as what was royalism; who were the royalists; what it meant to be a supporter of the King. After the classic studies

[27] Chalmers, *RWW*, 12.
[28] Major, *Literatures*, 2.

by Hardacre and Underdown,[29] historians such as G.E. Aylmer sought to divide royalists into binary groups such as Catholic and Protestants; Constitutionalists and absolutists; soldiers and civilians; members of the aristocracy and self-made men yet as Major has written this 'taxonomical methodology' is now considered 'anachronistic'.[30] More recently, scholars have taken up the conversation about the manifold varieties of political royalism, its origins, pre-civil war history and what constituted the royalist party in the early war years and during the interregnum. In the first of two watershed studies, Jason McElligott and David L. Smith undertake 'the task of recovering the royalist experience of the Civil Wars and Revolution' as they deal comprehensively with a nuanced examination and discovery, or re-discovery, of political royalism as an altogether more fluid and contingent concept than has hitherto been recognized.[31] This timely volume of essays also stresses the need for scholars 'to be clear' as to what exactly the term 'royalism' means, points to a neglect of the royalists of the 1650s, a neglect of the tropes of retreat in relation to politics, literature and classic studies such as Miner and Wilcher, and emphasizes the merits of a historicist reading, all issues to which this study attends.[32] In their second study, McElligott and Smith look to expand this investigation into the interregnum years to further redress the scholarly imbalance and explore the 'broad church' that is royalism in its various political as well as cultural guises, as they argue royalism was not 'a monolithic ideology' but rather a 'variegated, complex and heterogenous' entity, which in the 1650s

[29] Classic studies on royalism and politics that preceded the naughties include C.H Firth, 'The Royalists Under the Protectorate.' *English Historical Review*, 52 (1937), p. 634–48; Hardacre, Paul, *The Royalists during the Puritan Revolution* (The Hague, 1956); Underdown, David, *Royalist Conspiracy in England, 1649–1660* (New Haven: Yale University Press, 1960); Hutton, Ron, *The Royalist War Effort, 1642–1646* (2nd edn, 1999); Smith, David, L., *Constitutional Royalism and the Search for Settlement, 1640–1649* (New York: Cambridge University Press, 1994).

[30] Major, *Writings*, 14. See E,G., Aylmer, 'Collective Mentalities in mid-seventeenth-century England: II Royalist Attitudes' *Transactions of the Royal Historical Society*, 37 (1987): 1–30.

[31] McElligott and Smith, *Royalists and Royalism during the English Civil Wars* (Cambridge: Cambridge University Press, 2007), 2. Hereafter cited as *RRECW*. In particular, see respectively chapters by Malcom Smuts and Barbara Donagan which detail the role of the court and courtiers in the formation of royalism and the varieties of royalism that constituted its 'rainbow coalition'(Donagan, p. 66). See also David Scott, "Rethinking Royalist Politics: Faction and Ideology" in *The English Civil War, 1640–49: Conflict and Contexts* (Basingstoke, Palgrave Macmillan, 2009), 37, 44 for more traditional definitions of royalists.

[32] McElligott, Jason & Smith, David, L., *RRI*, 8.

represented not so much a 'single unitary phenomenon as a spectrum of different attitudes and beliefs'.[33] In particular, they pose a series of important questions regarding definitions of royalism which resonate with the study here. Specifically, they query how royalists defined themselves as such: is mutual recognition a factor; if identity is subject to change, what remains royalist; what 'words, deeds and beliefs' are considered essential and, are there patterns, among other questions of identification.[34] It is to these expanding and evolving ideas of royalism that this book turns, as it moves away from politically dichotomous ideas of royalism or factional royalism, to explore what happens to royalism as exile and diaspora cuts across all domains of its subjects' existence, particularly in Chap. 4, as it considers how local and transnational constructions and appropriations of royalism compare to each other.

If there was an imbalance in work on political royalism, there were fewer still full-length investigations focusing on the literary history and culture of royalists. Earl Miner's classic work on the cavalier mode is described by him as an 'attempt to discriminate Cavalier poetry from other seventeenth century alternatives, and to discriminate the major features within it'.[35] Miner pays close attention to those who were, and are, considered as 'the sons of Ben' as he traces the cavalier aesthetic, however, even though 'the times' are consistently referred to throughout, the study feels somewhat unmoored from its socio-political history. More recently still, there has been a move towards integrating the disciplines of History and English as scholars show an increasing interest in the value of reading literary works alongside its political and historical contexts.[36] As an example, Lois Potter explores the royalist psychological need for secrecy,[37] and astutely indicates that historically scholars have leapt the period 1640–60 on the grounds that the intervening period belonged to the history of politics and religion and not literature,[38] while she also notes that 'comparatively little attention has been paid to the writers of this group'.[39] James Loxley traces the development, and deployment, of a

[33] Ibid., 3,4.

[34] McElligott & Smith, *RRI*, 9.

[35] Miner, *The Cavalier Mode*, vii.

[36] See Major, *Writings*, 14–18 for an engaging bibliographic appraisal of developments.

[37] Potter, Lois, *Secret Rites and Secret Writing, Royalist Literature 1641–1660* (Cambridge: Cambridge University Press, 1989), xiv.

[38] Ibid., xi.

[39] Ibid., 3.

politically instrumental, and self-reflexive, poetics from the early years of Charles I's rule to beyond the regicide and enquires as to what this cultural reapplication of traditional forms means when set in context of construction of 'verse practice in accordance with partisan needs'.[40] His endeavours to explore the relationship between royalism, literature and cultural survival assert that 'the war of the pen' made panegyric poetry 'a literature of engagement, a textual form of fighting' which might 'exceed the determining reach of the territorial struggle'.[41] Hence, Loxley underscores the importance of literature as a means through which the royalists could establish and safeguard their cultural and even political interests. While I corroborate Loxley's assertion of retreat as a rhetorical gesture, the study here moves decidedly away from the idea of retreat as a sign 'of failure of the spirit'[42] to assert its value as an rhetorical tool of resistance and as a coping mechanism which unified royalists and in fact buoyed the spirit.

Valuable as these studies are to the understanding of royalist literature, especially when considered in tandem with contemporary partisan requirements, they do however have their limitations. As Hero Chalmers has written:

> even the efflorescence of compelling new studies specifically addressed to the topic of royalist literature has marginalized female authors and failed to recognize the degree to which women were shaping and participating in a kind of royalist political coding which motivates a number of these studies.[43]

An exception here is *The Writing of Royalism* by Robert Wilcher which maps of the journeys of male writers, such as William Davenant, Abraham Cowley, Jeremy Taylor, John Berkenhead and John Denham, across the decades as they respond to 'unfolding events which slowly reshape the religious and political landscape in which they live' while also charting the different kinds of writing that emerged to meet the challenges to

[40] Loxley, James, *Royalism and Poetry in the English Civil Wars: Drawn Sword* (Basingstoke: MacMillan, 1997), 3.

[41] Ibid., 214.

[42] Ibid., 209/10.

[43] Chalmers, *RWW*, 6.

traditional resources of literature posed by a changing political environment.[44] Weaving military events and literary response together, Wilcher charts a chronological narrative investigating the 'war of words'[45] that characterizes the years of military quarrel and defeat and rightly, albeit briefly, argues against the notion of Katherine Philips as an apolitical poet and defines the Cavendish sister's manuscript as 'redolent of a more political royalism'.[46]

While initial unevenness in scholarship led to omissions of royalist political and cultural narratives and questions of what royalism was from the historiographies of the period, with relatively few specific studies on royalist literary history, fundamental aspects regarding royalist identity have been similarly overlooked. Recently, however, Jerome de Groot has taken up the challenge of defining 'not was royalism was, but what it wanted to be'.[47] de Groot begins his book by questioning whether it is possible to talk of 'Royalist' identity or 'identities' and ends by considering royalist responses to the death of the king in 1649, and the 'refraction of loyalist ideology into a set of more contingent and problematic 'Royalisms''.[48] Throughout the war years, de Groot argues, royalism 'desired stable completeness', however, 'in the presence of great trauma, and particularly after the execution of the King, this was impossible'.[49] This trajectory is mirrored somewhat by the study here as I read royalist literature and entertainments, as well as cultural and personal identity, not only as a response to these traumas and as signifiers of a culture in crisis but also of a culture in evolution due to displacement. While the subjects of this book shared a common history, common culture and common national identity, the event of diaspora initiated an identity crisis which was at once the source of pain and possibility, opening up 'the chance the explore alternate modes of belonging' and representation.[50] Working from the premise that culture

[44] Wilcher, Robert, *The Writing of Royalism 1628–1660* (Cambridge: Cambridge University Press, 2001), 6.

[45] Ibid., 229.

[46] Ibid., 333, 260.

[47] de Groot, Jerome, *Royalist Identities* (Hampshire & New York: Palgrave Macmillan, 2004), 3.

[48] Ibid., 1, 4.

[49] Ibid., 144.

[50] McLeod, John, *Beginning Postcolonialism* (Manchester: Manchester University Press, 2000), 249. Hereafter cited as *BP*.

is defined as 'an embodiment' or 'the chronicle of a group's history',[51] this book chronologically and theoretically charts the movement of initial royalist dispersion from the early 1640s to the eventual homecoming in the 1660s to frame its subject's lives and their cultural production within its specific disruptive yet highly informative contexts. Royalisms in this book, however, are not only borne out of textual manifestations, recasting of old tropes or generic reinvention, but also through the more personal aspects of family, marriage and status, as well as through the impact of cultural environment, relationship to place, the trauma of dislocation, displacement and movement across the borders of nation states. To borrow de Groot's terminology, this book, then, explores the refracted concept of royalism as it is altered through the prism of the personal, place, displacement, community relations and local cultures reflected across textual and cultural manifestation and a broad geo-political transnational territory. While de Groot leaves his exploration of royalist identity as it experienced the cataclysmic event of the 'physical sundering of the head of state from his body' directly leading to a 'crisis of representation' after 1649,[52] this study continues to consider these events and others throughout the 1650s and 1660s as nodes of opportunity for its subjects; fissures through which possibility emerges for both text and individual shaped by the seemingly opposing forces of belonging and difference.[53]

As they were impacted by displacement, dislocation and relocation, the gendered identities examined here were 'no longer reliant on fixed notions of home' to 'anchor them to a singular sense of selves'.[54] Rather, through dislocation they embark on yet another type of shift from royalism to royalisms—a hybridity which enables agency and potential for transcendence of the trauma of diaspora. If de Groot argues the ambiguity inherent in the term '[r]oyalism' is demonstrated by the complexity and the shifting dynamic of identity formation'[55] which took place during the fractious years of the civil war, this book pushes this idea of shifting identity formation further to question what happens to its subjects' identity as women,

[51] Brah, Avtar, *Cartographies of Diaspora: Contesting Identities*, 2nd ed. (London and New York: Routledge, 2002), 18.

[52] de Groot, 143.

[53] Chalmers provides excellent commentary on the importance of royalism to the emergence of Phillips, Cavendish and Behn as authors, 7.

[54] McLeod, *BP*, 254.

[55] de Groot, *Royalist Identities*, 2.

royalists and cultural generators as further pressures of displacement, diaspora and exile cut across all domains of their existence.

Thankfully royalism today is understood as being 'altogether more heterogenous, fluid and interesting', with loyalties more 'individuated' and 'literature more variegated',[56] however, to understand royalism's more cultural and literary history as well as royalist identity, more work needs to be done. While a fuller understanding of the period will undoubtedly come from a study of 'the conservatives as well as the revolutionaries',[57] this book offers up a new contextualization of women's cultural production which will also serve to widen our knowledge of this relatively unknown and amorphous 'group'. While Major correctly insists that the experiences of the royalists are 'essential to a wider comprehension of the period as a whole',[58] he also argues for a 'creed that resists distillation' as he echoes de Groot and insists that we must think in terms of 'royalisms' rather than 'royalists'.[59] This book, then, responds to its predecessors' call to avoid such collapsing of the term, moves from the seemingly static concept of royalism to a more fluid or contingent set of royalisms and explores the proliferation of these varied 'royalisms' throughout the media examined.

## Exiles

The experience of the royalists in exile was first written about by Paul Hardacre in 1953 who, in pioneering the exploration of different areas of royalist intellectual and cultural life and a process of transmission which he argues was 'accelerated by exile',[60] also astutely recognized that through many forms of writing royalist exiles found a voice while abroad 'that could not have been raised in [their] native land during these years'.[61] Even more poignant, and an area which, sixty-eight years later, has still not been examined fully by scholars is Hardacre's observation that 'the full impact of the period on the intellectual and cultural life of England after

[56] Major, *Literatures,* 3.

[57] Underdown, David, *Royalist Conspiracy in England* (New Haven: Yale University Press, 1960), viii.

[58] Major, *Literatures,* 2.

[59] Ibid., 3.

[60] Hardacre, Paul, 'The Royalists in Exile during the Puritan Revolution, 1642–1660' *HLQ* Vol.16, no. 4 (August 1953): 353–370, 364.

[61] Hardacre points to doctrines, revolutionary theories, vindications or histories as modes through which many sought to refute radical notions at home, 357.

the restoration has hardly been recognised'. Geoffrey Smith's *Cavaliers in Exile* (2003) detailing the exiled cavaliers as a 'varied crowd of fugitives' who were uprooted and scattered is a groundbreaking text offering insight into the experience of those royalists who went into exile on the continent just prior to the regicide and during the interregnum;[62] however, as a social history, Smith's study is void of any kind of intellectual, literary or cultural analysis. Examining the 'importance of exile to our understanding of prominent literature, philosophical and religious texts',[63] Christopher D'Addario's *Exile and Journey in Seventeenth Century Literature* (2007) prefers to explore the experiences of Milton, Hobbes and Dryden after the restoration, once again providing us with a largely all-male cast. His examination of the experience of exile by reading imaginative texts, and his interpretation of those texts as 'determiners of social and cultural exchange', most certainly strikes a cord with this book. However, the study here differs as it looks back to the beginnings of forced dispersion for Stuart supporters as the civil wars unfolded to trace the reified experience of marginal alterity that royalist exiles experienced. Philip Major's important collection of essays *Literatures of Exile in the English Revolution* (2010) has touched on many interesting aspects of writing as it is inflected by alterity and exile.[64] Exile, he argues, 'shapes an instability that leaves words unmoored from their former meaning and application, and makes them occupy, like the exiles themselves, a space of 'tantalizing liminality'.[65] This book is indebted to Major's view of the potentiality that is derived from the experience of exile for writers, and the way in which we might re-historicize, as well as theorize, the royalist experience through the lens of exile. The most recent contribution to our understanding of the relationship between royalism, exile and writing comes once more from Philip Major who writes that our circumscribed 'understanding of not only the exiles themselves but of the host communities in which they lived', and the 'rich… social, political and cultural potential…has all but been ignored'

[62] Smith, Geoffrey, *The Cavaliers in Exile 1640–1660* (Basingstoke &New York: Palgrave, 2003), 7.

[63] D'Addario, Christopher, *Exile and Journey in Seventeenth Century Literature* (Cambridge; Cambridge University Press, 2007), 4.

[64] Two notable chapters in Major's edited collection *Literatures of Exile* include Hughes, Ann and Julie Sanders, 'Disruptions and Evocations of Family amongst Royalist Exiles', p. 45–63, and Kebluesk, Marika, 'A Tortoise in a Shell: Royalist and Anglican Experience in Exile in the 1650's', 79–89.

[65] Major, *Literatures*, 4.

due to 'the residual Anglo-centricism of scholarship on 17th Century Britain' which 'has discouraged engagement with exilic literary material'.[66] My study thus aligns with Major's work as he sets out to retrieve and explore 'the manifold ares of enquiry into exile of the period' through a 'concomitantly rich variety of contemporary writings…to provide another window into the complex interface between literary construction and lived experience'.[67] Drawing on cultural production from Nottingham, Cardigan, Antwerp and The Hague, this study traces the ways in which its subjects reconcile themselves with their quotidian experiences of displacement, isolation or exile through poetry, song, letters, verse letters, prose fictions and theatrical entertainments. Other significant additions to scholarship on exile include chapters on royalist women, royalist culture and family in the context of exile, yet these remain minimal. Only one chapter dedicates itself to women and the subject of exile in McElligott and Smiths' later treatment of royalists and royalism during the interregnum.[68] In this chapter, Hughes and Sanders provide a summary overview of locations of interest on the continent for peregrinatious royalists and most certainly 'draws out the prominence of women within the exiled community as intermediaries, patrons and activists' while also highlighting the 'importance of place among exiled Royalists, not least in providing a setting for rituals and ceremonial displays that constituted acts of defiance towards the republican regimes'.[69] Hughes and Sanders feature once more in Major's *Literatures of Exile*, this time considering 'literary and visual constructions' juxtaposed with 'analyses of the various survival stratagems used by the Cavendishes, at home, and in exile'.[70] To be sure, we have here the beginnings of vital exploration in terms of women, allegiance and exile translating into cultural forms of cohesion and defiance at work on the continent, however, what is lacking throughout scholarship is a consideration, and engaged analysis, of their work in light of, not just their socio-political upheaval but of their personal sense of displacement as royalists, women and cultural generators as well.

In its contribution to early modern women's writing and studies of royalism and exile, this book is designed to attend to this gap in literary

[66] Major, *Writings*, 4/5.

[67] Ibid., 1/2.

[68] Hughes, Ann and Julie Sanders, 'Gender, Geography and Exile: Royalists and the Low Countries in the 1650's', in *Royalists and Royalism During the Interregnum*, p. 128–148.

[69] McElligott & Smith, *RRI*, 7.

[70] Hughes, Ann and Julie Sanders, 'Disruptions', 46.

studies of the decades in question, and especially offers a unique way to 'identify a distinctive and coherent character in the poetry and literature' of royalist exiles, which Timothy Raylor notes is usually read by 'reference to literature or philosophical developments in France'.[71] To do so, this study employs diaspora theory to consider a multiplicity of 'exiles' across expansive geographic territories, both internal and external—those exiled *from* and *to* locations across Britain; exiles at home and abroad—those located across the British Isles compared with those situated in Antwerp or the Hague. The term 'exile' is loosened out to include those who were affected by formal banishment, such as Margaret Cavendish,[72] and those who characterized their experience of geo-political exile as psychologically repercussive such as Katherine Philips, who, in the early 1660s living in Wales, grew 'dull' and experienced 'melancholy' and 'fear' while distanced from friends and the newly restored court in London.[73] Without this widening of the theoretical concept and frame, study of 'true' royalist exiles—that is those who were formally banished—would indeed produce a rather limited and, as Raylor has noted, 'self-contained' field of investigation.[74] However, by reading the royalist experience through the lens of diaspora and expanding the term exile appropriately within this frame, to comparatively explore differing experiences of 'exile', the study here fruitfully loosens, expands and complicates the usual inflexible frames by which we understand royalist exile more generally. Offering the first full-length study to characterize the royalist condition as one of diaspora and exile, this book also continues previous scholarly lines of enquiry into our understanding of the royalist exile 'as a watershed intellectual and cultural phenomenon'[75] and joins Major in the recovery of the 'apparent marginalization of exile in the historiography' of the period.[76] The intent of this book, then, is not to further the narrowing of scholarly trajectories but to provide and establish a perspective from which we can build a broader more

[71] Raylor, Timothy, 'Exiles, Expatriates, and Travellers: Toward a Cultural and Intellectual History of the English Abroad' in Major, *Literatures of Exile*, p. 15–43, 16.

[72] Margaret Cavendish went into exile with Queen Henrietta Maria's court in 1644, where in Paris, she met her husband, William, who had been on the continent since 1644 and had been formally banished since 1649. See Chap. 4 and fn 2 for more here.

[73] Philips, *Letters to Poliarchus*, Sir Charles Cotterell ed. (1664) XLI & XLIII, respectively.

[74] Raylor, 43.

[75] Major, *Literatures*, 12.See in particular, Raylor.

[76] Ibid., 1. See also Raylor, Timothy, 'Exiles, Expatriates and Travellers' in *Literatures of Exile* for discussion of intellectual and literary survey of royalists in exile on the continent.

comprehensive narrative of the period as a whole, and without question royalists and royalist exiles in all their various forms are fundamentally essential to such understanding.

## Context and Re-Theorizing the Event

> Thus Country|men you see how you and all yours, what ever is deare to any of you, hath beene bought and sold by these Gentlemen, who in stead of peace and preservation to the Countrey, have brought in War, Bloud|shed and ruine upon it[77]

Devised to rouse men whose spirits were quashed by the opposition forces of the parliamentarian army, this statement by William Cavendish, the King's northern general, deploys a rhetoric of betrayal and victimhood to insist that 'what ever is dear to any' of his troops has been reduced to commodity status. The intensity of this statement captures a sense of powerlessness and a recognition of the devastation which faced the King's troops in the mid-1640s. Moreover, it highlights, for his troops, the demoralizing reality that the 'preservation' of peace and country has been wantonly exchanged for 'War, Bloud\shed and ruine'. Indeed, the very title of this treatise indicates that oppression was felt and widely acknowledged by the King's supporters by this time. However, this unravelling of the fabric of English nationhood and the sense of 'Countrey' had begun some years previously.

The chronological sequence of events which led to the dispersal of royalists began as early as 1641. Geoffrey Smith notes that waves of exiles, eventually numbering up to 40,000, began with the 'clauses of exception from pardon' in 1642 and continued up to the suppression of Booth's rising in 1659.[78] Other events included the scattering of Queen Henrietta Maria's circle as parliament conducted interrogations, demanded arrests and petitioned for the banishment of court papists. The second group to flee after the papists were many from the army plot group. In 1644, after a series of military disasters, and finally his defeat at Marston Moor, William Cavendish fled to Holland. Thereafter, parliamentarian forces advanced into the royalist West Country and Wales. The subsequent fall of these last

[77] Cavendish, William, Earl of Newcastle, '*A Declaration by direction of the committee at Yorke to their deluded and oppressed countrey-men*', 1645.

[78] Smith, *Cavaliers*, 57.

royalist strongholds and defeat at Philiphaugh in 1645 led to a scattered exodus, some to the Isle of Man, some to the continent and some to Ireland. Oxford surrendered in 1646 prompting yet more royalists to leave. Add to this, the defeat at Preston in 1648, the suppression of royalist risings, the purging of parliament of those members deemed to be in favour of the King, the trials and executions of Charles I in 1649, and other leaders and what emerges, then, is a picture of devastation which ultimately led to the demoralization of those who supported the King.

While this series of catastrophic events prompted the flight of Stuart supporters, the landed gentry had meanwhile lost prestige and places at court. Geoffrey Smith writes that families and households went into exile; others were economic and political exiles; many were banished not only from London and Westminster but also from the nation state by punitive banishment acts and ordinances that sought to control and surveil the movements of royalists countrywide.[79] Within the court itself, different strands of royalism and the relationship between them were complicated and the formation of royalism was underway yet constantly changing.[80] The year 1655 saw 'a new wave of fleeing Cavaliers' as Penruddock's rising proved to be a flop.[81] Exile, writes Hardacre, was 'motivated by duty to caste and loyalty to monarchy' and others that fled included Roman Catholics apprehensive of puritan victory and agents of the King and Queen.[82] Banished literary leaders of the day included John Denham, William Davenant, Abraham Cowley, Edmund Waller and Thomas Killigrew.[83] These events and the ensuing exile of royalists, whether it be on the continent or that of internal exile at home, form the basis for what I term here as the 'royalist diaspora'. Moreover, I argue, that even those who were diasporised *in situ*—that is, those who remained at home yet felt alienated from it—experienced no less a marginal status than that of those who went abroad. By including internal dispersion as part of the diasporic environment, this study engages meaningfully with current diaspora theory and contributes another aspect to what Robin Cohen terms a

[79] See Chap. 2, for more on this.

[80] For discussion on the emergence of royalism, see McElligott, Jason and David, L., *Smith, Royalists and Royalism during the English Civil Wars.*

[81] Smith, *Cavaliers*, 141–3.

[82] Hardacre, 354.

[83] Ibid., 362.

'classical, victim diaspora' a 'dispersal following a traumatic event in the homeland, to two or more foreign destinations'.[84]

It is the defining misfortunes which characterize and constitute a diaspora. For the classical victim diaspora, 'being expelled by a tyrannical leader, or being coerced to leave by force of arms, mass riots'—or, in the case of the royalists, the trauma of civil war and banishments—are experiences that Cohen regards as 'qualitatively different phenomena from the general pressures of over population, land hunger, poverty or a generally unsympathetic political environment'[85] and thus they define the trigger which categorizes a group as a diaspora. Further to this, Cohen engages with diaspora theorist William Safran to outline a number of desiderata which Safran postulated as features shared by a minority community of expatriates and defines their status as a diaspora. Firstly, as Safran notes, they, or their ancestors, have been dispersed from an original 'centre' to two or more foreign regions; they retain a collective memory, vision or myth about their original homeland including its location, history and achievements; they believe they are not—and perhaps can never be—fully accepted in their host societies and so remain partly separate; their ancestral home is idealized and it is thought that, when conditions are favourable, either they or their descendants should return; they believe that all members of the diaspora should be committed to the maintenance or restoration of the original homeland and to its safety and prosperity; and, finally, that they continue in various ways to relate to that homeland and their ethno-communal consciousness and solidarity are in an important way defined by the existence of such a relationship.[86]

Before mapping these qualities or criteria onto the royalist experience and cultural production, some amendments made by Cohen are worthy of consideration and/or of inclusion and others are not applicable to the prototypical diaspora model used here. Cohen binds the first four of

[84] Cohen, Robin, *Global Diasporas* (London: Routledge, 2008), 11. Royalist dispersion spread to multiple locations on the continent included France (Paris, The Loire Valley, Normandy, Calais, Bologna), The Hague, Bruges, Brussels, Breda, Rotterdam, Spain and Italy. Hardacre notes other countries including Denmark, Sweden, Russia and Poland, Africa and the Far East, Turkey, Palestine and Egypt, especially Cairo, p. 356, 367. Still more travelled to New England. Investigation of these farther flung exiles across the British Atlantic is beyond the scope of the study here. For example, see Kate Chedgzoy, *Women's Writing in The British Atlantic World* (Cambridge: Cambridge University Press, 2007).

[85] Cohen, 2.

[86] Safran, 'Diasporas in Modern Societies,' 83–4.

Safran's criteria together insisting that they are 'concerned with the relationship of the diasporic group to its homeland'.[87] While not wishing to diminish what he considers as the vital 'importance of the homeland in defining one of the essential characteristics of diaspora', Cohen posits a number of other important factors as possible criteria for the recognition of a diaspora, criteria which will enable a nuanced reading of royalist writings, productions and entertainments which emerged throughout these years.[88] Amending the first feature, he suggests that 'dispersal from an original centre is often accompanied by the memory of a single traumatic event that provides the folk memory of the great historic injustice that binds the group together'.[89] It appears he has blended both first and second of Safran's points to produce his first criteria. As Safran notes, the moment of dispersion demarcates a 'collective memory, vision or myth about their original homeland'. Cohen goes further to insist that it is this memory and the 'traumatic event' which 'binds the group together'. Cohen's feature is a logical step in the right direction, indicating a natural bond that groups of this nature would experience under oppressive conditions of trauma and dispersion. The royalist media in this study exhibits many examples of 'collective memory, vision or myth' regarding their homeland. We will see that, collective memory becomes a form of community mediated through topographically orientated works saturated with 'royalisms'. For instance, in Chap. 2, the deployment of the Halcyon myth, although a pervasive characteristic trope throughout literature from both sides of the divide during the period, is appropriated by royalist writers as a crucial means of identification and differentiation, as well as cultural grounding for their scattered tribe at this chaotic time.

These conceptual factors that shape what constitutes a diaspora, Cohen then distils into his own list of common features:

1. Dispersal from an original homeland, often traumatically, to two or more foreign regions;
2. Alternatively, or additionally, the expansion from a homeland in search of work, in pursuit of trade or further colonial ambitions;
3. A collective memory and myth about the homeland, including its location, history, suffering and achievements;

[87] Cohen, 6.
[88] Ibid., 4.
[89] Ibid., 6.

4. An idealization of the real or imagined ancestral home and a collective commitment to its maintenance, restoration, safety, prosperity, even to its creation;
5. The frequent development of a return movement to the homeland that gains collective approbation even if many in the group are satisfied with only a vicarious relationship or intermittent visits to the homeland;
6. A strong ethnic group consciousness sustained over a long time[90] and based on a sense of distinctiveness, a common history, the transmission of a common cultural and religious heritage and the belief in a common fate;
7. A troubled relationship with host societies, suggesting lack of acceptance or the possibility that another calamity might befall the group;
8. A sense of empathy and co-responsibility with co-ethnic members in other countries of settlement even where home has become more vestigial; and
9. The possibility of a distinctive creative, enriching life in host countries with a tolerance for pluralism.[91]

These 'common features', Cohen remarks, are in no way monolithic. He states that he 'deliberately' uses the 'expression *common* features to signify that not every diaspora will exhibit every feature listed'.[92]

In the case of the 'royalist diaspora' all but the second feature are disseminated through poetry, prose and entertainments as endeavours of cultural projection, both at home and abroad. Features three and four will be outlined in Chap. 2 as I show the ways in which Katherine Philips and Margaret Cavendish invoke the myth of the Halcyon and the trope of retreat to idealize a lost time, a lost culture and simultaneously offers a symbolic *locus* of return through a poetics of order. Through their topographical work, they insist on order during chaotic times and reclaim the

[90] Cohen fails to define what exactly he means by 'a long time'. The intent of this study is to focus on a judiciously chosen twenty-nine-year span from 1640 to 1669, yet the extent of travels of other royalists, or indeed other English female authors, who ventured across the Atlantic or farther east, for example, would make for yet more interesting literary studies. See, for example, Chedgzoy, *Women's Writing in the British Atlantic World*; Gardina Pestana, Carla, *The English Atlantic in the Age of Revolution, 1640–1661* (Cambridge, Mass: Harvard University Press, 2004).

[91] Cohen, *GD*, 17.

[92] Ibid., 16.

very land from which they (royalists) have been physically and psychologically severed to offer textual sites of figurative and virtual reunion. Feature five, while not thoroughly the concern of this study, can be demonstrated by those royalists who had initially fled England but returned as conditions or opinion changed during the interregnum.[93] Feature six and seven is evident if we look at the royal courts of Queen Elizabeth of Bohemia and that of Mary of Orange. While the sister and daughter of Charles I were not technically part of the initial dispersion, they nevertheless provided, through entertainments and cultural events, a 'strong ethnic group consciousness' that was 'sustained over a long time' and which included the 'transmission of a common cultural' heritage. Most certainly, their production of *A King and No King* at The Hague in 1654 was in itself a form of resistance offering a 'riposte to those whose "starched outsides" (Puritans) would forbid theatrical performances' since the closure of theatres in 1642.[94] Coupled with its dissemination in English prints, this particular performance suggests a 'sophisticated interaction between texts and events, with an audience that is both in the theatre and also beyond its walls, so that the very fact of a performance takes on a highly charged political significance'.[95] While Elizabeth and Mary's contributions to the cultural and political cause agitated and galvanized royalists on the continent, back in the homeland, the Cavendish sisters who experienced the most distressing aspect of internal exile—the division of and separation from their family—sought to transmit and consolidate their allegiance to the monarchy and commitment to family through manuscript productions which connotes a belief in a 'common history' and a 'common fate'. In doing so, they were projecting and 'privileging' the family 'unit in contrast' to the oppositions of 'sin and debauchery',[96] as well as promoting the trope of the family as a way to reiterate important hierarchical

[93] Examples include philosopher, tutor and writer, Thomas Hobbes; poets William Davenant and Edmund Waller. See Smith, *Cavaliers in Exile*, Hardacre, 'The Royalists in Exile' & Norbrook, 'Identities'.

[94] Knowles, Robert, 'We've Lost, Should we Lose Too our Harmless Mirth?: Cavendish's Antwerp Entertainments,' *Royalist Refugees: William and Margaret Cavendish at the Rubens House 1648–1660* (Antwerp: BAI, Rubenianum, 2006), 70/1.

[95] Ibid., 75. Hardacre also writes that 'many exiles could appreciate and even cooperate in intellectual activities at home, for example, the editors of the Polyglot Bible employed Anglican clergymen in exile and sent sheets to Dr Morley in Antwerp, proving that the republic of letters not only survived the shock of civil strife but also thrived and operated across international borders', *The Royalists in Exile*, 361.

[96] de Groot, Jerome, *Royalist Identities*, 127.

traditions associated not just with the monarchy but also as an integral part of royalist identity. Features eight and nine emerge through the dynamic, progressive and integrative prose fictions by Margaret Cavendish which, discussed in Chap. 4, were undeniably influenced by her period of exile on the continent and, more specifically, in Antwerp and are acknowledged by scholars such as Kate Lilley as 'formally experimental', 'generically self-conscious' and 'ambitious', producing 'unexpected hybrids'.[97] Re-theorizing the royalist narrative through this decentralized geopolitical frame allows us to read afresh the history and culture of royalist mobility during the 1640s, 1650s and 1660s and reconsider already known works in yet more fruitful ways.

Another of Cohen's relevant features wishes to recognize 'the positive virtues of retaining a diasporic identity' more fully than Safran has indicated. Cohen notes that the 'tension between an ethnic, a national and a transnational identity is often a creative one'.[98] Here he cites examples of the Jews' responsibility for many advances 'in medicine, theology, art, music, philosophy, literature, science industry and commerce', while also reminding us of the extraordinary number of Nobel prizes won by Jews in the arts, sciences and medicine.[99] His call for the 'virtues rather than the dangers and traumas of diasporic existence' to be validated echoes Nico Isreal's observation that '[d]isplacement…wounds people—this ought not to be forgotten—but it need not be perceived as a condition of terminal loss' either.[100] This paradox of diasporic identity is precisely the focus of this study and will be more fully drawn out in Chap. 4, as I explore the ways in which the culturally nomadic Philips and Cavendish negotiated a 'triple identity' (composed of their gendered, royalist and exilic selves) as they searched for, defined and redefined, their subjective cultural and political identities within the 'tantalizing liminality' of the diasporic environment.

Speaking of cultural identity, Homi K. Bhabha's conceptualization of cultures and the hybridity that emerges on the borders of culture is particularly useful when discussing mobility of peoples. Bhabha posits that 'no culture is full unto itself' and that cultures are:

[97] Lilley, Kate, *Introduction to Margaret Cavendish, The Blazing World and Other Writings* (London: Penguin Group, 2004), xi.

[98] Cohen, *GD*, 7.

[99] Ibid., 7.

[100] Isreal, Nico, *Outlandish: Writing Between Exile and Diaspora* (Stanford: Stanford University Press, 2000) 17.

> only constituted in relation to that otherness internal to their own symbol forming activity which makes them de-centered structures-through that displacement or liminality opens up the possibility of articulating, *different*, even incommensurable cultural practices.[101]

This idea undermines and dissolves commonly believed structures that confirm, say, an Anglo-centric perspective, while also asserting that the very binary with which cultures insist they are different or opposite is one which weakens that imagined position: it 'denies the essentialism of a prior given original or originary culture'.[102] Thus, Bhabha insists that 'all forms of culture are continually in a process of hybridity'.[103] Second to this, Bhabha asserts that:

> hybridity is not to be able to trace two original moments from which the third emerges, rather hybridity to me is the 'third space' which enables other positions to emerge. This third space displaces the histories that constitute it, and sets up new structures of authority, new political initiatives.[104]

Thus, we have a scenario in which a culture is fluid, and its identity—formed by structures of authority, ideologies and political initiatives—is set free through the process of hybridity alone. Add to this the element of enforced dispersion and its result, exile, and what emerges is an exciting continuance of cultural flux which invites new ways of being, thus requiring 'new art of the present'[105] to document this being.

While regarding culture as 'intermingled and manifold',[106] a phenomenon experienced especially by those who are dispersed by diaspora, Bhabha goes on to define borders as the 'beyond' and outlines the impact on one's subjectivity thus:

> 'beyond' is neither a new horizon, nor a leaving behind of the past…we find ourselves in the moment of transit where space and time cross to produce complex figures of difference and identity, past and present, inside and

[101] Bhabha, Homi. K., 'The Third Space: Interview with Homi Bhabha' in *Identity, Community, Culture, Difference*. Jonathon Rutherford ed. (London: Laurence and Wishart, 1990), 210. This citation will be abbreviated to 'Interview' from here.

[102] Ibid., 211.

[103] Ibid., 211.

[104] Ibid., 211.

[105] McLeod, *BP*, 217. McLeod quotes Homi Bhabha's *Locations of Culture* here.

[106] Ibid., 218.

> outside, inclusion and exclusion. For there is a sense of disorientation, a disturbance of direction, in the 'beyond'.[107]

Hence, through the occupation of the 'beyond', shifting forms of 'representation emerge and the "in-between" spaces provide the terrain of elaborating strategies of selfhood'.[108] In negotiating these new hybridized identities, '[h]is or her subjectivity is deemed to be composed from variable sources, different materials, many locations—demolishing forever the idea of subjectivity as stable, single or 'pure''.[109] What occurs, then, is what Bhabha calls the action of 'restaging the past'; the exile is suddenly 'empowered to act as an agent of change, deploying received knowledge in the present and transforming it as a consequence'.[110] This process of hybridity has 'proved very important for diaspora peoples',[111] as it denies former binary patterns and suggests that the position of the 'beyond' stands as a 'place of possibility and agency for new ideas'[112]—that crucial locus of 'tantalizing liminality'. Thus, while Bhabha's seminal work *The Locations of Culture* addresses the situation of those who live on the borders or 'on the margins of different nations'[113] in the twenty-first century, his conceptualizations regarding the potential at the borders provide a useful way to read the disruptions of culture and identity caused by enforced dispersion during the years of the civil war and its aftermath.

## Terms of Negotiation

While negotiations of place, gender, community and projections of allegiance are central to the understanding of the world of the displaced royalist, it also is important to distinguish the difference between the sociological term and analytical tool, that is 'diaspora' and that of 'exile' and their applications in this study. The relationship between the two terms, 'diaspora' and 'exile', is dialectical and complicated. This study posits diaspora is the reason one becomes exiled. While exile, for some, is considered as

[107] Bhabha, Homi, K., *Location of Culture* (New York: Routledge, 1994), 2.
[108] McLeod, *BP*, 218.
[109] Ibid., 219.
[110] Ibid., 219.
[111] Ibid., 219.
[112] Ibid., 218.
[113] Ibid., 217.

possessing a 'frequently individualistic focus',[114] this study argues it is nevertheless still possible within the diasporic group. As Paul Gilroy notes, 'Diaspora yearning [group yearning] is transformed into a simple unambiguous exile once there exists the possibility of easy reconciliation with either the place of sojourn or the place of origin'.[115] James Clifford asserts that similarities between exile and diaspora include a presupposition of 'longer distances and a separation' including, as mentioned above, a 'constitutive taboo on return, or its postponement to a remote future'.[116] Although royalists could never have been certain of restoration, many nevertheless always hoped that there would be an eventual reinstatement of the monarchy and that they would return home. As Hardacre discovered, many had gone abroad in the expectation that 'their stay would be short and their preparations were accordingly scant'.[117] A prominent royalist exile, in a letter to his wife in May 1650, confided: 'seriously I do not in the least degree despayre that God Almighty will bring those rogues to confusion, and restore the Kinge'.[118] Thus, here we have an example of royalist yearning to see a reinstatement of the monarchy and an inherent eschatological impulse which trusts in divine intervention and 'some sudden revolution of providence' to make it so.[119] However, moving to describe the characteristics of a diaspora more fully, Clifford asserts that diasporas differ in that their cultural forms can never be:

> exclusively nationalist. They are deployed in transnational networks built from multiple attachments, and they encode practices of accommodation with, as well as resistance to, host countries and their norms. Diaspora is different from travel (though it works through travel practices) in that it is not temporary. It involves dwelling, maintaining communities, having collective homes away from home…[120]

[114] Clifford, James, 'Diasporas' in *Migration, Diasporas and Transnationalism*, Robin Cohen and Stephen Vertovec eds. (Glos & Massachusetts: Edward Elgar Publishing, 1999), 221.

[115] Gilroy, Paul, 'Diaspora', in *Migrations, Diasporas and Transnationalism*, Cohen and Vertovec eds (Edward Elgar Publishing, 1999), 293.

[116] Clifford, 'Diasporas,' 217.

[117] Hardacre, 355.

[118] Historical Manuscripts Commission, *Manuscripts of the Marquis of Bath*, vol. II (1907), 91 (Edward Hyde to Lady Hyde, 13 May 1650).

[119] *Compleat Collection of Tracts, by the eminent Statesman the right Honorable Edward, Earl of Clarendon*, (1747), 419, 421 (Psalm 18).

[120] Clifford, 'Diasporas,' 221.

That noted, Clifford asserts that this 'strong difference' experienced by those displaced, or 'this sense of being a "people" with historical roots and destinies outside the time/space of the host nation', is nevertheless 'not separatist'. He admits that whatever 'their eschatological longings, diaspora communities are "not here" to stay. Diaspora cultures thus mediate, in a lived tension, the experiences of separation and entanglement, of living here and remembering/desiring another place'.[121] Thus, while Clifford's interpretation intimates a group scenario in which multiculturalism may emerge and the group may settle in host countries, this study posits that while communities on the continent were indeed vital to the survival of royalist culture, there was an inherent desire to return to their native country. Moreover, as the subjects of this book wrote poetry, prose fiction, compiled manuscript or produced royal entertainments, their cultural acts of agency and politicized resistance co-existed alongside a host of other royalists who sought to undo the Commonwealth via alternative networks of spies or diplomatic and military organizers.[122] Reading this cultural agency alongside other political agencies of violence within host communities adds momentum to the idea that the royalist diaspora most certainly had designs on returning home. Hence, while some of these royalist women integrated to a certain extent, key to understanding their particular diaspora as one with exilic characteristics is to acknowledge that their constant hope was to eventually return home. For many royalists the act of living on the continent in no way diminished the 'remembering and desiring' of their true homeland which interestingly places them in yet another liminal space, as existing somewhere between diaspora and exile.

Diaspora is a hotly contested term; however, it is one which suits the experience of royalist displacement, and the recording of that experience through cultural means. Over previous years, Robin Cohen and Steven Vertovec have spent considerable time 'trying to arrest the tendency whereby the continuing potency of the term' diaspora 'is threatened by its misuse as a loose reference'.[123] I do not wish to do the term any injustice either and, while scholars like Nico Israel may not wish to 'domesticate

[121] Ibid., 311.

[122] See Smith's enlightening *Cavaliers in Exile*. See also: Smith, Geoffrey, *Royalist Agents, Conspirators and Spies: Their Role in the British Civil Wars, 1640–1660* (Farnham: Ashgate, 2011); Akkerman, Nadine, *Invisible Agents: Women and Espionage in Seventeenth-Century Britain* (Oxford: Oxford University Press, 2018).

[123] Cohen, *Migration, Diaspora and Transnationalism*, xvii.

cultural studies for the benefit of English departments',[124] I feel that any analytical tool which cultural studies deem useful in its efforts to understand society has much to offer literary scholars in our inexorable desire to comprehend all literary works as products of particular cultures and histories. Diaspora, then, is a concept called into service as a means to understand the phenomenon of royalist dispersion between the years 1640 and 1669. Not wishing to collapse the terms 'diaspora' and 'exile' into one, in this book one is viewed as a result of the other—exile as a result of diaspora. Ultimately, exile is the lens by which the literature itself is examined, arguing that literatures, and indeed theatrical entertainments, *of* exile have much to tell us about the broader experience and event of the 'royalist diaspora'.

As a historical and geographical concept, the term 'exile' refers to 'A banished person; one compelled to reside away from his native land' and/or 'Enforced removal from one's native land according to an edict or sentence; penal expatriation or banishment; the state or condition of being penally banished; enforced residence in some foreign land'.[125] Considering the experience of Stuart supporters of the 1640s, 1650s and 1660s, this term applies to many, who for various reasons sought solace elsewhere at home, throughout the archipelago, abroad on the continent or across the British Atlantic. Many royalists were officially exiled, Margaret Cavendish's husband, William Cavendish, being one of them,[126] yet, many left due to being unable to reconcile themselves with the new regime due to questions of principle and uncompromising loyalty to the monarch, as mentioned above.[127] After the regicide and the Treason act of 1651, Smith writes that some chose exile, some were forced, some were captured and released on condition they went into exile, others were fugitives on the run and some feared for their lives.[128] Many others felt it prudent to spend

[124] Isreal, *Outlandish: Writing between Exile and Diaspora*, 12.

[125] OED, http://www.oed.com.

[126] Cavendish felt he had no choice but to leave after the battle of Marston Moor, 1644. Sometime later, he had a price on his head, was viewed as a traitor and remained in Antwerp under threat of execution for treason for his role as military commander. Thus, he took up residency as a refugee in Antwerp. Ben Van Beneden. *Royalist Refugees.* Also see footnote no 2.

[127] Smith, *Cavaliers*, 61.

[128] Ibid.., 54–57. Other reasons to leave included employment opportunities, the impact of the dismantled court and lack of patronage, to some remaining appeared worse. Ultimately, some had no option but to go in order to survive, p. 59–60.

some time there while the storm raged at home. Yet, many more remained in England or Wales in a state of internal exile for the duration of the Interregnum. As Geoffrey Smith notes, the flight of royalist exiles was not an isolated and distinct event prompted by a single cause such as military defeat of Charles I's armies. Rather 'the exile may be seen as a series of waves' spanning the period between the meeting of the long parliament in 1640 to the restoration in 1660.[129] The fixed-term 'exile' begins to loosen out here as it begins to assume varying degrees of inference that could be applied to personal, partisan, geographical and even cultural predicaments alike.

At this point it may be useful to briefly distinguish differences between 'expatriates' and 'exiles' and how they relate to the women here. In modern usage, an expatriate is 'one who lives in a foreign country'.[130] This term, however, does not encompass the enforced and politicized nature of exile and instead suggests freedom of choice within an apolitical setting. The 'expatriate' is one who chooses freely to take to a period of living, or travelling, abroad. Contextually, the young men who embarked on the 'grand tour' prior to the civil wars would qualify more readily to be termed as such. The

> exile on the other hand is like a bird forced by the chill weather at home to migrate but always poised to fly back. He is political in that he has suffered the chill of official displeasure in some form or other, or at least he feels unwelcome, and waits passively for the weather to change.[131]

The enforced geo-political exile of the Stuart supporters during the war years and interregnum and their consequent endeavours to translate this state of being into literary and cultural forms is core to this study. Certainly, in this case, as literature stands as a social document which resists the erasure of geographical, historical and cultural differences, writers such as Cavendish or Philips, for example, will be seen to become what Azade Seyhan has termed 'chroniclers of the histories of the displaced'.[132] These 'waves' of royalists who set forth from England to the continent unable to reconcile with the political regime and those who remained alienated at

[129] Ibid., 4.
[130] OED, Http://www.oed.com.
[131] Gurr, Andrew, *Writers in Exile: The Identity of Home in Modern Literature* (Brighton: Harvester Press, 1981), 18.
[132] Seyhan, 12.

home by acts of banishment led to a displacement of a creed, a culture, and a diaspora of people, many of whom endeavoured to evade cultural annihilation and reconnect disbanded royalist exiles by writing poetry, prose fictions, compiling manuscripts or hosting royal entertainments.

Combining the approaches of historicist scholarship, post-structuralist concerns regarding theories of diaspora, narratives of exile and concepts of cultural hybridity, this study explores the ways in which the cultural productions that emerge from the diasporic experience transcend all notions of fixity, blurring the very boundaries by which their own previous power structures sought to maintain control. Employing theories of diaspora as a framework within which to locate its subjects, and reading their contributions in the light of conventions and tropes assigned to the literature of exile, this study offers a new way to understand the work of its subjects and the literary and cultural history of the royalist dispersion throughout the years in question.

By focusing exclusively on royalist women's cultural production, this study addresses a dual purpose. First, it situates these women within the unmapped terrain of 'royalist diaspora' and a variety of 'exiles' to produce gendered experiences of this overlooked historiography of British and European history. This book explores what this experience meant for women's identity as royalists uprooted, what might it have meant to them as women communicating that experience through various media and how these two components inflect and shaped royalist cultural productions during the period between 1640 and 1669. Second, as it considers their output as being informed by geographic *loci* and political allegiance, this book posits that these contributions importantly reflect the gendered experience of displacement as a lived tension between location and dislocation, as well as driven by the impulse for cultural, personal and political preservation. Choosing women of differing social ranks, ranging from a colonel's wife to the sister and daughter of Charles I, each of whom lived in disparate locations across the British Isles and the continent, this book not only offers opportunities for comparison of the ways in which defeat, exile and loss of self-identity is figured across a spectrum of ranks and through localized cultural expression but also presents a broader comprehension of 'royalism' as it was treated within cultural media across multiple geographic locations, as well as how those treatments may have varied or overlapped.

Through chronological exploration of these women's contributions, I trace a unique theoretical arc which outlines the royalist experience beginning with a series of initial ruptures and enforced dispersion caused by war, the acts for banishment and the regicide to the homecoming and eventual restoration of the monarchy in 1660, while simultaneously demonstrating the textual and cultural means by which these women sought to re-establish order during the chaotic war years, re-orientate themselves as a shattered community during the interregnum and eventually transcend the diasporic experience through cultural expression during the restoration years. Chapter titles, chronological sequence and development of each chapter present a series of sites which reflect their efforts at re-orientation through poetics of order in Chap. 2; renegotiation, cultural projection and protection through cultural *fora* of reunion in Chap. 3; literary and self-experimentation and expression within different diasporic environments in Chap. 4 and a re-working and negotiation of the return through prose fiction in Chap. 5. This theoretical and chronological trajectory also mirrors the shift from the more static concept of 'royalism' to the more fluid idea of 'royalisms' which allows us to embrace plurality and difference in the articulations of individuals' expressions of the experience of displacement, cultural identity and allegiance.

Most crucially, as this study employs a wider geographical focus to consider both exiles on the continent and those internally exiled at home it will reward us in two ways. First, as noted by Philip Major, it will lead to the discovery of ways in which 'exiles adapt to, or isolate themselves from, their new environment, a process which in turn reveals imperatives of assimilation, integration, acculturation and separation'.[133] Second, it allows for comparative engagement with differing literary and cultural survival strategies deployed both at home and on the continent: an approach by which we might, on a collective basis, extrapolate a royalist rhetoric of exile. Here the study builds upon Major's notion that displacement 'generates a paradoxically enabling marginal status: exile is a singularly extreme environment in which people behave in fresh and informative ways and its scrutiny therefore can be used to prise open traditional assumptions' as regards royalist identity and culture.[134] Further to this, a dual focus attends to scholars' calls to stop merely talking about the importance of Europe but to start showing its importance in practice[135] and draws on Jonathon

[133] Major, *Literatures*, 6.

[134] Ibid., 3.

[135] McElligott, Jason introduction to *Fear, Exclusion and Revolution: Roger Maurice and Britain in the late 1680s*. Jason McElligott ed. (Burlington, Aldershot: Ashgate 2006), 9. See

Scott's work who sees the seventeenth century as a unity and England as European.[136] However, perhaps more importantly, a dual focus on physical displacement in countries outside of England, but also including those who were diasporised *in situ* accommodates the inner, mental withdrawal of royalists who chose to remain at home in the 1640s and 1650s. Thus, this book shares Philip Major's view that a more 'holistic method allows for the complexity of the experiences and literary strategies of exile in these years to be more fully investigated' and 'leads to a wider, more nuanced comparison of responses to exile and defeat than would be possible if, say, consideration were given only to those who remained exiled abroad'.[137]

With the socio-political and ideological shifts that occurred in the 1640s, 1650s and 1660s, supporters of the King believed that their country had changed for the worse. As this study sets out to examine not only these decades but the years after the restoration as well, it shows that these decades cannot, and should not, be examined independently. By extending the focus prior to the regicide and beyond the restoration, this study blurs the 'arbitrary, artificial landmark created in part by a modern fixation on revolution', and disengage 'the modern (post-Marxist) assumption both of mid-century revolution and of revolution implying discontinuity' which 'has reinforced this division of the century into two halves'.[138] As Jonathon Scott posited, the Restoration period has been presented as 'artificially wedded to its future and severed from its past', in reality it is, on the contrary, 'uniquely under the shadow of its past'.[139] Hence, the nomadic sensibilities of this book which migrate beyond the temporal border of 1660s will prove that past trauma has indeed informed restoration writers. As Christopher D'Addario notes:

> as they walk in the present, these exiles, see, hear and smell both the immediacy of their newly foreign existence and the silhouette of the day before their exile' and that the desire to create for those in exile, 'comes from both the necessity of reorienting oneself somewhere between lost past and the immediate present.[140]

also, Major, *Literatures of Exile*, p. 8, fn2.

[136] Scott, Jonathon, *England's Troubles: Seventeenth Century English Political Instability in a European Context* (Cambridge: Cambridge University Press, 2000).

[137] Major, *Literatures*, 8.

[138] Ibid., 6. Major quotes Scott here.

[139] Scott, *England's Troubles*, 25–6.

[140] D'Addario, *Exile and Journey*, 2.

Thus, for subjects of diaspora and exile, the past cannot be severed from the present—both realms inform one another and any cultural product must be read with this in mind. As I explore the period beginning in 1640 through to 1669—a period during which royalists were forced from the public sphere by the sequestration of their estates, imprisonment, ejection from office, banishment or exile—I show their native country not only became a foreign territory but that through writing and royal entertainments, this territory was imaginatively transformed into many types of 'Englands of the mind'; a transformation which invites connection to and with a shared history.

Chapter 2 is concerned with they ways in which the experience of displacement and exile impacts on one's sense of place. As royalists were diasporised *in situ* by restrictive acts and ordinances set in place by various parliaments during the 1640s and 1650s, they were displaced not only to the continent but also throughout the British Isles. As it focuses on internal exile, this chapter shows how Katherine Philips and Margaret Cavendish ameliorated such disorientation and resisted political marginalization through the use of trope of retreat and the recognizable myth of the Halcyon. In doing so, they intersected with their male peers who were also engaged in the royalist cultural rebellion. As Christopher D'Addario posits, the experience of exile engenders the need to 'fashion a peaceful space in which the author can operate away from the unsettled difficult reality of daily life'.[141] Thus, we will see that these women writers conceived the symbolic spaces within their poetry as sites which could not only offer surrogate spaces of order juxtaposed to the anarchy and bedlam which prevailed outside but also provide a counter-exile narrative which resisted displacement and consolidated a relocated royalist authority.

Expanding on the theme of relocating power and re-establishing order, Chap. 3 focuses on cultural processes of re-orientation within communities both virtual and real, past and present. It examines the ways in which Philips, the Cavendish sisters and Elizabeth of Bohemia and Mary of Orange oppose geo-political marginalization through the creation of cultural *fora* of reunion. Building on the previous chapter, I argue the *fora* of Philips's coterie, the sister's manuscript compilation and the entertainments by Elizabeth and Mary represent alternate politically charged spaces of reunion which stand as a stern riposte to parliamentarian acts and ordinances which sought to control royalist gatherings, suppress stage plays

[141] Ibid., 2.

and ban cultural forms. James Clifford notes that for exiles any given culture and its ideologies, and its real manifestation that is '[c]ommunity can be both a site of support and oppression' but that diaspora communities 'articulate alternate public spheres, interpretive communities where critical alternatives...can be expressed'.[142] In this chapter, we will see that each cultural *fora* examined forms intellectual, cultural and ideological counter-public communities for scattered royalists; communities which could and did exist as culturally and politically different to the recently emerged and dominant parliamentarian sphere. Habermasian terminologies and the work of Nancy Fraser are also drawn upon to conceptualise how the circulation of royalist cultural media produced a counter-public sphere within which royalists could connect, communicate and correspond with each other.

In Chap. 4, I explore how the experience of displacement impacts directly on gender and identity through examination of the ways in which Cavendish and Philips negotiated disparate experiences of exile through the very different genres of prose fiction and letter writing. While working from the premise that women are naturally *expatria*ted in patria, I show how the added dimension exile allowed for further subversion and manipulation of arbitrary societal categorizations and proscriptions, incumbent upon women during the period, and I examine the ways in which these resilient women created dynamic, autonomous sites of exilic self-fashioning through their writing. As James Clifford asserts, diaspora, or exile could either 'reinforce or loosen gender subordination'.[143] He notes that:

> On one hand, maintaining connections with homelands, with kinship, and with religious and cultural traditions may renew patriarchal structures. On the other, new roles and demands, new political spaces are opened up by diaspora interactions.[144]

Thus, 'caught between patriarchies', women may 'find their new diaspora predicaments conducive to a positive renegotiation of gender relations'.[145] Hence, during this time of great socio-political, constitutional and religious upheaval, while these women encountered shifting ideological parameters as regards women and writing, including women's visibility in

[142] Clifford, 'Diasporas', 288, 314.
[143] Ibid., 313.
[144] Ibid., 313–4.
[145] Ibid., 314.

society and women's voice, they did, however, experience a complication of these prescribed ways of being through the experience of diaspora that paradoxically allowed for, not just literary experimentation but experimentation with and of the self.

Moving on from the formation and experimentation of identities within the diasporic environment, Chap. 5 concludes by examining the experience of the homecoming for both internal and external royalist exiles at the restoration of the monarchy in 1660. The homecoming for the exile is an event which can simultaneously produce both a sense of joy and engender feelings of disappointment. Michael Seidel has noted that upon return it is 'common enough' 'that the mental energy expended on the image of home in absence proves incommensurate with the reality of home as presence'.[146] Hence, despite the happy occasion of a culture and an ideology being restored, burgeoning disappointments concerning return to, and reintegration with, the newly restored regime at home nonetheless emerge. As royalists came to terms with the new monarchical regime, feelings of disappointment range from the political to the personal, and this chapter examines the ways in which Cavendish negotiated her new position in the homeland through her prose fiction *The Blazing World*. Within the fantasy locales of this prose fiction, this chapter argues Cavendish reaches a zenith moment as she crafts a social utopia and an absolute self to counter the disappointment of homecoming, thus we find that within this post-restoration work utopian worlds are juxtaposed with dystopian unrest and that the homecoming remains firmly under the shadow of the trauma of exile.

## Works Cited

### Books and Poems

Cavendish, Margaret, *The Preface of Natures Picture Drawn by Fancies Pencil to the life being several feigned stories, comical, tragical, tragic-comical, poetical, philosophical, historical, and moral: some in verse, some in prose, some mixt and some by dialogues*, London (1656).

Cavendish, William, Earl of Newcastle, *'A Declaration by direction of the committee at Yorke to their deluded and oppressed countrey-men'* (1645).

Philips, Katherine, *Letters to Poliarchus*, Sir Charles Cotterell ed. (1664).

[146] Seidel, 12.

Catalogues and Calendars

Historical Manuscripts Commission, *Manuscripts of the Marquis of Bath,* Vol. II (1907).

Compleat Collection of Tracts by Clarendon by the eminent Statesman the right Honorable Edward, Earl of Clarendon, (1747).

Secondary Sources

Akkerman, Nadine, *Invisible Agents: Women and Espionage in Seventeenth-Century Britain* (Oxford: Oxford University Press, 2018).

Battigelli, Anna, *Margaret Cavendish and the Exiles of the Mind* (Lexington: University of Kentucky Press, 1998).

Bhabha, Homi K., *Location of Culture* (New York: Routledge, 1994).

_____. 'The Third Space: Interview with Homi Bhabha' in *Identity, Community, Culture, Difference.* Jonathon Rutherford ed. (London: Laurence and Wishart, 1990).

Brah, Avtar, *Cartographies of Diaspora: Contesting Identities*, 2nd ed. (London and New York: Routledge, 2002).

Chalmers, Hero, *Royalist Women Writers 1650–1689* (Oxford & New York: Oxford University Press, 2004).

Chedgzoy, Kate, *Women's Writing in The British Atlantic World* (Cambridge: Cambridge University Press, 2007).

Chailand & Rageau, *The Penguin Atlas of Diasporas* (New York: Penguin Group, 1995).

Clifford, James, 'Diasporas' in *Migration, Diasporas and Transnationalism,* Robin Cohen and Stephen Vertovec eds. (Cheltenham, Northampton & MA, USA: Edward Elgar Publishing, 1999).

Firth, C.H., 'The Royalists Under the Protectorate' *English Historical Review*, 52 (1937): 634–48.

Cohen, Robin, *Global Diasporas* (London: Routledge, 2008).

D'Addario, Christopher, *Exile and Journey in Seventeenth Century Literature* (Cambridge: Cambridge University Press, 2007).

de Groot, Jerome, *Royalist Identities* (Hampshire & New York: Palgrave Macmillan, 2004).

Gilroy, Paul, 'Diaspora', in *Migration, Diasporas and Transnationalism*, Cohen, Robin and Stephen Vertovec eds (Cheltenham, Northampton & MA, USA: Edward Elgar Publishing, 1999).

Gurr, Andrew, *Writers in Exile: The Identity of Home in Modern Literature* (Brighton: Harvester Press, 1981).

Grundy and Wiseman, *Women, Writing, History 1640–1740* (London: Dotestios Ltd, 1992).

Hardacre, Paul, *The Royalists during the Puritan Revolution* (The Hague, 1956).

Hughes, Ann and Julie Sanders, 'Gender, Geography and Exile: Royalists and the Low Countries in the 1650's'in *Royalists and Royalism During the Interregnum*, Jason McElligott and David L., Smith eds., (Manchester & New York: Manchester University Press, 2010), pp. 128–148.

Hughes, Ann, 'Disruptions and Evocations of family amongst Royalist Exiles' in *Literatures of Exile, in the English Revolution and its Aftermath, 1640–1690.* Philips Major ed., (Surrey: Ashgate, 2010), pp. 45–63.

Hutton, Ron, *The Royalist War Effort, 1642–1646* 2nd edn. (London: Routledge, 1999).

Isreal, Nico, *Outlandish: Writing Between Exile and Diaspora* (Stanford: Stanford University Press, 2000).

Knowles, Robert, 'We've Lost, Should we Lose Too our Harmless Mirth?: Cavendish's Antwerp Entertainments,' *Royalist Refugees: William and Margaret Cavendish at the Rubens House 1648–1660* (Antwerp: BAI, Rubenianum, 2006).

Lilley, Kate, *Introduction to Margaret Cavendish, The Blazing World and Other Writings* (London: Penguin Group, 2004).

Major, Philip, *Literatures of Exile in the English Revolution and its Aftermath, 1640–1690* (Surrey: Ashgate, 2010).

______. *Writings of Exile in the English Revolution and Restoration* (Surrey & Burlington, Ashgate, 2013).

McLeod, John, *Beginning Postcolonialism* (Manchester: Manchester University Press, 2000).

McElligott, Jason, *Fear, Exclusion and Revolution: Roger Maurice and Britain in the late 1680s.* Jason McElligott ed. (Burlington, Aldershot: Ashgate 2006).

McElligott, Jason and David L., Smith, *Royalists and Royalism during the English Civil Wars* (Cambridge: Cambridge University Press, 2007)

_____. *Royalists and Royalism During the Interregnum* (Manchester & New York: Manchester University Press, 2010).

Mendelson, Sarah, *The Mental Worlds of Three Stuart Women: Three Studies* (Brighton: Harvester, 1987).

Miner, Earl, *The Cavalier Mode from Jonson to Cotton*, (Princeton: Princeton University Press, 1971).

Loxley, James, *Royalism and Poetry in the English Civil Wars: Drawn Sword* (Basingstoke: Macmillan, 1997).

Pacheco, Anita, *Early Women Writers: 1600–1720* (New York: Addison Wesley Longman, 1998).

Potter, Lois, *Secret Rites and Secret Writing, Royalist Literature 1641–1660* (Cambridge: Cambridge University Press, 1989).

Rees, Emma L.E., *Margaret Cavendish: Gender, Genre, Exile* (Manchester & New York: Manchester University Press, 2003).

Raylor, Timothy, 'Exiles, Expatriates, and Travellers: Toward a Cultural and Intellectual History of the English Abroad' in *Literatures of Exile in the English Revolution and its Aftermath, 1640–1690* Philip Major ed., (Surrey: Ashgate, 2010), pp., 15–43.

Ross, Sarah C. E., *Women, Poetry and Politics in Seventeenth Century Britain* (Oxford: Oxford University Press, 2015).

Rushdie, Salman, *Imaginary Homelands* (London: Granta Books, in association with Penguin Books, 1992).

Safran, 'Diasporas in Modern Societies,' in *Migrations, Diaspora and Transnationalism* Robin Cohen and Stephen Vertovec eds., (Cheltenham, Northampton & MA, USA: Edward Elgar Publishing Limited, 1999), pp. 364–380.

Scott, David, "Rethinking Royalist Politics: Faction and Ideology" in *The English Civil War, 1640–49: Conflict and Contexts* (Basingstoke, Palgrave Macmillan, 2009).

Scott, Jonathon, *England's Troubles: Seventeenth Century English Political Instability in a European Context* (Cambridge: Cambridge University Press, 2000).

Seidel, Michael, *Exile and the Narrative Imagination* (New Haven; London: Yale University Press, 1986).

Seyhan, Azade, *Writing Outside Nation* (Princeton, N.J. Oxford: Princeton University Press, 2001).

Smith, David, L., *Constitutional Royalism and the Search for Settlement, 1640–1649* (New York: Cambridge University Press, 1994).

Smith Geoffrey, *Cavaliers in Exile, 1640–1660* (Basingstoke & New York: Palgrave Macmillan, 2003).

______. *Royalist Agents, Conspirators and Spies: Their Role in the British Civil Wars, 1640–1660* (Farnham: Ashgate, 2011).

Whitaker, Katie, *Mad Madge: The Extraordinary Life of Margaret Cavendish, Duchess of Newcastle, the First Woman to Live by her Pen* (New York: Perseus Books, 2002).

Wilcher, Robert, *The Writing of Royalism 1628–1660* (Cambridge: Cambridge University Press, 2001).

Wilcox, Helen, 'Selves in Strange Lands: Autobiography and Exile in the Mid-Seventeenth Century', in *Early Modern Autobiography: Theories, Genres and Practices* (Michigan: University of Michigan Press, 2006).

Underdown, David, *Royalist Conspiracy in England, 1649–1660* (New Haven: Yale University Press, 1960).

CHAPTER 2

# Retreat Not Defeat: Politicized Topographies and a Poetics of Order

For my own part I begun to think we should all like Abraham live in tents all the days of our lives.[1]

Between 1646 and 1660 various parliaments issued no less than eighteen legislative socio-legal acts, ordinances and proclamations seeking the 'removal', 'putting out' and the 'expulsion' of 'papists', 'delinquents' and 'malignants' from the cities of Westminster and London.[2] On 23 February 1650, a particularly punitive banishing act insisted that 'all Papists, and all Officers and Soldiers of Fortune and Divers and other Delinquents … depart out of the cities of London and Westminster, and late Lines of Communication,[3] and all other places within twenty miles of the said late

[1] Fanshawe, Lady Ann, The Memoirs of Anne, Lady Halkett and Ann, Lady Fanshawe, John Loftis ed. (Oxford: Clarendon Press, 1979), 111.

[2] C.H Firth and R.S. Rait (eds.), *Acts and Ordinances of the Interregnum*, 1642–1660, Collected and edited by C.H., Firth & R.S., Rait, for the statute law committee, 3 Vols. (Abingdon: Professional Books, 1978). Dated 7 May 1646; 17 December 1647; 9 July 1647, respectively.

[3] In 1642–1643 an extensive defence circuit or enclosure surrounding London, Westminster and Southwark was built. See Smith Victor and Peter Kelsey in *London and the Outbreak of the Civil War*, Stephen Porter ed., (Hampshire: Macmillan Press, 1996), 117–145.


S. Cronin, *Women, Royalisms and Exiles 1640–1669*,
https://doi.org/10.1007/978-3-030-89609-6_2

Lines' or 'such persons shall be apprehended and imprisoned without bail or manprize'.[4] As suspicion and fear of royalist rebellion increased, from March 20, 'frequent searches' for royalists occurred throughout the cities and across 'several counties', and, after October of the same year, confinement orders came into effect which saw royalists ordered to remain on their estates not permitted to 'pass or remove five miles from thence', lest they face 'Imprisonment, and Sequestration of all their Estates Real and Personal'.[5] These orders and the enforced removal of all royalists from London and Westminster caused waves of internal exiles to be dispersed throughout Britain. Philip Major determines that 'the subject of internal exile … during this period has remained comparatively understudied' and that the literary response to this 'Act for Banishment' is to be found in many a royalist or Cavalier poem.[6]

As royalists encountered both political and martial defeat during the 1640s, the socio-legal restrictions and measures meted out through these acts and ordinances further compounded these destabilizing losses resulting in disorientation and a crisis of identity. Banished from their power base of London, royalists now perceived the city to be a *locus* brought low by the wars and the new political regime. Key recreational spaces such as Hyde Park or Spring Garden were no longer places for royalist ostentation or socializing but were now occupied by their enemies; the Whitehall masquing house had been demolished; the practice of Anglican religion outlawed; there was no royalty to set the social tone and so the city had a 'plebian feel'.[7] An early experience of the disorientation and dislocation felt by royalists as the wars intensified and many were displaced and relocated within Britain comes from memoirist Lady Anne Fanshawe who writes that after her father's London home at Bishop Gate Street was 'plundered' in 1642.[8] Later in 1643, Anne writes, the 'Long Parliament plundered him out of what remained' and 'sequestered' the entire estate which led to the family

[4] C.H. Firth and R.S. Rait (eds.), *Acts and Ordinances of the Interregnum*, 1642–1660, vol. ii. 26 February 1649/50, p. 349.

[5] Ibid., 350, 351.

[6] Major, Philip, "Twixt Hope and Fear': John Berkenhead, Henry Lawes, and Banishment from London During the English Revolution'. *The Review of English Studies, New Series* 59.239 (2007): 270–280. Major's paper is a very interesting departure point when considering those who did not take to exile on the continent; however, his paper deals only with male writers.

[7] Whitaker, *Mad Madge*, 135/6.

[8] Fanshawe, *Memoirs*, 111.

being relocated to Oxford to join the court.[9] Here, residing in a 'baker's house in an obscure street', subsisting on 'one dish of meat' and 'with little mony', Anne and her family found themselves 'like fishes out of water' as they bore witness to the lassitude of 'perpetual discourse of gaining and losing towns and men' and 'at the windows' observed 'the sad spectacle of war'.[10] Other royalists endured similarly restrictive measures as they were confined *within* London upon suspicion. Philip Major has written that royalist poets such as Richard Lovelace were saved seven weeks of imprisonment on condition that he *not* move outside the lines of communication except with a pass; Richard Fanshawe was sent *to* London and ordered to stay there, and after spending eight months in the tower, Mildmay Fane was released provided he stay confined to his house at Bartholemew Close.[11] For others, such as Robert Herrick, expulsion *from* locations in the country *to* London was also a common event. In 1647, due to his royalism, Herrick was expelled from living in his vicarage in Dean Prior, Devonshire, and went to London.[12] For many others, such as Henry Vaughan, residence in the country was the only option for those who perceived taking flight for the continent as desertion or simply a task too onerous to undertake.

Focusing on internal exile, this chapter argues that Katherine Philips and Margaret Cavendish positively reconfigure their marginality and the negative aspects of the royalist experience of enforced displacement through a poetics of order as they sought to reclaim sites of Englishness for their royalist readers. As Jerome de Groot notes, not only did royalists attempt to control the trauma through writing but also felt compelled to denounce what he terms 'the locus of mistake'.[13] We will see that through topographical poetry and evoking specific royalist topoi, Philips and Cavendish could simultaneously condemn London as the hub of parliamentarian vice yet re-anchor royalism to the very places from which they had been ejected. Meanwhile, they could also figure retreat as a virtuous move and position the countryside as an alternative *locus* of royalist power. While this chapter examines these women's appropriations of the trope of retreat as a rhetorical stance from which they could comment on events, strengthen cultural resistance and devise literary spaces of peace and order

[9] Ibid., 111.

[10] Ibid., 111.

[11] Major, *Writings*, 134.

[12] Corio, Ann, 'Herrick's Hesperides: The Name and the Frame'. *ELH* Vol. 52.2 (Summer 1985): 311–336, 311.

[13] de Groot, Jerome, 'Chorographia: Newcastle and Royalist Identity in the Late 1640s'. *Seventeenth Century* 18.1 (April, 2003): 61–75, 68.

to counter contemporary socio-political chaos, it also positions them alongside their male contemporaries such as Richard Lovelace, Robert Herrick or John Denham who were also using literature to resist, as well as transcend, parliamentarian oppression. Moreover, as Philips and Cavendish appropriated the myth of the Halcyon to return readers to the pre-lapsarian days of Charles I's personal rule, we will see that they re-inscribed and reenergized notions of royalism, as well as reasserted the image of the nation itself. Further, by illustrating the ways in which each writer returned or retreated to the period before the civil war through invocation of the halcyon myth, this chapter highlights commonalities across these women's works which support Safran's theory that the subjects of diaspora retain a collective memory, vision or myth about their original homeland, including its location, history and achievements.[14] For those of the prototypical diaspora, outlined by Cohen above, the impulse to connect with each other and maintain a sense of belonging via collective memory is strong. Hence, this chapter considers the ways in which each of these womens' experiences of exile bids them to look back and re-suture the rupture of disconnection with the true homeland and how this long perspective shapes their literary output during these unsettled years.

Reassertion of order during the war years and shortly after the trauma of regicide was paramount for both of these women writers who each experienced unique and disruptive aspects of the royalist diaspora. Philips lived in Cardigan in Wales since her marriage in 1648,[15] yet often travelled to London to visit friends while her husband dealt with parliamentary affairs.[16] Cavendish experienced external exile on the Continent for most of the interregnum, except between the years 1651 and 1653 when she spent eighteen months in England petitioning for her husband's estates.[17] Disparate as they were, each of these women wrote and emerged as writers within a climate of uncertainty which was conditioned by displacement of royalists from the powerbase London, yet despite this imposed marginality both women positively re-configure the trope of retreat as they relocate

[14] Safran, *Diasporas*, 83–4.

[15] Philips lived in Wales since the marriage of her mother to Sir Richard Phillips of Picton Castle, Pembrokeshire in 1646. Once married, she went to live in the priory house in Cardigan, one of the finest houses in the area at this time. See, Souers, Philip Webster, *The Matchless Orinda* (Cambridge: Harvard University Press, 1931), 20–21. See below in this chapter for more biographical information.

[16] See Chap. 3 below for more biographical information on James Philips.

[17] For more biographical information on Cavendish, see Chap. 4 below.

royalist power and resist geo-political exile. In her retirement poetry, we will see Philips offers up a new homeland to royalist friends writing about the 'noise of Towns' contrasted with the value of retirement to the 'real State' of Wales.[18] Meanwhile, in cavalier fashion, Cavendish will be seen to insulate royalists altogether as she attempted to stop time in multiple enclosure poems such as "Of an Island", "Of a Garden", "Of an Oake in a Grove".

A homeland decimated by war and an enforced dispersal of their creed across expansive geo-political territories led these women to write topographical poetry through which they sought to both reclaim sites of England's war-torn nation and flag their allegiance to the Stuart cause. James Turner writes that topographical poetry was 'often used for specifically political purposes' during the period.[19] Thus, while specific *loci* in poetry could correspond to actual locations, such as the countryside and valleys of Wales or symbolic gardens and groves, they not only served as a conduit to a more ordered and coherent past but through these textual *loci* sites of Englishness are reappropriated in an act of political reorientation, as well as a re-articulation of belonging and preservation of royalist culture.[20] For instance, in "On the Welch Language", Philips portrays Wales as a *locus* imbued with qualities which could well serve a displaced royalist community and Cavendish sets out to recreate the vestiges of the lost court within the mystical grove in her poem "Of an Oake in a Grove". By utilizing components of topographical poetry, Philips and Cavendish could anchor royalism and all it stood for to the very land from which it had been metaphorically severed, thus effecting a textual reclamation and recuperation. Turner further writes that topographical poetry could go even further to insist 'on the irrelevance of the world' suppressing 'its painful contradictions by interrogating, transforming or inverting it'.[21] Indeed, it will be seen that poems such as Philips's "Retir'd Friendship to

[18] Philips, Katherine, "Invitation to the Country". NLW. MS. 775B.

[19] Turner, James, *The Politics of Landscape: Rural Scenery and Society in English Poetry 1630–1660* (London: Basil Blackwell, 1979), 1, 6.

[20] de Groot explores another strand of this endeavour to re-assert identity, allegiance and the re-gaining of England for royalists. He notes '*Chorographia* shows how loyalists might reassert the Royalist delineation of national spaces and thereby reaffirm the role of the King in constructing and structuring England', 61, 63.

[21] James Turner notes that rural poetry 'flourished in the crisis of 1630–1660'; that the theatre also 'introduces landscape scenery and creates a topographical genre during this period'. Long 'descriptions of imaginary landscape are introduced into fiction, either as similes or as settings for amorous retreat'; that 'rural and topographical imagery is central to the poetry of this period', 1–2.

Ardelia" and Cavendish's "Of an Island" offer symbolic *loci* within which Wales and the Island of Britain are re-inscribed and re-ordered into altogether more pleasant places where 'Peace did well/No noise of war, or sad Tale could it tell'.[22] Moreover, as if to completely shield the royalist consciousness from external trauma, we find that within Cavendish's "Of a Garden" 'winter nere comes'[23] and anything that is not harmonious within the scene developed in the poem is not just flawed but eschewed altogether.

While royalist writers drew on both topographical theories of poetry and landscape to reclaim their homeland, we will see they also looked to the Halcyon myth to further fortify their rhetorical position. Robert Wilcher writes that 'this nostalgia for the decade of rule without parliament had a cultural as well as political dimension'.[24] Moreover, given the tremulous political milieu of the 1640s 'such an idealization of the past was natural enough', particularly among the gentry class which enjoyed a 'period of prosperity' during the 1630s'.[25] In addition, Dolores Palomo points out that 'early in the period the halcyon myth is invoked to describe England's peace and prosperity in contrast to the wars raging on the continent'.[26] Later in the 1640s, the storm element of the myth pervades contemporary poetry with imagery of whirlwinds, floods, noise, shipwreck, fire and a world turned upside down drawn from the less positive side of the halcyon myth during the war years.[27] Rather than focus on the destructive qualities of the myth, I show how Philips and Cavendish draw on the myth of the halcyon to override and invalidate the trauma of the present and in doing so re-script the broken royalist narrative of rupture and displacement. Cavendish, for instance, repeatedly invokes imagery of edenic peacefulness and abundance to describe England as 'an Island rich by Natures grace', 'fertile, rich and faire'[28] and even a protective 'Mother'[29]

[22] Cavendish, Margaret "Of an Island", *Poems, and Fancies written by the Right Honourable, the Lady Margaret Newcastle* (1653).

[23] Cavendish, "Of a Garden", *Poems and Fancies.*

[24] Wilcher, *Writing of Royalism*, 7.

[25] Ibid., 8. Wilcher cites Wormald, Clarendon, 181.

[26] Palomo, Dolores, 'The Halcyon Moment of Stillness in Royalist Poetry.' *Huntington Library Quarterly* 44.3 (Summer, 1981): 205–221, 207.

[27] Examples include: Mildmay Fane's "How to Ride out a Storm"; Jasper Mayne's "The Amorous Warre"; Thomas Stanley's "Hammond"; Abraham Cowley's "Ode Upon his Majesties Restoration and Return."

[28] Cavendish, Margaret. "Of an Island".

[29] Ibid.

figure which prior to the wars had been 'the envy of Europe'.[30] In doing so, she reverts to the vision perpetuated in the masques of Inigo Jones, Carew, Jonson and Townsend which generated other means of vital cultural assertion and preservation during the period of Charles I's personal rule.

If the Halcyon myth was common to literature prior to and during the wars, so too was the concept of retreat. The narrative of retreat, writes James Loxley, is one of the most enduring tropes of English literary history,[31] and, given the experience of enforced dispersion for royalists of the 1640s and 1650s, it is hardly surprising that we find the literature of royalism saturated with ideas of withdrawal, retirement and contemplative patience.[32] Moreover, as traditional pastimes such as maypole dancing and the celebration of Anglican feast days or Laudian ritual forms were suppressed along with the monarchy itself, there emerged coping mechanisms that involved recasting old ceremonies in private forms and surrounding them in cryptic language.[33] Certainly, Stuart entertainments had long since pastoralized the court itself, however, during the civil war, this 'amiable sentiment for the country life' became 'a grim necessity' and as a result the defence of the old pastimes went underground.[34] Thus, royalist poets concerned with cultural survival depicted the 'public mirth' and 'liberty' of open spaces as being associated with anarchy and vulnerability, while 'orderly and ordering rituals are found rather in protective enclosures such as estates, gardens, mystical groves'.[35] I show here, how Philips's "A Country life" and enclosure poems by Cavendish such as "'Of a Garden" and "Of an Oake in a Grove" provide their readers with a conduit through which they could reassign the royalist experience of retreat and removal from court as instrumental for empowerment. For instance, Philips offers friendship itself and the bowers of Wales and Cavendish

[30] Anselment, 'Clarendon and the Caroline Myth of Peace,' *Journal of British Studies*. 23.2 (Spring, 1984): 37–54, p. 39.

[31] Loxley, *The Drawn Sword*, 202.

[32] During these decades royalists returned to ideas of stoicism as they endeavored to rationalize and cope with what they perceived as an interminable battle between good and evil. Re-invention and renewal of cultural ideals of stoicism provided a justificatory stance for actions such as withdrawal, whilst also offering a model of integrity which set royalists above their enemies. See: Allen, David, *Philosophy and Politics* (East Linton: Tuckwell, 2000), 11.

[33] Marcus, Leah, *The Politics of Mirth: Jonson,Herrick, Milton, Marvel and Defense of the Old Holiday Pastimes* (Chicago and London: University of Chicago Press, 1986), 213.

[34] Ibid., 214.

[35] Ibid., 214.

offers a garden 'Paradise'[36] as recuperative surrogate spaces in place of the disbanded court. These spaces of withdrawal within the literature of the interregnum that also came from such poets as Henry Vaughan, Richard Lovelace, and Abraham Cowley were invested with ideas and images of private withdrawal that found 'delight in a private world of inner peace and piety' often foregrounding the countryside 'where strength was drawn from God, family and friends'.[37] Thus the spaces of retreat within royalist literature became positive places in which reinforcement of old values, social ties and safe havens could be accessed amid the crisis of civil war.

The poetry discussed here not only draws on topographical conventions and utilizes both the narrative of the halcyon as well as the trope of retreat to re-assert order and relocate royalist power but is further inflected by characteristics common with literatures of diaspora and exile. Azade Seyhan notes that the literature of displacement or diaspora 'is always a re-presentation … a making present that which no longer is,' and diasporic writing inevitably 'articulates a real or imagined past as a community in all its symbolic transformations'.[38] Thus, as royalists were forced into a state of alterity, the home they each knew prior to the wars becomes a place only reachable through the art of writing. Through a combination of memory and imagination, writers could reconnect with their lost homeland or recreate new fantasy locales through which they might, as Seidel puts it, 'transform the figure of rupture back into a figure of connection'.[39] It is this memory of the homeland, and the exiles' imagination, which provides solace through conceptualized locales, characters and events that are irrevocably resonant of the homeland, patria or country of origin. Via memory, allegorical elsewheres and substitutes for home emerge and the 'memory of home becomes paramount in narratives where home itself is but a memory'.[40] Through their appropriations of the trope of retreat and the myth of the Halcyon, we will see that Philips and Cavendish provide rich examples of this nostalgic longing and imaginative re-scripting of a culture and a nation as they seek to reify England's 'Golden Age' once more. Thus, diaspora gives way to a literature which seeks to reconnect with the past and as Philips and Cavendish looked back to anchor them-

[36] Cavendish, "Of a Garden".

[37] Smith, *Constitutional Royalism*, 285. For example of poems, see Henry Vaughan, "The Retreate"; Richard Lovelace, "The Grasshopper"; Izaak Walton, "The Angler".

[38] Seyhan, 16.

[39] Seidel, *Exile and the Narrative Imagination*, x.

[40] Ibid., 11.

selves in the present, they created 'Englands of the mind', past Englands and a possible future Englands, which undeniably attest to Seidel's idea that 'even the most remote and distant projections, the imaginative "nowhere" of exilic writings, are versions of a "somewhere" already there'.[41]

## 'Spaces of Retir'd Integritie'[42]: Relocation of Home in the Poetry of Katherine Philips

Katherine Philips was hailed by members of the royalist literati as 'the English Sappho'.[43] In the preface to the Herringman edition of her works, Charles Cotterell wrote:

> she of all the female Poets of former Ages, being for her verses and her virtues both, the most highly to be valued; but she has called herself. ORINDA, a name that deserves to be added to the number of the muses, and to live with honor as long as they.[44]

To be sure, Cotterell was not the only fan of this young, talented poet. Edward Phillips said of her in his *Theatarum Poetarum* that she was 'the most applauded at this time, poetess of our Nation, either of present or former Ages'.[45] Sir Edward Dering, husband of childhood friend Mary Harvey, refers to his 'admiration for Philips as a constant theme'[46] in his letter book. For example, in a letter written to Philips on 3 January 1662, he writes of 'Orinda's pen, whose every line gives more lasting honour than Egyptian pyramids though they alone of all the wonders of the world,

[41] Ibid., 3.

[42] Philips, Katherine, "A Country-life" in *The Collected Works of Katherine Philips: The Matchless Orinda*. Vols 1–2, Patrick Thomas ed., (Brentford: Stump Cross, 1990), 162.

[43] In Corneille, Pierre, *Poems by the most deservedly admired Mrs. Katherine Philips, the Matchless Orinda; to which is added, Monsieur Corneille's Pompey and Horace, Tragedies; with several other translations out of French* (1678).

[44] Cotterell, Charles, The Preface, *Poems* (1678).

[45] Thomas et al., *The Collected Works of Katherine Philips*, Patrick Thomas, G. Greer and R. Little eds. 3 vols. (Brentford: Stump Cross Books, 1990–3, Vol. I), 24.

[46] Hageman, Elizabeth, 'The Matchless Orinda: Katherine Philips,' in *Women Writers of the Renaissance and Reformation*. Katharina M. Wilson, ed. (Athens & London: The University of Georgia Press, 1987), pp. 566–607, 571.

seem to despise the injuries of time'.[47] During her life, she also received praise from Henry Vaughan and an elegy after her death.[48] Thus, many 'of her closest connections were Londoners [and indeed] royalists'.[49]

As the wife of Colonel James Philips, an active parliamentarian in Wales,[50] Katherine Philips sympathized with the royalist cause. Born in London to Katherine Fowler, nee Oxenbridge, and James Fowler, a prosperous London cloth merchant,[51] her family had strong puritan and parliamentarian connections.[52] Philips nonetheless had childhood friends who were royalists: Mary Aubrey, daughter of Sir John Aubrey, leading Glamorgan Royalist[53] and Mary Harvey Dering, who played a significant role in Philips's expanding literary career. Mary served as a 'catalyst between Philips and the Royalist musicians and poets surrounding Lawes',[54] such as John Wilson, Francis Finch, John Berkenhead and Henry Vaughan. By 1651, she was an established member of royalist literary circles and in that year together with Francis Finch contributed to William Cartwright's posthumous volume of plays and poems, as did John Berkenhead and Henry Vaughan, the musician Henry Lawes and their

[47] Hageman cites from the Letter-book of Sir Edward Dering, Archives and Rare Books Department, University Libraries, University of Cincinnati. The quotations are from letters 4 and 37 in part I of the letter-book.

[48] Post, Jonathon. *English Lyric Poetry: The Seventeenth Century* (London: Routledge, 1999), 247.

[49] Hageman, 'The Matchless Orinda', 570.

[50] At sixteen Katherine was married to Philips. Robert Evans describes Philips as 'a fifty four-year old Welshman who loyally served the Commonwealth and Cromwell' and who 'often helped suppress royalist dissent.' Evans, Robert, C. 'Paradox and Poetry: Katherine Philips in the Interregnum' in *The English Civil Wars and the Literary Imagination*. Claude J Summers and Ted-Larry Pebworth eds. (Columbia and London: University of Missouri Press, 1999), 174/5.

[51] Hageman, '*The Matchless Orinda*', 566. Hageman also offers insightful information about Katherine's school years at Mrs. Salmon's Presbyterian school for girls near Hackney. See also Thomas, Patrick. *Writers of Wales* (University of Wales Press, 1988). Another classic source for biographical information on Philips is Souers.

[52] As a young girl, Katherine grew up praying to God to take the Bishops from the Kingdom of England. Her mother remarried to Philip Skippon, a parliamentarian Major General, her uncle was Oliver St John, a peer of Cromwell's, one of the most powerful men during the commonwealth and against the King at every turn, and a first cousin of her husband was Col. Thomas Wogan who was a regicide. See Souers, 20, 29.

[53] Thomas, Patrick, *Writers of Wales*, 4.

[54] Limbert, Claudia, A., "The Unison of Well Tun'd Hearts': Katherine Philips's Friendships with Male Writers" *English Language Notes* 29 (1991): 25–37, 26.

mutual acquaintance Edward Dering.[55] It was Philips's poem which headed the publication described by scholars as a 'collection of commendatory verses prefacing the posthumous—and politically significant—edition' of the works of Cartwright.[56] Further, she had songs set to music by Henry Lawes who in 1655 in his *Second Book of Ayres and Dialogues* published work by Philips, Francis Finch and other members of the royalist circle. Additionally, one of the five songs by Berkenhead in the 1655 volume was addressed to Lucasia,[57] thus emphasizing the strong connections between Philips, her closest friend, Anne Lewis Owen (Lucasia) and the polemicist and royalist spy John Berkenhead. Thus through her work and her friends, Philips became part of a network of esteemed royalist writers who strove to maintain royalism and stay connected through cultural means.

Many scholars are quite willing to accept that Philips's work has a political dimension.[58] Susan Wiseman, for example, notes that Philips blended a 'fusion of loyalty and wit, rendering aesthetics indistinguishable from politics' which 'marked her poetry as Royalist and aligned her with others who longed to reinstate the monarchical golden age'.[59] Others, however, are not so convinced. James Turner, for example, consigns her to domesticity when he suggests that she is 'unconcerned' with politics as she writes from her 'secure' country dwelling in Wales. Moreover, while he admits she 'embodies an opinion of a country life', he insists she is apolitical as he reads her poetry in the context of her suppression as a married woman, arguing that she 'herself' is 'a sequestration' by her husband.[60] Nearly a

[55] *Comedies, tragi-comedies, with other poems, by Mr William Cartwright, late student of Christ-Church in Oxford, and proctor of the university. The ayres and songs set by Mr Henry Lawes, servant to His late Majesty in his publick and private musick.* (Humphrey Moseley at the Prince's Arms, St. Pauls, 1651.)

[56] Sant, Patricia, M. and James N. Brown, 'Two Unpublished poems by Katherine Philips' *English Literary Renaissance*, 24.1 (1994): 211–28, 214. Sant and Brown refer here to Philips's poem 'To the memory of the most Ingenious and Vertuous Gentleman Mr. Wil: Cartwright, my much loved friend' in *Comedies, Tragi-Comedies, With Other Poems, by Mr. William Cartwright.* 1651.

[57] Hageman, 'The Matchless Orinda', 576.

[58] For example, see Chalmers (above); Wilcher (above); Barash, Carol. *English Women's Poetry 1649–1714*; Smith, Nigel. 'The Rod and the Canon' *Women's Writing* 14.2 (2007): 232–245; Evans, C. E. 'Paradox in Poetry and Politics'.

[59] Wiseman, Susan, 'Woman's Poetry' in *Cambridge Companion to Writing the English Revolution.* N.H.Keeble ed. (Cambridge, Cambridge University Press, 2001), 127–147, 130.

[60] Turner insists that her poetry is designed to express 'freedom of spirit' as a means 'to transcend the material base of her existence', thus he links Philips's work to that of her per-

decade later, Ellen Moody wrote that 'Mrs. Philips was apolitical'.[61] She further asserts that 'Orinda was sincere … in her dislike of any kind of public market place or politics'.[62] While Moody may be aiming to be sensitive to what could be construed as the ambiguous nature of Philips's poetry, this observation overlooks Philips's contribution to numerous published royalist volumes and her plentiful royalist connections and dedications within her own works.

This section, therefore, joins Carol Barash in her endeavour to recuperate Philips's work which has been lost in reductive readings that assume her poetry is little more than 'innocent little verses' about her life in Wales.[63] This section places Philips alongside cavalier writers and positions her as a writer who sought to uphold her loyalty to her royalist friends despite her domestic and geographical predicaments. Further, it proposes that her experience of marginalization, prompted by Philips's residency in Cardigan, west Wales, unlocks for her a very specific symbolic *locus*, or paradise regained during the interregnum years. Linking Philips to her royalist counterparts by examining her poetry of retreat within the distinct context of royalist displacement, this section argues that this relatively small group of poems, which evoke a longing for a lost golden age associated with Charles I's personal rule, have much to tell us about Philips's complicated relationship with royalism and how she, as a royalist sympathizer, established for herself and her royalist friends a means by which they could resist enforced dispersion and marginalization. Thus, the section examines the regaining of order through emphasis on place and retirement to that symbolic place, while arguing that these poems of retirement stand as a defiant riposte to what Philips saw as a violently 'scorching Age'.[64]

To re-establish order for her community of royalist friends in England during the interregnum and after the act for banishment, Philips revives and manipulates meta-narratives of English history. By combining both the meta-narratives of the ancient Britons with the Caroline myth of peace, Philips transforms the difficult present into a space of order and provides

sonal predicament and overlooks her loyalty to royalism and the potentially rich political readings of her work. pp. 3, 4.

[61] Moody, Ellen. 'Orinda, Rosania, Lucasia et Aliae: Towards a New Edition of the Works of Katherine Philips' *Philological Quarterly* 66 (1987): 325–354, 329.

[62] Ibid., 334.

[63] Barash, *English Women's Poetry 1649–1714*, 56.

[64] Philips, "A Retir'd Friendship. To Ardelia, 23rd Aug 1651". NLW. MS. 775B.

royalist friends with a substitute for the homeland they have been dislocated from. Through invocation of the past and meta-memory of that past, she suggests Wales as an alternative seat of nobility and thus presents for her readers a site of stability within the disorientating present. This is seen most vividly in her poem entitled "On the Welch Language" which revives Wales's mythological power and offers what was the last royalist stronghold as a refuge for royalist friends. Further, as Philips appropriates Wales as a substitute *locus* for the halcyon days she evokes conventional literary topoi of those happier times of Charles I's personal rule to support this. The poem presents Wales as a site of comfort from the experience of political defeat; it is the locale by which Philips may transcend the disruptions of war to re-imagine days of peace, prosperity and cultural richness and provide for her friends a *locus* by which she can 'transform the figure of rupture back into the figure of reconnection'.[65] Evoking great civilizations past, Philips draws parallels between 'the Roman and the Grecian State' observing that similarly 'the British fell, the spoil of Time and Fate'.[66] As Philips attempts to unearth this common history of the Britons, she first looks to a time preceding the emergence of the Welsh language to restore her readers to a past in which all Britons were unified by their native tongue. The Welsh language emerged during the fifth and sixth century after the withdrawal of the Romans. However, its origins lie with the branch of Brythonic languages which forms one of the two branches of the insular Celtic language family. The insular Celtic language known as British was spoken by all ancient Britons from the Iron Age 1200 BC to 400 AD. By foregrounding the 'British language' in this poem as the language spoken by all Britons, Philips dissolves linguistic boundaries which inhibit and alienate those who are displaced or dislocated, including herself, and she succeeds in valorizing the ancient origins of the British language at a time when identity hung in the balance.

We are told that British was the language of the 'sacred Bards of old', the language through which 'their thoughts did unfold'. Indeed, through this great language, the bards are identified as having 'civilz'd and taught the listening Swains'. Further, it is stated that the British language was the tongue of the nobility in ancient times as the poetic voice asserts 'This

[65] Seidel, x.

[66] Philips, "On the Welch Language". NLW. MS. 776B.

Merlin spoke',[67] 'This spoke King Arthur' too 'who, if Fame be true/ could have compell'd Mankind to speak it too'. It is further suggested that 'In this once Boudicca valour taught'. Thus, as the legendary Queen Boudica of the Britons instructed her warriors in the British language, we are told she 'spoke more nobly' than the 'soldiers fought' thus notions of great civilization and learning are revealed to be preferred over that of warfare and bloodshed. Moving backwards through the annals of ancient British history, we are told 'This spoke Caractacus' when he was facing death as a military prisoner of the Romans and the power of the language was such that it compelled the Roman emperor Claudius to release him, since 'He it so decently and nobly wore'. As Philips evokes the idea of language as something to be worn, like clothes, or colours which may be the mark of one's allegiance, she thus insists on language as an integral part of the matrix of identity. For those displaced, language is a referent of one's identity and through the experience of displacement, it is the one element which may constantly remind one of one's foreignness.[68] However, within this poem Philips inverts this seemingly disempowering aspect of displacement to recuperate England's past glory. Hence, despite contemporary disruptions and the disorientating event of the regicide, indeed, despite 'the Language hath the beauty lost' it is argued that 'she has still some great Remains to boast'. Moreover, by establishing the 'British language' as the tongue of the original Britons, and linking the British language to great ancient personae, Philips revives the noble identity and ancient narratives of the Britons, thus providing royalists with an alternative angle with which to reconcile themselves with their reality.

Having exploited the meta-narratives of mythological and ancient empowerment to re-orientate her royalist friends, Philips then dips into this vast well of royalist cultural history as she focuses on aspects of the Caroline myth to provide her royalist friends with recognizable referents, further enhancing the notion of her literature as sites of order and familiarity amid the chaos of the interregnum years.[69] Through utilizing aspects of the Caroline myth of peace, Philips's work resonates with royalisms and her return to pastoral havens and the emphasis on nature is a signature of the time. Poems such as "A Country Life", "Invitation to the Country" and "A retir'd Friendship, to Ardelia" valorize the theme of retirement

[67] Philips, "On the Welch Language".

[68] D'Addario, 5.

[69] The Caroline myth of peace referred to an imaginative return to an era of innocence and peace manifest in the bower of bliss or Eden.

which would have appealed greatly to royalists who saw no other option than to take flight to the country as the trauma of civil war and the horror of regicide proved distressing and disorientating. Drawing on cultural trends and literary topoi also deployed by such royalist writers as Richard Lovelace in "Aramantha", for example, Philips invites her friends to 'this bower',[70] a symbolic edenic place within the broader geo-site of Wales and in doing so turns to the convention of the *locus amoenus*. This convention draws on the imagery of magical gardens, island paradises and zones of pastoral ease which all come from within the renaissance epic landscape and beckoned the hero to rest from toil.[71] As Anthony Welsh has written, demoralized cavaliers looked to fictions to escape to Arcadia: an elegiac golden world far from the disappointments of war.[72] Through her retirement poems, Philips suggests Wales is a pastoral haven of repose and contemplation set against the turmoil of the city, that 'boisterous World beyond'.[73] In this manner, Philips's work reflects implicit royalisms through the deployment of Wales not only as a site of repose but also as a metonym for the old order. It is this sense of place in Wales which Philips foregrounds as her *locus amoenus*, and it is through the development of this symbolic *locus* that she endeavours to reconnect with, or re-establish, a type or order reminiscent of a pre-lapsarian time specifically that of Charles I's personal rule.

In her aim to present the countryside of Wales as a place of pastoral retreat, Philips's stacked quatrains in a Country-Life manifest a positively edenic space which can be re-instated as a *locus* of royalist power in contrast to dishonour and turmoil which reign in the city:

How Sacred and how Innocent
A Country-life appears,
How free from Tumult and Discontent,
From Flattery or Fears![74]

The language of the first couplet sets up the image of a country life not only as uncomplicated, but as something sacrosanct and devoid of the

[70] Philips, Katherine. "A retir'd Friendship. To Ardelia, 23d Aug, 1651". NLW. MS. 775B.

[71] Welsh, Anthony, "Epic Romance: Royalist Retreat and the English Civil War," *Modern Philology* (Feb 2008) 105.3: 570–602, 572.

[72] Ibid., 571.

[73] Philips, "A Retir'd Friendship".

[74] Philips, "A Country life". NLW. MS. 776B.

anarchy and disorder evoked in the second couplet. Through the poetic structure of statement and counter-statement, the poetic vision of the Welsh countryside as a *locus amoenus* is then built upon to evoke ideas and imagery associated with the golden age of Charles I's personal rule prior to the outbreak of the civil wars. Philips then draws on this nostalgic longing to reinforce her argument:

That Golden Age did entertain
No Passion but of Love;
The thoughts of Ruling and of Gain
Did ne'er their Fancies move....[75]

Thus, the 'Golden Age' is presented as a time of order, peace and 'Love', not to be overrun by passions driven by desire for power and empty ambition. It was an era of temperance not swayed by the fickle or the greedy. Further, the poem offers the reader specific *loci* of peace and order into which one may retire. 'Solitude' itself is presented as a 'space' into which one can retreat; 'Silence' and 'Innocence' are also interior or psychological arenas of peaceful quiet; 'A Cottage' and a 'Hermitage are offered as material abodes which instil a sense of secluded serenity and reflection.[76] Drawing on both positive and negative aspects of the halcyon myth, these spaces of retreat and order are juxtaposed with spaces and imagery reminiscent of Hades itself, a 'World' of 'Fire and Sword', a 'stormy World', the sites of 'War and Strife'. Even topographical sites of significance in London are now left to the Parliamentarians as royalists are urged to turn away from such distemper in their city:

When the inviting Spring appears,
To *Hide-Park* let them go,
And hasting thence be full of fears
To lose *Spring-Garden* shew.
Let others (nobler) seek to gain
In Knowledge happy Fate,
And others busie them in vain
To study ways of State.[77]

[75] Ibid., "A Country life".

[76] Philips chimes with Lovelace here—in the final stanza of "To Althea, From Prison", the innocent mind itself is presented as a hermitage, line 28/9.

[77] Ibid., "A Country life".

Hence, driven by the desperation for order and peace, and the desire to be free of the 'Vice' and Vanity'[78] which persists in the city, the speaker implores who 'In such a Scorching Age as this ... would not ever seek a shade'.[79] Through form, language and imagery, Philips renders a scenario in which the malignancy of London is juxtaposed with the calm of the country. Moreover, through he invocation of topographical sites within London, Philips denounces the 'locus of mistake' and urges her friends to 'Come' to the protective 'Bower' or *locus ameonus* that is Wales.

As Philips presents Wales as metonymic of the true homeland, or indeed of England itself for royalists, she emphasizes the importance for both herself and her royalist friends of withdrawal to counteract the experience of politicized marginalization. As Earl Miner has noted, 'the most distinctive feature of the cavalier response to the times was retreat'.[80] Thus, turning once again to this topical theme among many cavalier poets, Philips also valorizes the theme of retirement, recasting politicized royalist retreat as logical principled action. Moreover, linking her poems with the politicized royalist retreat, Philips intimates that there is not just consolation but also a virtue to be found in retreat. Reading these poems in sequence allows for a unique appreciation of not only Philips's complicated political position but of her moral enterprise as well.

Within "A Country-life", Philips sets up her *locus* of retreat, offers a definitive moral stance and completes this movement to within, providing her readers with a textual tool for defiant resolution and autonomous reflection. During this time of great uncertainty, 'not only self-sufficiency but sanity in a mad world' was 'required' and turning in on oneself and away from the world in order to be free was preferred by many a cavalier poet.[81] Within this poem, Philips strongly encourages this movement and offers not just virtue and moral elevation as a reward for acting thus but also detachment from the negative aspects of ideological influence. Emphasizing the simplicity to be found in the country, the act of being 'content'[82] in simple abodes such as a 'cottage' or a 'hermitage', mentioned above, Philips asserts it is 'from hence our Peace doth flow'. Using

78 Philips, "Invitation to the Country". NLW. MS. 775B (the pages which contain this poem begin from the reverse of the manuscript).

79 Philips, "A Retir'd Friendship".

80 Miner, *The Cavalier Mode*, 79.

81 Ibid., 91–92.

82 Philips, "A Country-life".

the first-person pronoun in this poem, Philips's own voice may be clearly heard advocating the country as a less oppressive place than the city:

I have a better Fate than King's,
Because I think it so.
When all the stormy World doth roar
I cannot fear to tumble lower
Who never could be high.
Secure in these unenvi'd walls
I think not on the State,
And pity no mans case that falls
From Ambitions height.

Here, she is 'secure,' here she has freedom of thought, is autonomous and lives in an independent state. Reverting to the humility *topos*, she asserts that those who covet power and ambition are likely to fall, however, here in her 'unenvie'd walls' she is unreliant on the state and so articulates an air of defiance and self-sufficiency effecting an inversion of her cultural and political peripheral position. Thus, through this disassociation with 'the locus of mistake', Philips highlights the advantages of her peripheral vantage point iterating that this space has allowed her mind to be free. Distancing herself from the centre of action, she states that 'while others revel it in State', 'Here' she'll 'contented fit'. Indeed, it would seem that she believes that anyone caught up in politics, consumed by the 'Exchange' 'will never know a noble Flame' and that all have been reduced to 'Sport', a point scoring exercise or sort of one-upmanship, which is ultimately an empty endeavour. Once again, resorting to *pro et contra* statements in these couplets, she commands the moral high ground when she avows—'While Vanity plays all their Game, / Let Peace and Honour mine'. Another distancing device emerges at the close of the poem as Philips outlines her own determination to retreat both physically and psychologically from what she perceives to be a vainglorious maelstrom:

But I, resolved from within,
Confirmed from without,
In Privacy intend to spin
My future Minutes out.
And from this hermitage of mine
I banish all wild toys,
And nothing that is not Divine.

Shall dare to tempt my Joys
There are below but two things good,
Friendship and Honesty,…

In this retir'd and humble seat,
Free from War and Strife,
I am not forc'd to make retreat,
But chuse to spend my life.

Here, Philips is resolute, and the recent events in London have also 'Confirmed from without' that there is no value to be found in the city anymore. Like Henry Vaughan, whose poem "The Retreate" also completes that movement to within and within which we find 'the cavalier mode is displaced by the metaphysical',[83] here Philips turns inwards and chooses 'Privacy' as the *locus* within which she imagines her 'future Minutes' spinning 'out'. Joining her cavalier counterparts once more, Philips's treatment of time as a 'suggestion of death'[84] resonates through the first four lines, of this section above, within which both acquisition *and* loss of the good life exist in momentary harmony.[85] However, this journey to solitude and eventual death is complicated by these 'two things good'—'Friendship and Honesty'. "A Country-life" not only highlights the virtue to be found in retirement, but also points to the creation of a metaphysical commune, through which royalists may undertake a complete rejection of events and recede into a pre-lapsarian world, wherein one can think autonomously, free from ideologies, and socio-political strife. The multiple points of removal within the poem, along with the structure of the couplets and quatrains, not only set up recurrent images of chaos versus peace and honour versus vanity but also reveal the tension generated by dislocation and a fractured sense of belonging. Hence, Philips constantly weighs one against the other, always negotiating the dichotomy of here versus there as she articulates a desire for order.

From this marginal place of solace, Philips looks back to consider the city and her friends who may remain there as she offers a temporary vantage point from which to contemplate recent events. This consideration and her solution are evident in the very title of "Invitation to the Country", which draws on traditional conventions of the pastoral poem, however, its

[83] Miner, *The Cavalier Mode*, 180.

[84] Ibid., 104.

[85] See Miner for discussion on the cavalier treatment of time in poetry, particularly 104/5.

main concern is with the latest developments in the metropole, London. Shifting between personal caution and political concern, the poem urges royalist friends to quit the city and find virtue in retirement as it also offers short-term virtual retreat to contemplate recent political upheaval. The opening of this poem sees a personal plea by Philips who prophetically cautions her royalist friend Mary Aubrey,—her 'dear Rosania'—that her royalism 'will become thy Penance too' and urges her to be wary of the trappings and vices of city life at this time.[86] Indeed, Philips not only denounces the 'locus of mistake' here, but warns Rosania that 'Titles, Honours, and the World's address/ Are things too cheap to make up Happiness'. She explicitly iterates that virtue and honour are not to be found in 'Towns' and that they are mere expressions of the current 'giddy race', those town-based parliamentarians. Further, advocating for the integrity to be found in retreat, the speaker reminds 'Rosania' that 'For a Retirement from the noise of Towns, / Is that which for some Kings have left their Crowns', clearly aligning the movement of retreat with a sense of majesty and rationalizing the King's choice to leave the city in the face of irreconcilable political differences.

However, the poem then shifts from the personal to the universal and embarks on a sociological musing, or ideological interrogation of recent events. Referring to the top-down monarchical system, Philips notes that in spite of their flaws those 'With Titles burthen'd and to greatness chained' understood the system and their role within it; despite that 'they alone enjoy'd what they possest' they 'relisht most and understood it best'. Philips here appears to suggest that for all its faults the monarchy knew how to maintain the status quo and even justifies such hegemony since we are told when necessary they enabled the 'empty swift dispatch of all below'. The reader might, at this point, consider that this is a clear indication of Philips's sense of allegiance to the Stuart cause, and a longing for past order, especially since she then writes that 'even that Tyrant (sense) doth these [Cromwell] destroy' and that this move has been 'more officious to [the nation's] Grief than Joy'. Thus, Philips acknowledges that the curtailment and defeat of the monarchy has brought more grief than relief yet curiously seems to intimate that both administrations are not beyond infallibility. Yet more ambivalence creeps in as we work our way through this survey of the post-royalist landscape. It is

[86] Philips, "Invitation to the Country". Mary Aubrey was married to John Montagu, a parliamentarian judge, in London in 1648, which may explain her mobility in and around the city.

noted that that as 'man' appears unconcern'd' and the king remains a slave to his 'own passions hurl'd', questions concerning the stability of future leadership in this new world emerge. Within the parameters of this ideologically dense poem, then, Philips betrays a poetic manifestation of her own complicated position as she is caught between two political poles. Philips appears to weigh monarchism against the alternative. On one hand, she suggests that 'Titles', 'Honours', and the volatility of the passions of Kings—and by extension monarchy and royalism—are empty assignments and queries their moral depth and stability, yet, on the other hand, indicates that parliamentarian tyrants are not the solution either. The speaker then advocates for contemplation and insists that the 'Country-life assists this study best / Where no distractions do the Soul arrest'. Insisting that readers should search for a higher spiritual force, the poem encourages a focus on 'Nature and its Author too' for answers to this current state of affairs. Shifting to the present tense, Philips suggests that from the aspect of the country a more objective stance may enable clarity of thought 'possest with Freedom and a real State', that from here they may look down on 'Vice and Vanity and Fate' and 'pity the folly which the World controuls' . Thus, as this poem represents a metaphoric or imaginative shift from the grievous epicentre, London, to peripheral Wales, it presents a complex weaving of socio-political context, personal concern and spatial oscillation between these two locations reflecting the very real psychic and physical experience for royalists during these years. As the reader navigates the language of opposition, themes of corruption in contrast to the virtuous also augment the speaker's moral perspective on these events and sociological measured thought replaces that of the passions of Kings; an entirely modern shift which seems to subtly query ideologies of power and contemplate the possibility of the emergence of a new world order.

Foregrounding the demise of monarchy coupled with a movement towards objective reflection is then complicated by "A Retir'd Friendship to Aredelia". The date of this poem—23 August 1651—positions it as a post-regicide poem. In response to the regicide, Philips here chooses not to deal with the tensions directly but rather constructs a more conceptual space into which she and her royalist friends may retreat. Speaking of cavalier poetry of the age, Miner observes that the 'movement to within marks their poetry',[87] and once again, we find Philips drawing on contemporary literary trends as she endeavours to come to terms with recent events. "A

[87] Miner, *The Cavalier Mode*, 63.

Retir'd Friendship", once more in the tradition of the pastoral poem, invites one to 'Come' to a place of pastoral peace.[88] Again, Philips utilizes the image of the *locus ameonus* in opposition to the 'outside' world as she 'denies proximity to turmoil'[89] and devises a poetic arena of order into which royalist friends may metaphorically retreat. '*Here* is no quarreling for Crowns', '*Here*'s no disguise or Treachery', '*Here* let us sit and bless our Stars'[90] [my emphasis] are lines which invite the reader away from the politically charged world. Then, the lines 'Why should we entertain a fear', 'We wear about us such a charm', remove one from the proximity of danger and figures friendship as a talisman with protective, or even supernatural, qualities. Moreover, the virtuous tone of this retirement poem, which can barely contemplate why anyone 'In such a Scorching Age… would not ever seek a shade' deploys dichotomous language to highlight the stark contrast between these two moral vantage points. Meanwhile, the form of the poem in the regulated stanzas dictates the pace and large gaps between stanzas in contrast to the block form of the previous poem create an air of measured calm and room for pause. This promotion of moral virtue to be found in retreat fits with the royalist propensity to seek shelter amongst the ideals of stoicism and the use of the pronoun 'we' sets it up as a work which seeks to address all royalist friends, and, as Robert Evans has described, Philips's diction is rooted in general ethics and moral psychology rather appealing to all.[91] Moreover, as a poem of enclosure, "A retir'd Friendship" appropriates the notion of friendship as a device or medium through which one may imagine a sort of commune. The poem metaphorically reaches its arms out towards and around those 'mingling souls'[92] to protect its members from 'having their own peace betrayed', while it overcomes the petty strife of war through offering a more sociologically based solution focused on union and integrity, free from ideological prescriptions or political policy.

For Philips, the royalist experience of enforced dispersal and diaspora due to the acts for banishment provided fertile territory for writing. While her work was circulated among royalist coterie members, who were scattered across North and South Wales, as well as in and around London, the

[88] Philips, "A retir'd Friendship". *NLW*, MS 775B.

[89] Prescott, Sarah, 'Katherine Philips and the Poetic Spaces of Welsh Retirement', *Philological Quarterly* 88.4 (Sept 2009): 345–364, 356.

[90] Philips, "A retir'd Friendship".

[91] Evans, 'Paradox in Poetry', 181.

[92] Philips, "A retir'd Friendship".

publication of some poems in both the Cartwright and Lawes volumes turned her writing into a balancing act, which left her in a precarious position as a royalist sympathizer married to a Parliamentarian Colonel. While not wishing to upset or shame her husband, she nevertheless wished to reach out to royalist friends and offer them comfort. Advocating retreat as the only way to absorb the horrors of their age, Philips skilfully drew on contemporary literary trends and evoked multiple aspects of the lost monarchy for royalist friends in a bid to provide them with recognizable referents of order undeniably resonant of their homeland. She evoked the halcyon days associated with Charles I's rule and offered Wales as the true homeland, for displaced royalists—a pastoral haven and a site of 'Felicity'.[93] Further, as Philips urged the action of retreat, she advanced a set of guidelines, a virtual map or a set of moral co-ordinates by which royalist friends may achieve integrity in retreat, a means by which they may negotiate the shifting socio-political terrain while seeing out the storm.[94] Moreover, the multi-directional nature of her work renders it as a medium through which she could redeem the fractured pieces of her war-torn nation. While reaching back to the past to anchor the present she simultaneously remained cautious about the future insisting that retirement to the country, and more specifically Wales, was the only option that may provide the space required to contemplate the magnitude of recent events. Philips, then, positioned the countryside, and by extension Wales, as not only a last bastion of nobility and civilization but of Englishness itself; it was a place in which the greatest elements of the nation could be recaptured

[93] Philips, "A Country-life".

[94] "On the Welch Language" appears in another manuscript—Cardiff City Library MS. 2 1073, derived from verses compiled between February and December 1651. "Invitation to the Country" comes from NLW MS. 775 (commonly called the Tutin manuscript and is considered to contain Philip's poetry composed during the interregnum) and is undated. "A Retir'd Friendship" is also from the Tutin MS. and is dated 1651 in the title, while "A Country Life" also appears in the Dering MS, *The University of Texas as Austin, Harry Ransom Humanties Research Centre, Misc*HRC 151PhilipsMS 14, 937.* Patrick Thomas has stated that it 'seems probable that Dering copied many poems from the poet's own MS during the latter months of her stay in Dublin' (Patrick Thomas, Texts, in *Poems*, Vol. I, 45). Thomas also suggests that this manuscript provides an important guide to the text of many poems that do not appear in the Tutin manuscript and dates the poem's composition to 1650. While it is very possible that all of these poems were composed within a year of one another, my reading is not based on their chronology, rather it is based on what appears to me to be a development of Philip's ideas and philosophies pertaining to country retreat as a means to ameliorate royalist trauma and disorientation.

imaginatively. As she revived ancient mythological Wales Philips not only blurred temporal and geographical boundaries to invoke the idea that Wales is the true seat of English power, but also assuaged the royalist ego transforming retreat from defeat into a positive action, and, as she did so, she effected an imaginary relocation and recuperation of home for royalist friends. Philips's poetry of retreat offered her royalist friends a space within which they could be unburdened by the ravages of the era, a space within which they could exchange—as she articulates it in "A Country life"—'War and Strife' for 'Friendship and Honesty'.[95] As 'individual citizens strove to come to terms with what was happening inside themselves as the familiar world turned upside down'[96] through a poetics of order, Philips offered metaphorical safe havens not only for her unmoored royalist friends but a place within which she too could re-suture the rupture in her own life and envision a society for 'mingling souls'[97] 'free from Tumult and Discontent'.[98]

## Retreat to the 'Well of Helicon'[99]: Enclosures of Order in the Poetry of Margaret Cavendish

Unlike Philips, who dwelt in Britain as a marginalized Stuart supporter during the interregnum, Margaret (née Lucas) Cavendish, connected to the court of Queen Henrietta Maria as a maid of honour, had been on the continent since 1644. However, between the years of 1651 and 1653, Cavendish journeyed to England with her husband's brother, Sir Charles Cavendish, to petition for her husband's estates. This visit to her homeland in the wake of the 1650 banishing act, mentioned above, would prove disappointing in two ways. First, the committee denied her petition, declaring that her husband was 'the greatest traitor to the state' and that as he had not been married before the war but only 'since he became a delinquent' they argued that at the 'time of marriage he had no estate'.[100]

[95] Philips, "A Country-life".

[96] Wilcher, *Writing of Royalism*, 6.

[97] Philips, "Invitation to the Country".

[98] Philips, "A Country-life".

[99] Cavendish Margaret, 'To the Reader', *Poems and Fancies, Written by the Right Honourable, the Lady Margaret Newcastle* (London: T.R. for J. Martin, and J. Allestrye, 1653).

[100] Cavendish, *The Life of William Cavendish, Duke of Newcastle: To which is added the True Relation of My Birth, Breeding and Life.* Charles Harding Firth ed. (New York: Scribner and Welford, 1886), 167.

Second to this, the news that her husband had been granted by his creditors 'all manner of provisions and necessaries for his further subsistence'[101] compounded Cavendish's sense of rejection and marginalization in her homeland. These sentiments emerge when she writes that her 'Lord was then in a much better condition amongst strangers, than we in our native country'[102] and, more damningly still, that her native peoples had 'hearts as hard' as her 'fortunes' and 'natures as cruel as' her 'miseries'.[103]

This sense of marginalization was further exacerbated by the radical change which had occurred in London since the regicide. For Cavendish, as for many royalists, 'the customs of England being changed as well as the laws'[104] rendered their sense of cultural validity redundant. Hence, though many influential royalist writers such as William Davenant, George Suckling, Abraham Cowley and Edmund Waller had 'crossed the channel',[105] many had chosen internal retreat, surrounding themselves with friends and allies, and, in 'a few private country homes ... the prewar court culture of art, music, drama, and literature' was 'kept alive'.[106] It was here, during this time that Cavendish went with her 'Lord's brother to hear music in one Mr. Lawes his house'.[107] Here she was immersed in a culture of male and female singers, musicians, poets and composers, and, with such support and inspiration, Cavendish began to write her first volume of poetry, *Poems and Fancies*. She went on to publish this volume while in England, and, as Hero Chalmers notes, it is this circle that 'appears to have played a significant role in Cavendish's bold decision to print her works at all'.[108] Thus, this visit to London proved to be a pivotal moment in Margaret's life, particularly that of her literary career. It was in her own homeland that she was first inspired to write, and, I argue here that it was her unique 'plurality of vision'[109], as both internal and external exile, which

[101] Cavendish, *The Life*, Firth ed., 298.
[102] Ibid., 298.
[103] Ibid., 296/7.
[104] Ibid., 298.
[105] Miner, 179.
[106] Whitaker, *Mad Madge*, 136.
[107] Cavendish, *True Relation*, 302. Cavendish is referring to Henry Lawes here.
[108] Chalmers, *RWW*, 17.
[109] Said, Edward, W., *Reflections on Exile and Other Essays* (London: Granta, 2012), Said posits that most 'people are principally aware of one culture, one setting, one home; exiles are aware of at least two', 150.

conditioned her production of heavily encoded poetry much of which has been undervalued as valid social and political commentary by many critics.

Modern criticism has mostly concentrated on Cavendish's dramatic oeuvre[110] and has tended towards gender performativity readings of the works arguing that Cavendish was a type of proto-feminist creating feminist utopias.[111] Generally, Cavendish is not viewed as a writer who engages directly with the political milieu of her day. For example, Susan Wiseman argues that she 'has little of Philips's sense of Royalist endeavor expressed in a shared vocabulary'[112] and Jonathon Post derisively describes her poetry as 'fanciful woodnotes' which may have 'absorbed and participated in the radical social upheaval of the civil war, although not its radical politics'.[113] As described by such scholars, Cavendish's poetry may not bear the outward characteristics of political activism, yet we will see that her enclosure poetry not only provides sites of ordered security into which royalists may retreat but that this poetry also engages with the political sphere through use of the trope of retreat as a counter exilic strategy which denies marginality and reorientates royalist power. Moreover, this section will show that Cavendish's poetry does indeed share a comparable set of tropes and metaphors not only common to Philips's work but that of the wider network of cavalier writers. As Alan Rudrum reminds us, we must remember to consider the text and its significance as a speech act in the

[110] Cavendish, *Playes and Orations of Divers Sorts* (1662) & *Plays Never Before Printed* (1668).

[111] For example, see Smith, Hilda, *Reason's Disciples: Seventeenth-Century English Feminists* (Urbana, Ill.: University of Illinois Press, 1982); Gallagher, Catherine, "Embracing the Absolute: The Politics of the Female Subject in Seventeenth-Century England", *Genders* I (Spring, 1998): 24–39; Bonin, Erin. L. "Margaret Cavendish's Dramatic Utopias and the Politics of Gender" *Studies in English Literature 1500–1900* 40.2 (2000): 339–254. http://www.luminarium.org/sevenlit/bonin.html; De Monte, R., 'Making a spectacle': Margaret Cavendish and the staging of the self, *A Princely Brave Woman: essays on Margaret Cavendish, Duchess of Newcastle*, Ed Stephen Clucas (Hampshire: Ashgate, 2003), 109; Kellet, Katherine. R. "Performance, Performativity, and Identity in Margaret Cavendish's The Convent of Pleasure", *Studies in English Literature* 48.2 (2008): 419–442; Mosher, Joyce Devlin, 'Female Spectacle as Liberation in Margaret Cavendish's Plays', *Early Modern Literary Studies* 11.1 (May, 2005) 7:1–28; Tomlinson, Sophie, "'My brain the stage': Margaret Cavendish and the fantasy of female performance", *Readings in Renaissance Women's Drama Criticism, History and Performance 1594–1998.* S.P. Cerasano & Marion Wynne-Davis eds. (London: Routledge, 1998), 272–292.

[112] Wiseman, Susan, 'Women's Poetry', 130.

[113] Post, *English Lyric Poetry*, 210, 241.

circumstances into which it was published.[114] Thus, the very fact that this volume was published not long after the regicide, rather than circulated in manuscript form, marks it not only as a work which may have been intended for the public sphere but as one which may have been intended to make a particular impact in Puritan England, while also generating the much-needed funds to ensure the Cavendishes survival in exile.[115]

Many scholars have debated the ambiguous and inconsistent nature of Cavendish's political philosophies in an attempt to understand her views more clearly.[116] For Hilda Smith, the uncertainty lies within the contradictory nature of her work, and she finds it thus impossible to draw any distinctions.[117] For Hero Chalmers, the concern is to show how Cavendish's 'cultural and historical positioning as a royalist shapes and catalyses her emergence as a highly visible author.'[118] However, she is careful to point out that it would be reductive to view this fortuitous positioning as a 'Trojan horse in which to conceal their [female authors] ambitions' and insists that this interpretation would 'belittle the strength of their political commitment'.[119] While Chalmers' study must be hailed as a watershed moment in the study of royalist women writers and their contribution to the political sphere, it should be noted that she too only covers Cavendish's drama, in the main.[120] More recently, Deborah Boyle has argued that it is

[114] Rudrum, Alan, 'Royalist Lyric' in *The Cambridge Companion to Writing of the English Revolution.* N.H Keeble ed. (Cambridge: Cambridge University Press, 2001), 183.

[115] The publishers of the 1653 edition were John Martyn and James Allestare, and the printer Thomas Roycroft (most famous for their publication of the polyglot Bible).

[116] See for example Smith, Hilda, 'A General War Amongst the Men ... But None Amongst the Women: Political Differences Between William and Margaret Cavendish' in *Politics and the Political Imagination in Later Stuart Britain* (Rochester: University of Rochester Press, 1997), 143–60; Suzuki, Mihoko, *Subordinate Subjects: Gender, the Political Imagination and Literary Form in England 1588–1688* (Aldershot, Hampshire: Ashgate, 2003); Holmesland, Oddvar, 'Margaret Cavendish's The Blazing World: Natural Art and the Body Politic', *Studies in Philology* 46(1999); Ankers, Neil, 'Paradigms and Politics: Hobbes and Margaret Cavendish Contrasted' in *A Princely Brave Woman: essays on Margaret Cavendish, Duchess of Newcastle.* Stephen Clucas ed. (Aldershot, Hampshire: Ashgate, 2003); Norbrook, David, 'Margaret Cavendish & Lucy Hutchinson: Identity, Ideology and Politics' *In-Between: Essays & Studies in Literary Criticism Vol. 9* [1 & 2] 2000: 179–203.

[117] Smith, 'A General War Amongst the Men', 151.

[118] Chalmers, *RWW*, 9.

[119] Ibid., 8.

[120] Chalmers briefly discusses *The Blazing World*, and mentions *Natures Pictures* as a textual reconstitution of scattered royalists, *RWW*, 131.

possible to distinguish and 'piece together a consistent core of political views' and insists that 'the textual evidence seems to show that for Cavendish the goal for human society is the promotion of peace and stability'.[121] However, there has still been too little sustained analysis of Cavendish's poetry and what it might tell us about her experience as a marginalized and uprooted royalist and her political views while she was visiting England during this pivotal year and a half.

Given Cavendish's personal experiences during the wars, her multiple exiles and her coming of age during a time which saw civil wars, regicide and the destruction of socio-political structures previously known to her, a desire for stability is hardly surprising.[122] Moreover, as a subject of diaspora and exile, her response through topographical poetry focused on Britain or scenes of Britishness seems yet another natural response. Driven to look back, idealise and re-imagine her homeland, much like Philips, Cavendish deploys tropes of retreat and the myth of the halcyon as a means to elide the broken royalist narrative and recreate a sense of linear history. This section reads "Of an Island", "The Ruin of an Island", "Of a Garden" and "Of an Oake in a Grove" as poetry of political engagement specifically conditioned by the context of radical political change and the consequent displacement of thousands of royalists. Sharing Ree's sentiments that Cavendish's work is politically charged and that she invented ways of circumventing censorship by agitating expected generic norms, this section argues that Cavendish devised heavily coded poetry, which once read directly within the context of the post-war environment, and royalist diaspora has much to tell us about her political sentiments. Importantly, it will be seen how Cavendish, like Philips, intersected with and contributed to a set of already established conventions within works such as John Denham's "Cooper's Hill", Robert Herrick's halcyonic *The Hesperides* (1648) and Richard Lovelace's *Lucasta* (1649) within which

[121] Boyle, Deborah, 'Fame, Virtue and Government: Margaret Cavendish on Ethic and Politics', *Journal of the History of Ideas* 67.2 (April 2006): 251–290, 254, 258.

[122] Margaret's family had experienced the tough end of destructive forces during the wars. In 1642 rioters ransacked their family home at St. John's, breaking windows, spoiling gardens and demolishing walls in their attempt to pull down the house. Her brother was shot at the order of General Fairfax after the siege at Colchester in 1648; her mother's tomb was broken into, and her mother's bones scattered about during the siege by Commonwealth Troops. Her multiples 'exiles' include her removal from home, from Oxford when Queen Henrietta Maria fled to the continent, and her distance from family while living abroad until after the restoration.

the vanished court and its culture was protected, at least in literary terms. This section will show that, like her contemporaries, Cavendish turned to these royalist literary trends, tropes and metaphors to rationalize and reconfigure her experiences of personal, cultural and political chaos into a poetics of order. Thus, we will see that these heavily encoded poems are a direct consequence of her experience of war, displacement and exile and, as with Philips, though her work may be cultural in origin it should be read as a politicized response.

In her letter to the reader, Margaret Cavendish writes 'I went to the Well of Heilcon, and by its Wells side I have sat and wrote this worke'.[123] From the outset, Cavendish aligns her work and by extension royalism with Humanist models of philosophy wherein classical antiquity offered invaluable sources of excellence. As David Norbrook has argued, 'royalists tended to see their enemies as base born philistines and saw the monarchy as a natural guardian of the arts'.[124] Thus through deploying the Greek myth of Helicon in the opening paratext of her book, Cavendish immediately establishes a link between the great classics and her work, and by extension not only elevates her own work but royalism as well. Moreover, her figurative retreat to sit by the well of Helicon to seek artistic inspiration reminds the reader that in order to cope with the stress of the times one had to withdraw inwards, whether it be literally or metaphorically. In this manner, the formal presentation of the volume presents to its readers a retreat into order and away from disorder.

Moving into the volume, Cavendish establishes order amid chaotic times by deploying imagery of peace and tranquility within the safety of enclosures evoked. In form as well as content, Cavendish appears to appropriate the already widely used trope of the halcyon moment of stillness,[125] as a device by which she may arrest the disintegration of her culture and reach back to happier times preceding displacement and political marginalization. Like Philips, she too provides for her readers compensatory arenas within which they can indulge in a re-representation of the past in an

[123] Cavendish, *Poems and Fancies, Written by the Right Honourable, the Lady Margaret Newcastle* (London: T.R. for J. Martin, and J. Allestrye, 1653). Helicon—a site of inspiration, a mountain in Greece regarded by the ancient Greeks as the abode of Apollo and the muses.

[124] Norbrook, David, *The Penguin Book of Renaissance Verse* (London: Penguin Books, 1992), 35.

[125] Palomo, 'The Halcyon Moment'.

effort to re-establish order and insist on cultural and political preservation. We will see that "Of an Island" looks back to the halcyon era and celebrates England as a blessed island, while "The Ruin of an Island" points to religious sedition as the reason for the wars and the fall of the monarchy. Meanwhile, we will also see that other enclosure poems such as "Of a Garden" and "Of an Oake in a Grove" exalt the court and attempt to recreate its previous order, while providing metaphoric enclosures of solace for embattled royalists just after the event of regicide in 1649.

"Of an Island" offers Cavendish's readers an idyllic island kingdom; a symbolic *locus* of pre-war halcyonic England into which royalist readers may imaginatively retreat from the disruptive experiences of displacement and its attendant disorientation. Dolores Palomo reminds us of the appropriateness of the halcyon myth being applied to an island kingdom noting 'the halcyon's nest is an island floating in the sea'.[126] "Of an Island" sees England as both a protected space and is itself a protector of its peoples. Nostalgic remembrance is evoked as the speaker reminds readers England 'was the sweetest place', an island surrounded by waves who 'do her homage, and her feet do Kisse'.[127] We are also told that in both past and present times these waves served as a natural barrier to the rest of the world for 'in a Ring they circle her about, /Strong as Wall, to keep her Foes still out'. Indeed, the waves are not the only protectors or celebrants of this Fair Isle since the 'Windes' and 'Cloudes' also 'serve as scouts'. Thus, enforced by the language of enclosure the island is presented as a safe, protected space and the image of the halcyon nest—the island of England—as a protective microcosm is firmly established.

To fortify this image of England as a protected isle and reach back to the happier times of Charles I's personal rule, the island is represented as an Arcadian idyll redolent of celebratory halcyonic overtones. The winds do not only act as scouts but they 'serve' to glorify and celebrate the kingdom 'blowing their trumpets loud on every side'. The birds further exalt this alternative England and 'with delight do sing'; the flowers too are 'fresh, and gay with mirth' as they dance [like virgins] 'upon the lap of Earth'; even the woods 'Thrive with joy, this Isle their Roots do feed' and they too 'Dance with the Windes, when they do sing, and blow'. Through anthropomorphism not only do the natural elements deify the island of England but they also create the sense of pageantry. These celebratory

[126] Ibid., 214.

[127] Cavendish, Margaret, "Of an Island", *Poems and Fancies* (1653).

aspects of the poem are not only reminiscent of pre-war court masques but also restore royalists to the memory of civic holidays and country pastimes now banned by parliament.[128]

To further enhance this image and the collective myth of the idyllic halcyon days, the island is also presented as a place endowed with great natural abundance, fecundity and order. It is a pastoral paradise 'where beasts that chew their cud, in Pleasure lye,' a bucolic idyl in which the grass 'grows to the belly' of the cows. James Turner notes that during the mid-seventeenth century, the 'traditional *locus amoenus* ... is transformed into an ideal landscape; the pleasure it yields develops at the same time from simple joy in grass, flowers and water to a complex structured emotion—pleasure of ownership, pleasure in the well-managed estate, pleasure of seeing everything in its proper place'.[129] Indeed, during the mid-century in particular, the 'proper use of landscape' could establish 'the poet's authority' and utilization of the 'panoramic view allows him/or her to appear clear without plainness, inspired without fantasy, pious, visionary but strong on facts'.[130] Certainly, Cavendish turns to this authoritative method of re-casting the island of England in this poem to stand as a place endowed with celebratory aspects yet also presents it as a place of order with each natural element contributing to the general pleasure and stability of the nation. Chiming with John Denham's topographical poem "Cooper's Hill" in which he writes the eye 'which swift as thought contracts the space',[131] the speaker in Cavendish's poem asserts the 'Landskips' here are ordered and pleasing to the eye by 'Prospects and Rills that run about', and 'hills o're tops of Dales, which level be'.[132] Thus, in Cavendish's carefully constructed landscape, the very act of surveying, looking or seeing brings with it its own sense of order and clarity. Additionally, even the seasons within this poem are tempered by Apollo as he 'never brings hot Reantes, to do her harm, nor lets her take a cold'.[133] To be sure, this personified Nature has endowed this island with a temperate climate in which the island's inhabitants enjoy 'soft Aire' which 'line

[128] For example, Jonson, Ben & Inigo Jones, *The Golden Age Restored* (1616); Jonson, *The Fortunate Isle and their Union* (1625); Jonson, *The King's Entertainment at Welbeck* (1633); Jonson, *Loves Welcome* (1634).

[129] Turner, *Politics of Landscape*, 39.

[130] Ibid., 44.

[131] Denham, John, "Cooper's Hill", *Poems and Translations* (1668), line 13.

[132] "Of an Island".

[133] Ibid.

them all within, / As furrs in Winter, in Summer Satten thin.' The island here is at once a protective enclosure, a *locus* of gaiety and harmony—a place within which there is 'no noise of war' and as such represents a symbolic riposte to puritan austerity during the uncertain years of the early interregnum. Within this poem, Cavendish alludes to the pre-war era of Charles I's personal rule and idealizes the now corrupted homeland. As she does so, she creates an England of the mind, and, much like Philips, she creates a metaphoric safe haven; a simultaneous 'idyll and a model, an escape and a solution' of what she hopes will become once more 'a form of reality—a version of the world'.[134] "Of an Island" becomes a virtual conduit through which she may create and revision the island of England as a site of order or at least give the allusion of order in an otherwise chaotic world.

In addition to the creation of an idyllic enclosure protected and celebrated by its natural assets, Cavendish furthers her stratagem to restore her readers to the ordered, peaceful era of the halcyon days by exploring the dichotomy between concord and discord. Having established this allegorical England as an Arcadian idyll in "Of an Island", Cavendish moves to set up recurrent notions of concord versus discord not only to remind her readers of the loss they have just endured but also to suggest possible causes for such devastation in the present and a means to avoid it in the future. The pastoral haven within "Of an Island" is thus juxtaposed with the chaos within the next poem, "The Ruin of an Island".

As we have seen, in the first of these dialogic poems, the island of England, in "Of an Island", is presented as a pastoral haven, an edenic site of temperance and order redolent with halcyonic overtones. However, the presence of temperance and order is juxtaposed and much complicated with the following poem in which Cavendish presents the island as an enclosure which, once out of favour with the gods, is a *locus* of ruin and destruction. Quite apart from the telling title—"The Ruin of an Island"—the opening lines clearly identify the religious sedition which has led to such a fall from 'Gods' grace:

> This Island liv'd in Peace full many a day,
> So long as She unto the Gods did pray.
> But she grew proud with Plenty, and with Ease,
> Ador'd her selfe, so did the Gods displease,

[134] Turner, *Politics of Landscape*, 48.

She flung her Altars downe, her owne set up,
And she alone would have divine Worship.
The Gods grew angry, and commanded Fate,
To alter, and to ruine quite the State.[135]

Though considered to be a largely secular writer, these lines go some way to elucidate Cavendish's contradictory religious outlook.[136] The poetic voice here makes it manifestly clear that religious debate, factions and dissenting religious thought and practice is responsible for England's fall from grace and the ruin of the island. However, while on one hand Cavendish appears to be conservative in condemning these religious rebels, on the other hand, she deviates from royalist orthodoxy altogether in her determination to speak of God in the plural which was, as David Norbrook has written, 'quite extraordinary' in the seventeenth century.[137] Moreover, gendering the island seems to be the only way Cavendish can account for such damning religious arrogance, conceit and rebelliousness. We are told that '*She* flung *her* Altars downe and *her* owne set up'[my emphasis], '*she* alone would have divine Worship' and as a result the island suffers with 'Vapour bad from all the Earth', 'Poyson', 'Venome' and 'Malice boyl'd with ranor, Spleen and Spight'.[138] Thus, through this feminization Cavendish condemns those who apostasize as weak, yet paradoxically aligns her own sex with the nation's state of disorder. Moreover,

[135] Cavendish, "The Ruin of an Island".

[136] Norbrook writes that although Cavendish was a 'practising Anglican who frequently asserted her unquestioning belief in that faith … her true religious feelings were open to question', 'Identity', 317. Norbrook provides excellent commentary on contractions inherent in Cavendish's religious, ideological and political opinions.

[137] Norbrook, 'Identity', 188.

[138] On 4 Jan 1645, the Elizabethan prayer book was replaced by a new directory of worship and on 13 Jan the Commons adopted a system of parochial Presbyterianism. Wilcher writes that Henry Ferne 'spelled out the nature of a Presbyterian system and the dangers it entailed for the religious and civil well-being of the Kingdom'; Edward Symmons, army chaplain, related hard and fast evidence that the prisoners he interviewed in Shrewsbury 'who were suffered to preach, did abuse and pervert Gods word to their own purposes'. Cavendish would have been present in Oxford during these unsettling times as maid to Queen Henrietta Maria. More evidence of what Cavendish terms as a relationship with God twisted out of shape was further echoed by Quarles in pamphlet responses—during 1644, parliamentarians were viewed by some as 'masterlesse journey men' ready 'for a halfe a Crown a week' to 'fly in the face of God's Viceregent [the King]'. Wilcher quotes Quarles. Those who have gone against the King have done so at a cheap price, debasing themselves. Wilcher, *The Writing of Royalism*, 230, 231, 232.

having already established the concord which the island enjoyed prior to the fall in the previous poem, Cavendish not only provides its antithesis here, but goes further to experiment with trends of landscape theory. Rather than set up an image of past and present in one poem, which would serve to make one image of a 'perpetual and beneficent status quo opposed to the perennial forces of evil',[139] Cavendish creatively utilizes two poems to achieve her 'model of truth'.[140] I want to suggest here that Cavendish's presentation of these dialogic poems derives from her experience of having being exiled abroad. Her position, as she wrote this particular volume, is informed by being both an external exile and an internal exile. Her perspective as an external exile 'gives rise to an awareness of simultaneous dimensions'[141] which internal exiles may not experience in the same way. Such 'contrapuntal'[142] positioning enables Cavendish to produce work that at once reaches back via the myth of the halcyon to re-suture the rupture caused by displacement but simultaneously renders an allegorical present which captures the shock of recent events.

In the second poem, the island and people are conflated, their idolatrous actions condemned and consequently both will suffer the wrath of the fates, commanded by the 'Gods'. Through these poems the happier imagery of times past is set in direct juxtaposition with times present, hence 'time is landscaped as well as space',[143] and Cavendish replaces the optical elements of a utopian, or pre-lapsarian, world in the previous poem with all the 'Malignity'[144] of a dystopian, post-lapsarian world in the second. In this present world humanity's relationship with God has been contorted; it has 'To Parents Children unnat'rally grow/ And former Friend-ship now turn'd cruell Foe'. Further, during this preposterous time of rebellion not only has the nations' relationship with religion been distorted, but there has occurred an unholy inversion of the status quo which undermines the sacred institution upon which society and the monarchy itself is built. The reader is reminded that 'Religious men were thought to be stark mad' and 'Extortions, Bribes thought to be most just', a declaration which at once stresses the preposterous nature of the times

[139] Turner, *Politics of Landscape*, 44.
[140] Ibid., 45.
[141] Said, 142.
[142] Ibid.
[143] Turner, *Politics of Landscape*, 44.
[144] "Ruin of an Island".

and brings its greedy passions to the fore.[145] Obliquely critiquing those who follow the parliamentarian regime, Cavendish didactically insists that:

> those who keep the Lawes of God on high,
> Shall live in Peace, in Craves shall quiet lye.
> And ever after like the Gods shall be,
> Injoy all pleasure, know no Misery.

Notably using 'God' in the singular here, Cavendish refers to 'Lawes' concerning divine right and in doing so infers that those who do not question the King and adhere to royalist orthodoxy—those who do not question the divine right of God's appointed on earth—'shall live in Peace ... Injoy all pleasure' and 'know no Misery'. Thus, she supports royalism and its founding principles concerning the King as religious and political head of the country. Reading these poems side by side reveals how Cavendish supplies not only a site of order and comfort by invoking all that is reminiscent of peace times and Charles I's personal rule, but, she also supplies the apocalyptic alternative. Moreover, in these dialogic poems Cavendish appropriates the topographical fabric of England to assert her political message thus intersecting with literary trends through which 'landscape may be termed panegyric topography'... 'the visible scene and the political message may support each other'.[146] Certainly, couched in contemptuous language which chimes with royalist polemical writers, Cavendish reveals strong political feeling and provides a stern warning to anyone who may be having doubts concerning necessary order to be found under monarchical rule. Moreover, as Cavendish asserts her political message, she also draws on pervasive strategies by writers of diaspora and exile. Through memory she idealizes the lost patria, she fantasizes about the future and she creates for herself and fellow royalists a reinvigorated, metaphorical space and community, at once imagined and real.

Having offered her readers an indelible image of England as a site of order, endowed with nature's blessings and then exploring the reasons for the loss of this Eden in the following poem, Cavendish then returns to

[145] Context for these exhortations comes again from 1644. Wilcher notes that 'ministers of religion are undergoing the worst persecution since 'a bloody cloud' hung over the church during the reign of Queen Mary', they have to bear the jibes of every 'hackney pamphleteer, every mercenary scribler' that sees profit in casting 'blots on their faces' and adding 'affliction to the afflicted', *The Writing of Royalism*, 224.

[146] Turner, *Politics of Landscape*, 48.

reassure fellow royalists with a more intimate natural enclosure. Unlike the tendency for gardens to be equated with activity within the country house poem, Cavendish devises an alternatively quiet garden to assert a sense of stability and provide order for beleaguered royalists. Drawing on contemporary literary trends concerning idealized retreats, the space of the garden offers shelter from 'the ravages of historical time' thus Cavendish continues to successfully craft 'safe places where one can enjoy the fruits of nature'[147] and draw strength from its eternal rhythms.

Within "Of a Garden" Cavendish opts to recreate much of the opulence and sensual overload one might find at court as it evokes a microcosm of edenic pleasure for the senses; a virtual pleasure paradise wherein all elements are synonymous with the wished for ordered state. Within the first few lines of the poem, the sight is calmed by the 'azure sky' 'alwaies bright and cleare' while 'no grosse thick vapours in the Clouds appeare'.[148] On one hand, Cavendish may be inferring a reference to the royal garter and the cult of Saint George, popular during the Caroline period suggestive of amelioration to be found in pre-war traditions directly connected to the royal family. However, on the other hand, one can also enjoy 'various colours by Nature intermixt, / Direct the eyes, as no one thing can fix', suggestive perhaps of the invigorating and kaleidoscopic effect of courtly entertainments. One's aural senses are also relieved in this garden paradise. Dispensing altogether with the disruptions of war 'No noyse is heard' in the garden and even one's sense of smell is comforted as 'Up through the Nose bruis'd Flowers fume the braine/As Honey-dew in balmy showers raine'. Much like Lovelace's "Aramantha" which looks to the behaviours of songbirds as other representations of Stuart manners, the poem also brims with the chorus of countless songbirds. The 'chirping Sparrow, and the singing Lark', the 'nightingale', the 'blackbird' and the 'pleasant Thrush … which sing in every bush' also appear to rebel against the parliamentarian ban on many country pastimes. Furthering the aural pleasure to be found in this harmonious garden, the poem is laden with classical figures who serve to play the sweet sounds of aires on the wind. Music by the Greek gods, Zephyrus, Apollo and Orpheus may be heard, yet each gracefully 'yeelds, and not contends with spight', thus once more providing appropriate models for the royalist sensibility, civility and order.

[147] Palomo, 'Halcyon Moment', 218.
[148] Cavendish, "Of a Garden".

Hence, both visually and aurally respite from the turmoil of the outside world is offered to Cavendish's readers.

Additionally, we find that the garden is infused with imagery which evokes what Dolores Palomo has termed 'the halcyon moment of stillness', a more than an 'apt metaphor expressing the mid-century desire for peace and its nostalgic recollection of lost tranquility'.[149] In this garden, time is indeed brought to a halt and Cavendish carefully crafts the image of eternal life triumphant over death and decay when she writes 'No weeds are here, nor wither'd leaves, and dry,/but ever green , and pleasant to the eye'.[150] Further, the cold of the cavalier winter cannot be felt in this refuge as there is:

> No Frost, to nip the tender buds in birth,
> Nor winter snow to fall on this sweet earth.
> For here the Spring is always in her prime,
> Because this place is underneath the Line:
> The Day, and Night, equall by turnes keep watch,
> That theevish time should nothing from them catch.

If Robert Herrick acknowledges yet supplants the presence of the cavalier winter in the title and the opening line of "Farewell Frost, Or Welcome the Spring" when he writes the snows are replaced by 'lusty spring', Cavendish's poem denies the existence of winter altogether. This poem instead offers protection from the inexorable march of time, the cold realities of the cavalier winter and instead offers the monarchical 'Line' as a shelter under which the shattered royalist community may weather the external storm. Moreover, sustained by 'the dew' which 'all over spreads' the royalists are a blessed and well-nourished tribe, kept going by the 'biblical manna ... Gods gift to sustain life when the usual means are taken away'.[151] Hence, the poem asserts royalist self-sufficiency, safety within this enclosure, and offers the garden as a type of edenic 'refuge against the ravages of time' and 'a way of capturing the [longed for] stilled moments' of the chaotic interregnum years.[152] Along with this halt of time and the compounding imagery of sensuous tranquility, the speaker also states 'No

[149] Palomo, 'Halcyon Moment', 206.
[150] Cavendish, "Of a Garden".
[151] Palomo, 'Halcyon Moment', 218.
[152] Ibid., 218.

fruites are there, but what the taste invites'.[153] Thus, as Cavendish offers a space of sensuous solace, she pushes further to offer royalist friends a guilt-free pre-lapsarian space in which no sin can occur. The removal of the device by which man first sinned acts as both a *tabula rasa* and as a form of damage control in this poem; the absence of temptation resets history as much as it prevents future falls from grace. This poem offers the ideal—there is only what one wants here, thus it stands as not only the ultimate ordered space but also the ultimate safe paradisical refuge.

The third natural enclosure Cavendish poetically invokes is a grove. "Of an Oake in a Grove" represents for Cavendish a zenith moment of cultural inscription and, once more, she turns to current literary trends as she endeavours to devise a space not only ordered but sacred, into which royalists might imaginatively retreat. As Leah Marcus states, 'one of the commonest, yet most enigmatic images of royalist poetry of the late civil war and immediate postwar period is the image of a grove'.[154] The image of a grove in the literature of the period was that of no ordinary grove—the grove would be 'charged with visionary intensity, its shape suggesting the architecture of a church or a palace and harbouring emblems of one or both of those institutions in their prewar form'.[155] Certainly, Cavendish's grove is no commonplace grove with the opening couplet intimating an ordered venerated space describing 'A Shady Grove' where 'trees grew in equall space' to form 'a consecrated space'.[156] Employing ecclesiastical language, the status of this space is stressed, and moving into the poem this image of a sanctified space is developed further as emphasis is placed on the ways in which the 'quivering light' breaks in:

> Much like to Glasse, or Christall Shiver'd thin:
> Those pieces small on a Green carpet strwe'd,
> So in this wood, the light all broken shew'd.

Here, the image of light streaming in through stained glass windows is inescapable, and this light only serves to enrich the groves blessed atmosphere, infusing it with a serene tranquility. However, it is Cavendish's deployment of the royal oak tradition which truly positions this poem as one which is not only a work extracted from a literary culture seeking to preserve and honour the monarchy but it places this poem firmly within

153 Cavendish, "Of a Garden".
154 Marcus, *Politics of Mirth*, 218.
155 Ibid., 218.
156 Cavendish, "Of an Oake in a Grove".

the realms of political commentary. As Cavendish contemplates the demise of the King, she cannot articulate it in real terms, so turns the metaphor of the 'tree'. This resonates with Jerome de Groot's assertion that writers turned to the deployment of a 'rhetorical trope that consciously uses the insubstantiality of language to defer the pain of the real', thus as Cavendish deploys this 'metaphor to occlude the real' and seeks 'refuge in the tropes of language',[157] she joins the royalist effort to come to terms with the loss of their King through writing. Using the grove as a hieroglyph of the court, or the church, each of which the King is head, and drawing on the tradition of the royal oak which 'is the arboreal species traditionally associated with the monarchy ... a symbol closely tied to King Charles I and his family',[158] Cavendish has indeed entered a space of veneration and bids her readers to follow.

Deploying the device of prosopopoeia, the King is written into this panegyric as 'an ancient Oake stood there, /Which heretofore did many Offerings beare'.[159] Speaking in the past tense the speaker lists the virile features of this kingly oak as having in 'his younger years' many 'Acornes he did beare', thus aligning the King with prosperity and fecundity, at once a generous benefactor and father figure. The King's virility is further underscored through the imagery of this oak's physique. This royal oak bears no 'Dandriffe, Mosse' but a 'crown' that 'was thick, and:

> bushy was his head,
> His stature tall, full breasted broad and big,
> His body round, and strait was every twig.

The past tense of the description, along with the shift in tone to one of pathos renders this poem as semi-elegiac. There is no formal indication of change, only the juxtaposition of this image of youth followed by an acceptance that 'youth, and beauty, which are 'shadows thin,/ Doe fade away, as if they ne're been'. The imagery at this point grows darker and what was once a glorious crown 'has now grown bald' with thievish 'time' and 'now weak and feeble he doth grow, /That very last blast is apt him down to throw'. Chiming here with the cavalier treatment of time as a metaphor for death, Cavendish's poem now presents the King, who stood

[157] de Groot, *Royalist Identities*, 171.

[158] Marcus, *Politics of Mirth*, 220.

[159] Cavendish, "Of an Oake in a Grove".

as a living symbol of what God's appointed can achieve on earth, once full of 'The liquid sap, which from the root did rise' is now 'all drunke up' and cannot avoid time which 'doth ruine' and 'brings all to decay'. Dichotomous imagery of life versus decay is utilized to gently urge her readers to accept the death of their King, yet once more, the use of nature to relay this message gives it an authority and an aramanthine promise. As Cavendish provides an ordered space of mourning for the dead King, its symbolic representation manifest in nature, she also appears to be asserting the faith that just as nature decays only to be renewed so too will royalism be renewed in time. In the depths of the forest, Cavendish provided a specifically sacred poetic mausoleum of order into which royalists may enter to remember or grieve for their slain King, thus she not only turns to contemporary trends and tropes that provided solace in the eternal cyclical character of nature, but, most importantly, she engages with the transmission of common cultural and religious heritage so important to subjects of diaspora.

As Cavendish drew on contemporary cultural and literary trends and tropes, she provided imaginative spaces of order for royalists during the disorientating early years of the interregnum. Within "Of an Island" she turned to the landscape of England as an 'instrument of thought, a useful analogue for personal and social values'[160] and reached back to the halcyon era to present an edenic space of harmony, temperance and celebration. "Of a Garden" offered an enclosed space of repose, which simply erased all trace of an outside world thus dispensing altogether with any notions of disruption. The garden also offered a space of serene stillness, a pocket in time, which is suspended from all trauma invoking the 'halcyon moments of stillness' which nourished 'the spirit in time of deprivation and despair'.[161] "Of an Oake in a Grove" also offered a space of order for royalists grieving for their slain King, while intimating the possibility of recovery from the loss and gesturing towards the future for royalists. Within these poems, Cavendish turned to nature and the significance of a series of natural spaces such as islands, gardens and groves, to rationalize and relay the royalist need for order and cope with the traumatic demise of the English court. As Leah Marcus notes, during the interregnum many poets tended to discover the 'cryptic vestiges of the lost court and its

[160] Turner, *Politics of Landscape*, 36.

[161] Palomo, 'Halcyon Moment', 218.

ritualism in the midst of the country landscape'.[162] Contributing to this literary trend, Cavendish invested her poems with images and emblems which resonate of pre-war courtly ideals and entertainments, as she reconstituted a world which existed prior to the upheaval of diaspora. Like her literary peers, such as Lovelace, Howell or Vaughan, she too was concerned with the immediate problem of cultural survival. As Lovelace repeatedly 'imbeds rituals and symbols of the vanished court in protected rural enclosures as a way of perpetuating vestiges of the culture that was lost'[163] Cavendish too sought not only to perpetuate old ideals but went further to write recuperative poetry which provided a sense of order for herself and fellow royalists. Within these loyal poetic repositories, Cavendish appeared to be set on presenting 'everything as natural harmonious and unified' as opposed to the other side which is simply accepted as 'violent, chaotic and therefore against nature'[164] as is rendered in "The Ruin of an Island". It would seem that, her aim as a royalist poet was focused on creating an 'imaginary kingdom of nature' which 'is manifestly more coherent than the real political world'.[165] In this manner, Cavendish joins her diasporic family as they revisioned their shared history through a common poetic language and in common forms.

With various acts and ordinances, which sought to control and marginalize the King's supporters, deterritorialization and alienation became a reality for Philips and Cavendish and their royalist cohort. Linked by their political allegiance and the experience of politicized marginalization within the homeland, both of these women writers intersected and engaged with contemporary poetic forms to maintain cultural survival of royalist values and traditions, through narratives of retreat and virtuous patience, constancy and withdrawal and private self-protection in the face of 'irreconcilable differences'.[166] As Philips reached back to the past to transform marginality into centrality, she turned to what Azade Seyhan terms the 'cultural memory bank' as 'an act of lending coherence and integrity to a

[162] Marcus, *Politics of Mirth*, 214.
[163] Ibid., 215.
[164] Turner, *Politics of Landscape*, 114.
[165] Ibid., 102.
[166] Allan, *Philosophy and Politics*, 13.

history interrupted, divided, or compromised by instances of loss',[167] and in doing so she re-scripted history *as* it was interrupted thus invalidating 'the locus of mistake'[168] and all those connected with it. Moreover, she displaced the *locus* of present disruptions entirely by replacing it with a new homeland, Wales. In addition, her work conveys themes usually found in literature associated with the experience of exile such as centralized spaces, for example the bower; friendship; solidarity; interiority—as well as actively sought seclusion.[169] As a survival strategy, Philips, as a royalist sympathizer, transformed her poetry into a political device that would gather her royalist friends up from their parliamentarian enemies and reconnect them with a lost world, while concurrently offering her own personal *locus amoenus*, Wales, as an impartial space for new beginnings. In the meantime, Cavendish too dispensed altogether with the distressing realities of daily life through the creation of enclosures which re-established order for disorientated royalists during the chaotic years of the interregnum and in some, she ironically effected a complete banishment of all the distressing elements of recent events. Similar to Philips's idealization of alternate spaces, each of Cavendish's poems discussed here are invested with themes of exile. For instance, the island makes present that which no longer is,[170] while it evokes harmony and union as well as the possibility of pastoral meditation. The garden offers a centralized space of retreat and invokes notions of actively sought seclusion, while, the grove endeavours to heal wounds in space and time by the exercise of memory concerning the dead King.

Most crucially, as each of these women re-scripted the variant landscapes within their poems, imagined locales—or non-places—turned into imaginatively reenergized places. The literature of diaspora, then, yields to a literature of 'elsewheres' or more plainly, place. Therefore, as Philips and Cavendish turned to topographical sites of Englishness, sites of rural withdrawal or sites of symbolic order extracted from the natural world, they

[167] Seyhan, *Writing Outside Nation*, 4.

[168] de Groot, 'Chorographia', 68.

[169] For example, Sidney's *Arcadia*—the nobles retreat to a zone of pastoral ease; Exiled from Florence in 1302, Dante refers to 'bowers' in the 'Paradise' section of *The Divine Comedy*, *Canto XXIII*; Ovid's *Ex Ponto* and *Tristia* sees the exiled Ovid seek solidarity via the act of writing; The Bible, an exilic text, contains a bower in the form of Eden; Plutarch's *Moralia* on exile infers a bower type locus as a green and shaded place, a source of calm.

[170] Seyhan, *Writing Outside Nation*, 16.

re-inscribed their world and provided landscapes from which to begin anew. Moreover, through the celebration of the Golden Age combined with such use of topographical poetry they flagged their allegiance to the Stuart cause and re-sutured royalism and royalists to the very places from which they were banished. From their respective marginal positions within the royalist diaspora, these writers projected their new desired reality away from the unsettling realities of quotidian life, and, within these newly inscribed places they succeeded in transforming metaphors of loss and defeat into metaphors of empowerment and political agency; a defiant 'making present that which no longer is',[171] at least in textual form.

## Works Cited

### Book and Poems

Cavendish, Margaret, 'A True Relation of My Birth, Breeding and Life' in *The Life of William Cavendish, Duke of Newcastle: To which is added the True Relation of My Birth, Breeding and Life.* Charles Harding Firth ed. (New York: Scribner and Welford, 1886).

______. *Orations of Divers Sorts* (1662).

______. *Plays Never Before Printed* (1668).

[Cartwright, William], *Comedies, tragi-comedies, with other poems, by Mr William Cartwright, late student of Christ-Church in Oxford, and proctor of the university. The ayres and songs set by Mr Henry Lawes, servant to His late Majesty in his publick and private musick.* Humphrey Moseley at the Prince's Arms, St. Pauls (1651).

[Philips, Katherine], *Poems by the most deservedly admired Mrs. Katherine Philips, the Matchless Orinda; to which is added, Monsieur Corneille's Pompey and Horace, Tragedies; with several other translations out of French* (1678).

### Secondary Sources

Allen, David, *Philosophy and Politics* (East Linton: Tuckwell, 2000).

Ankers, Neil, 'Paradigms and Politics: Hobbes and Margaret Cavendish Contrasted' in *A Princely Brave Woman: essays on Margaret Cavendish, Duchess of Newcastle.* Stephen Clucas, ed. (Aldershot, Hampshire: Ashgate, 2003).

Anselment, Raymond, 'Clarendon and the Caroline Myth of Peace', *Journal of British Studies* 23.2 (Spring, 1984): 37–54.

[171] Ibid.

Barash, Carol. *English Women's Poetry 1649–1714* (Oxford: Oxford University Press, 1996).

Bonin, Erin L. 'Margaret Cavendish's Dramatic Utopias and the Politics of Gender.' *Studies in English Literature 1500–1900* 40.2 (2000): 339–254 http://www.luminarium.org/sevenlit/bonin.html.

Boyle, Deborah, 'Fame, Virtue and Government: Margaret Cavendish on Ethic and Politics.' *Journal of the History of Ideas* 67.2 (April, 2006): 251–290.

Chalmers, Hero, *Royalist Women Writers* (Cambridge: Cambridge University Press, 2004).

Corio, Ann, 'Herrick's Hesperides: The Name and the Frame.' *ELH* Vol. 52.2 (Summer 1985): 311–336.

de Groot, J. 'Chorographia: Newcastle and Royalist Identity in the late 1640s.' *Seventeenth Century* 18.1 (April 2003): 61–75.

______. *Royalist Identities* (Hampshire & New York: Palgrave Macmillan, 2004).

D'Addario, Christopher, *Exile and Journey in Seventeenth Century Literature* (Cambridge: Cambridge University Press, 2007).

De Monte, Rebecca, "Making a spectacle': Margaret Cavendish and the staging of the self,' in *A Princely Brave Woman: Essays on Margaret Cavendish, Duchess of Newcastle*, Stephen Clucas, ed. (Hampshire: Ashgate, 2003).

Evans, Robert C. 'Paradox and Poetry: Katherine Philips in the Interregnum,' in *The English Civil Wars and the Literary Imagination*. Claude J. Summers and Ted-Larry Pebworth, eds. (Columbia and London: University of Missouri Press, 1999), p. 174–185.

Firth, C.H., and R.S. Rait (eds.), *Acts and Ordinances of the Interregnum*, 1642–1660, Collected and edited by C.H. Firth & R.S. Rait, for the statute law committee, 3 Vols. (Abingdon: Professional Books, 1978).

Loftis, John, *The Memoirs of Anne, Lady Halkett and Ann, Lady Fanshawe* (Oxford: Clarendon Press, 1979).

Gallagher, Catherine, 'Embracing the Absolute: The Politics of the Female Subject in Seventeenth-Century England.' *Genders* I (Spring, 1998): 24–39.

Hageman, Elizabeth, 'The Matchless Orinda: Katherine Philips' in *Women Writers of the Renaissance and Reformation*. Katharina M. Wilson ed. (Athens & London: The University of Georgia Press, 1987), p. 566–607.

Holmesland, Oddvar, 'Margaret Cavendish's The Blazing World: Natural Art and the Body Politic', *Studies in Philology* 46 (1999): 462.

Kellet, Katherine R, 'Performance, Performativity, and Identity in Margaret Cavendish's The Convent of Pleasure.' *Studies in English Literature* 48.2 (2008): 419–442.

Limbert, Claudia A. "The Unison of Well Tun'd Hearts': Katherine Philips's Friendships with Male Writers" *English Language Notes* 29 (1991): 25–37.

Loxley, James, *Royalism and Poetry in the English Civil Wars: The Drawn Sword* (Basingstoke: Macmillan, 1997).

James, Susan, *Margaret Cavendish: Political Writings* (Susan James, ed.). (Cambridge: Cambridge University Press, 2003).

Major, Philip, "Twixt Hope and Fear': John Berkenhead, Henry Lawes, and Banishment from London During the English Revolution". *The Review of English Studies, New Series* 59.239 (2007): 270–280.

______. *Writings of Exile in the English Revolution and Restoration* (Surrey and Burlington: Ashgate, 2013).

Marcus, Leah, *The Politics of Mirth: Jonson, Herrick, Milton, Marvel and Defense of the Old Holiday Pastimes* (Chicago and London: University of Chicago Press, 1986).

Miner, Earl, *The Cavalier Mode from Jonson to Cotton* (Princeton: Princeton University Press, 1971).

Moody, Ellen, 'Orinda, Rosania, Lucasia et Aliae: Towards a New Edition of the Works of Katherine Philips' *Philological Quarterly* 66 (1987): 325–354.

Mosher, Joyce Devlin, 'Female Spectacle as Liberation in Margaret Cavendish's Plays', *Early Modern Literary Studies* 11.1 (May, 2005) 7: 1–28.

Norbrook, David, *The Penguin Book of Renaissance Verse* (London: Penguin Books, 1992).

______. 'Margaret Cavendish and Lucy Hutchinson: Identity, Ideology and Politics.' *In-Between: Essays & Studies in Literary Criticism* Vol. 9 [1 & 2] 2000: 179–203.

Palomo, Dolores, 'The Halcyon Moment of Stillness in Royalist Poetry.' *Huntington Library Quarterly* 44.3 (Summer, 1981): 205–221.

Post, Jonathon, *English Lyric Poetry: The Seventeenth Century* (London: Routledge, 1999).

Rudrum, Alan, 'Royalist Lyric' in *The Cambridge Companion to Writing of the English Revolution*. N. H. Keeble, ed. (Cambridge: Cambridge University Press, 2001).

Safran, William, 'Diasporas in Modern Societies' in *Migration, Diaspora and Transnationalism*, Robin Cohen and Stephen Vertovec eds. (Cheltenham & Massachusetts: Edward Elgar Publishing Limited, 1999), p. 364–380.

Said, Edward W., *Reflections on Exile and Other Essays* (London: Granta, 2012).

Sant, Patricia M. and James N. Brown, 'Two Unpublished poems by Katherine Philips.' *English Literary Renaissance* 24.1 (1994): 211–28.

Seidel, Michael, *Exile and the Narrative Imagination* (New Haven & London: Yale University Press, 1986).

Seyhan, Azade, *Writing Outside Nation* (Princeton, N.J., Oxford: Princeton University Press, 2001).

Smith, Hilda, *Reason's Disciples: Seventeenth-Century English Feminists* (Urbana, Ill.: University of Illinois Press, 1982).

______. 'A General War Amongst the Men … But None Amongst the Women: Political Differences Between William and Margaret Cavendish' in *Politics and the Political Imagination in Later Stuart Britain* (Rochester: University of Rochester Press, 1997), p. 143–160.

Smith, Nigel. 'The Rod and the Canon' *Women's Writing* 14.2 (2007): 232–245.

Smith, Victor and Peter Kelsey, *London and the Outbreak of the Civil War*, Stephen Porter ed. (Hampshire: Macmillan Press, 1996).

Smith, David L., *Constitutional Royalism and the Search for Settlement 1640–1649* (New York: Cambridge University Press, 1994).

Souers, Philip Webster, *The Matchless Orinda* (Cambridge: Harvard University Press, 1931).

Suzuki, Mihoko, *Subordinate Subjects: Gender, the Political Imagination and Literary Form in England 1588–1688* (Aldershot, Hampshire: Ashgate, 2003).

Prescott, Sarah, 'Katherine Philips and the Poetic Spaces of Welsh Retirement.' *Philological Quarterly* 88.4 (Sept, 2009): 345–364.

Thomas, P., et al., *The Collected Works of Katherine Philips*, Patrick Thomas, G. Greer and R. Little, eds. 3 vols. (Brentford: Stump Cross Books, 1990–3, Vol. I).

Thomas, Patrick, *The Collected Works of Katherine Philips: The Matchless Orinda*. Patrick Thomas, ed. (Brentford, Stump Cross, 1990).

______. *Writers of Wales* (University of Wales Press, 1988).

Tomlinson, Sophie, ''My brain the stage': Margaret Cavendish and the fantasy of female performance' in *Readings in Renaissance Women's Drama Criticism, History and Performance 1594–1998*. S. P. Cerasano & Marion Wynne-Davis, eds. (London: Routledge, 1998), p. 272–292.

Turner, James, *The Politics of Landscape: Rural Scenery and Society in English Poetry 1630–1660* (London: Basil Blackwell, 1979).

Welsh, Anthony, 'Epic Romance: Royalist Retreat and the English Civil War.' *Modern Philology* 105.3 (Feb 2008): 570–602.

Whitaker, Katie, *Mad Madge: The Extraordinary Life of Margaret Cavendish Duchess of Newcastle, the First Woman to Live by her Pen* (New York & Basingstoke: Basic Books, 2002).

Wilcher, Robert, *The Writing of Royalism 1628–1660* (Cambridge: Cambridge University Press, 2001).

Wiseman, Susan, 'Woman's Poetry' in *Cambridge Companion to Writing the English Revolution*. N. H. Keeble ed. (Cambridge, Cambridge University Press, 2001), p. 127–147.

CHAPTER 3

# Processes of Re-orientation: Cultural Fora as Sites of Reunion

Thou best of Men and Friends! we will create
A Genuine Summer in each others breast;
And spite of this cold Time and frosen Fate
Thaw us a warme seat to our rest.[1]

As we have seen above, the war years and its aftermath provoked much uneasiness for the various parliaments who sought to dispense with royalist presence within the city of London and Westminster. During the 1640s and 1650s, while parliament purged London of the King's supporters, they were also deeply concerned by royalist social gatherings and communications, and as early as 1643 an act was issued to prevent 'disorderly assemblies' of royalists throughout England.[2] Certain other acts and ordinances were further intended to control those who might take 'liberty to convene together…wandring and shifting from place to place, become Spyes and Intelligencers for the Common Enemy' as well as those who 'continue personal Correspondancies each with other'.[3] To counter this threat,

[1] Lovelace, Richard, "The Grasse-hopper".

[2] Firth, C.H., and R.S. Rait, *Acts and Ordinances of the Interregnum*, 1642–1660, Vol. I (5, March, 1642–1630, Jan, 1649), (Abingdon: Professional Books, 1978), 'An Ordinance to supresse all Riotous and disorderly persons in and above Meere, Shafstbury, and Brome, Selwood in the county of Somerset, Dorset and Wilts', 3 May 1643, 139.

[3] Firth, C.H., and R.S. Rait. *Acts and Ordinances of the Interregnum*, Vol. II (9, Feb, 1649–1616, March, 1660), 'Act for removing all Papists, and all officers soldiers of fortune, divers other Delinquents removed from London and Westminster…', 26 February 1649/1650, pp. 349–354, 350. This act has a further clause in the margins which reads



S. Cronin, *Women, Royalisms and Exiles 1640–1669*,
https://doi.org/10.1007/978-3-030-89609-6_3

several acts of parliament were 'prolonged' and 'public meetings on pretence of recreation… were prohibited lest they should afford an opportunity for the gatherers of conspirators, the ripening of their counsels, and the break out of rebellion'.[4] While these acts and ordinances sought to restrict mobility and communication among royalists, this chapter shows that literary and cultural responses can be seen to range across the various cultural *fora* of manuscript circulation, coterie meetings and theatrical entertainments, with each articulating cultural and community networks at a time when royalists strove to 'create a Genuine Summer in each others breast'.

Philip Major has written that during the period 'much of the cavalier poetry…waxes on the consolatory joys of royalist fellowship for those who are confined to their estates', yet he also points out that, being confined to estates did not necessarily mean peaceful seclusion for royalists; that some estates were in some senses retreats but to the 'security conscious government they were far from impenetrable' and 'confinement, then, does not automatically facilitate a life of peaceful retirement'.[5] Under such conditions royalists had to find rather more surreptitious means to connect and remain connected. This chapter argues that through their cultural productions royalists formed alternate localized yet interconnected communities, not only in England but on the continent as well, to establish and maintain the bonds of fellowship and solidarity beyond the control of parliamentarian acts and ordinances. It examines the ways in which Lady Jane Cavendish, Lady Elizabeth Brackley, Katherine Philips, Queen Elizabeth of Bohemia and Mary of Orange created sites of reunion via their cultural production, strengthening both personal and cultural identity as well as preserving royalist heritage, customs and traditions during the war years and interregnum. As this chapter examines virtual and real inter-connective spaces created by forms of song, poetry and theatrical production, it asserts that these cultural *fora* provide sites through which physical absence of particular individuals was overcome and a cultural consolidation was achieved across the royalist diasporic community. This chapter also shows the ways in which these women intersected with widespread royalist cultural resistance and how their work represents what Robin Cohen identifies as a

'Further regulations for papists etc., from the 1 October 1650 for the prevention of conspiracies', 350.

[4] *Calendar of State Papers, Domestic*, 1651, p. viii.

[5] Major, Philip, *Writings of Exile in the English Revolution and Restoration* (Surrey & Burlington: Ashgate, 2013), 129, 131.

'strong ethnic group consciousness sustained over a long time and based on a sense of distinctiveness, a common history, the transmission of a common cultural and religious heritage'.[6] These cultural modes and the spaces they generate are readable as expressions of royalist society at a particular historical moment conditioned by the struggle to overcome the rupture of war, enforced dispersion and diaspora. Finally, this chapter examines the ways in which exiles operate within this culture, and how cultural and political identity becomes elaborated within these *fora*, all the while asserting that cultural productions unique to royalists at this time are necessitated by the need to create a *locus* of reunion for dislocated royalists.

Situating these women's cultural productions within the context of parliamentarian restrictions in England and the heated socio-political milieu occurring at The Hague, I re-evaluate their contributions as products of diaspora. James Clifford notes that 'diaspora discourse articulates, or bends together, both roots and routes to construct...alternate public spheres, forms of community consciousness and solidarity that maintain identifications outside the national time/space in order to live inside, with a difference.'[7] We will see that the Cavendish sisters' compilation of their family manuscript, Katherine Philips's coterie and Queen Elizabeth of Bohemia and Mary of Orange's entertainments stand as articulations of substitute communities or spheres in which critical alternatives to the world they inhabit are expressed, or voiced, and cultural heritage successfully preserved. Moreover, the study of '[d]iaspora provides valuable cues and clues for the elaboration of a social ecology of cultural identity and identification. The pressure to associate, remember or forget varies with changes in the economic and political atmosphere'.[8] Hence, each example of royalist community and cultural heritage examined here is uniquely conditioned by its location, proximity to localized politics and any frictions therein. For instance, the Cavendish sisters generated an opposing operational sphere of cultural production through manuscript compilation and circulation within which they memorialized their aristocratic familial heritage and flagged allegiance to the monarchy while under house arrest at Welbeck Abbey in 1644; Katherine Philips initiated and managed to remain connected to her coterie despite possible domestic tensions and volatile local political conditions in West Wales, and Queen Elizabeth of

[6] Cohen, *GD*, 17.
[7] Clifford, James, 'Diasporas' in *Migration, Diasporas and transnationalism*, 221.
[8] Gilroy, Paul, 'Diaspora', 295.

Bohemia and Mary of Orange staged performances and theatrical entertainments which formed a strong community consciousness, solidarity and a *locus* of identification for royalists not only within and around the politically unstable hub at The Hague but which proliferated throughout the continent and back across the channel to England through widespread prints.

Jurgen Habermas provides another way to conceptualize these cultural *fora*. Habermas's idealized "public sphere", or the locus of exchange of ideas, was centred on three specific criteria—a disregard of status, a domain of common interest and the inclusivity of all people regardless of class or gender. Nancy Fraser has since pointed out that the public sphere was in fact constituted by a number of exclusions and that specific marginal groups, such as women, were excluded on the basis that they did not possess the rhetoric to engage in relevant debates. She suggests that in reaction to their exclusion these marginal groups developed their own counter-public sphere. While these terms themselves are anachronistic, the conceptual framework provides a heuristic tool with which to understand divisions of inclusion and exclusion in the republic of letters.[9] More importantly, Norbrook writes that the 'model' is in any case valuable precisely as it encourages a move beyond the rather narrow empiricism and localism of some tendencies in British historiography' and that the model offers 'a framework against which we may interrogate the norms of public dissuasion at particular moments in history'.[10] Hence, while the revolution enabled an initiation of a political consciousness and the public sphere in England, the historical moment of diaspora for royalists led them to create counter-public spheres, or alternative communities within the broader diasporic community, within which they could gather to share cultural bonds and maintain allegiance to the monarchy.

Further to re-contextualizing its subjects' cultural production as products of diasporic counter-publics, this chapter examines individual loss as

[9] See: Habermas, Jürgen, *English Translation, The Structural Transformation of the Public Sphere: An Inquiry into a Category of Bourgeois Society*, Thomas Burger ed. (Cambridge, MA: The MIT Press, 1989), 36; Fraser, Nancy, 'Rethinking the Public Sphere: A Contribution to the Critique of Actually Existing Democracy', in *Habermas and the Public Sphere,* Craig Calhoun ed. (Cambridge MA: MIT Press, 1992), pp. 109–142. For application of these theories to the seventeenth century, see Norbrook, David, 'Women, the Republic of Letters, and the Public sphere in the Mid-Seventeenth Century'. *Criticism* 46.2 (Detroit, Spring): 223–241.

[10] Norbrook, 'Women', 1.

mimetic of collective loss and explores the dialectical relationship between the two. It will show how the Cavendish sisters transmitted and consolidated their allegiance to the monarchy and commitment to family through manuscript productions, an act which connotes a belief in a 'common history' between royalists. In doing so, they were projecting and privileging the unit of the family as a means to provide much-desired 'stability'.[11] Through poetry, the sisters promoted the trope of the family as a way to reiterate important hierarchical traditions associated not just with the monarchy but also as an integral part of royalist identity. Further, I argue for the political valency of the Cavendish sisters' use of song throughout the manuscript and suggest that such frequent appearance of the genre points to both an act of political subversion and urges defiant reunion which sought to surmount distance between daughters, their father and the wider royalist family. Meanwhile, Katherine Philips, friend and loyal supporter of many royalists, engaged in clandestine modes of epistolary verse during the interregnum. Not only did her coterie act as a medium through which royalists could communicate with one another, but it will be seen that specific poems were remodelled to produce a kind of epistolary verse which furthered royalist requirements for secrecy. Through this generic appropriation, her focus on friendship and advocacy for self-sufficiency, Katherine Philips nurtured her disbanded and distant friends, while protecting their identity and avoiding censures at a time when the hope of establishing lines of communication with fellow royalists was vital. Meanwhile, it will be seen, that on the continent at the courts of Queen Elizabeth of Bohemia and Mary of Orange, royalist culture and heritage were maintained through entertainments reminiscent of those of the Caroline court. I show how the theatrical productions of Queen Elizabeth of Bohemia and Mary Stuart served to overcome the absence of both the King and royalist friends in defiant reaction to the English parliament's closure of theatres. As it re-contextualizes these women's cultural outputs, this chapter argues that all three *fora* of cultural reunion were highly subversive due to their defiance of parliamentarian acts and ordinances, while recurring themes such as resistance, self-sufficiency and insularity mark them as politically other. Just as poetry became sites of order in the previous chapter, the cultural *fora* explored in this chapter become crucial counter-public sites of reunion for displaced and disorientated royalists.

[11] de Groot *Royalist Identities*, 7.

## Lady Jane Cavendish and Lady Elizabeth Brackley: Manuscript, Song and the Royalist Family

Pox on this grief, hang wealth, let's sing
Shall's kill ourselves for fear of death?
We'l live by th'aire which songs do bring,
Our sighing does but wast our breath.[12]

For royalist poet and songwriter Alexander Brome, spirits could be roused by singing and hard times transcended—songs were the very things which could breathe life into flagging royalists during the dark days of the mid-1640s. Song was indeed a popular mode of resistance for royalists despite parliamentary acts and ordinances which sought to penalize 'the maker, writer or composer of any such unlicensed Book, Pamphlet, Treatise, *Ballad*, Libel sheet or Sheets of News' [my emphasis] by imposing fines of 'forty shillings or being imprisoned in the common Gaol for the county or Liberty where the offence is committed'.[13] Operating within this oppressive climate of surveillance during which parliament banned meetings, feastings, pastimes, dancing or games of any kind, royalists sought comfort in song culture.[14] Forms of resistance and reunion through song culture are manifest in the numerous examples of drinking ballads, prison poems and clandestine concerts that took place in and around London.[15] These musical communities, such as Lawes' society discussed above, formed among both disheartened internal exiles and exiles on the

[12] Alexander Brome, *Songs and Poems.* Pub. 1661. 'The Royalist', written 1645, 43.

[13] *Acts and Ordinances.* Vol. I. An Ordinance Against unlicensed or Scandalous Pamphlets and for the better regulating of Printing, 30 Sept 1647, 1021/1022.

[14] For example, see: an Ordinance concerning stage-plays dated 2 September 1642, Vol. I, 26; An Order for the burning of the Book of Sports dated 5 May 1643; An Ordinance for better observation of the Lord's day dated 8 April 1644 in Firth & Rait, *Acts and Ordinances of the Interregnum*, vol. I.

[15] Anselment, Raymond A., "Stone Walls' and 'I'ron Bars': Richard Lovelace and the Conventions of Seventeenth-Century Prison Literature'. *Renaissance and Reformation* 29 (1993): 15–34; Kebluesk, Marika, 'Wine for Comfort: Drinking and the Royalist Exile Experience, 1642–1660' in *A Pleasing Sinne: Drink and Conviviality in Seventeenth Century England.* Adam Smyth ed. (Cambridge: D.S. Brewer, 2004); Major, Philip. *Writings of Exile in the English Revolution and Restoration*; Spink, Ian, *Henry Lawes: Cavalier Songwriter* (New York & Oxford. Oxford University Press, 2000). For literary example, see: Lovelace, "To Althea, From Prison"—there is emphasis on 'cups', 'draughts' and 'health' as a means to rouse the spirits and toast the King in such trying times.

continent, offering a 'chance for discreet interaction between key figures...and the performances created communal solidarity in the face of uncomfortable times'.[16]

The Cavendish sisters worked within a traditional literary system of composition and circulation of poems and plays 'presented to them by their father's earlier literary environment'.[17] However, the socio-political climate in which they compiled one of only two manuscripts was vastly different to that of the 1630s.[18] Arthur Marotti reminds us that, within the manuscript tradition, texts written by 'non-publishing coterie authors...ought to be examined in terms of the specific historical conditions in which they were produced and received'.[19] For Jane and Elizabeth, civil war, oppression by opposition forces and house arrest led them to turn to writing not just for entertainment but to find solace and for reasons of personal, familial and political continuity, connectivity and preservation. In the case of the Cavendish sisters, a number of responses to social-political turmoil, separation from their father and the experience of house arrest emerge from the manuscript which coalesce to form a rhetorical counter-public of resistance wherein networks are asserted and statuses affirmed, values celebrated and cultural forms preserved.

The conditions of war, oppression and internal exile paradoxically provided the Cavendish sisters with the space to compose and compile a reactionary and highly politicized manuscript. Situating their work alongside other cavalier forms of cultural resistance concerned with confinement and internal exile, this section shows the intention of this manuscript was not only to celebrate family but also to preserve royalist cultural forms as they were systematically suppressed and banned by parliament in the early 1640s. This section posits the manuscript represents a textual performance

[16] Knowles, James, 'We've Lost, Should we lose our Mirth too?', 74.

[17] Coolahan, Marie Louise, 'Presentation Volume of Jane Cavendish's Poetry. Yale University, Beinecke Library Osborn Ms b. 233', in *Early Modern Women's Manuscript Poetry*. Jill Seal Millman and Gillian Wright eds. (Manchester & New York: Manchester University Press, 2005), 85. See also Ross, *Women Poetry and Politics*, pp. 100–134.

[18] I will be citing from the Bodleian Library copy of the Cavendish sisters work. MS Rawl. Poet 16. There is however another manuscript at Yale University, Beinecke Library Osbourne MS. B. 233. It has been argued that this manuscript predates the Bodleian copy by Alexandra Bennet, 'Now Let my Language Speake': the Authorship, Rewriting, and Audience(s) of Jane Cavendish and Elizabeth Brackley.' *Early Modern Literary Studies* 11.2 (September, 2005): 1–13.

[19] Marotti, Arthur, *Manuscript, Print and the English Renaissance Lyric* (New York: Cornwall University Press, 1995), 9.

of these cultural forms which, in the absence of any physical performance, replaces those which were curbed by parliament. Thus, the manuscript functions as a virtual *locus* of reunion as much as it stands as a repository for shared royalist cultural heritage and identity. Further, this section argues that through song the Cavendish sisters simultaneously confront their own confinement and the absence of their father, while also offering communal riposte to puritan austerity and parliamentarian restrictions. However, most crucially, this section argues that their songs, hitherto unexamined, qualify as a type of prison poetry as they convey the reality of living in a garrison and then under house arrest. I argue the manuscript stands as both a cultural artefact that records a specific moment in the history of the royalist diaspora, and, that for the diaspora group it provides, in its more private form, a crucial counter-public sphere of specific cultural and political expression. Moreover, as a virtual forum of reunion, which through circulation could reach out to unite both immediate family members and the wider royalist 'family', it contributed to a broader network of royalist cultural resistance at work in England during the early war years.

Scholarship on the works of Lady Jane Cavendish and Lady Elizabeth Brackley has tended to focus on their better-known play from the manuscript, *The Concealed Fancies*, first brought to light almost a century ago by Nathan Comfort Starr.[20] Since then, while his assessment of this play has been rescued from the notion that the play is 'practically without value', the bulk of scholarship has tended towards yet more readings of that particular play with little attention given to the remainder of the manuscript.[21] Margaret Ezell's comprehensive study of the entire manuscript stands

[20] Comfort Starr, Nathan, 'The Concealed Fancies: a Play by Lady Jane Cavendish and Lady Elizabeth Brackley.' *Publications of the Modern Language Association* 46 (1931).

[21] Starr, 837. See, for example, Warren, Robin, 'A Partial Liberty: Gender and Class in Jane Cavendish and Elizabeth Brackely's the Concealed Fancies' in *Renaissance Papers*. T.H. Howard-Hill and Philip Rollinson eds. (Rochester, NY: Camden House, 2000); Findlay, Alison, 'She Gave you the civility of the House': Household Performance in the Concealed Fancies' in *Readings in Renaissance Women's Drama: Criticism, History and Performance 1594–1998*. S.P. Cerasano and Marion Wynne Davis eds. (London, NY: Routledge, 1998); Burroughs, Catherine, 'Hymen's Monkey Love': The Concealed Fancies and Female Sexual Initiation.' *Theatre Journal* 51 (1999); Findlay, Alison, 'Playing the Scene-Self: Jane Cavendish and Elizabeth Brackley's The Concealed Fancies' in *Enacting Gender on the Renaissance Stage*. Viviana Comensoli and Anne Russell eds. (Urbana & Chicago: University of Illinois Press, 1999). For a recent exception, see Ross, *Women, Poetry and Politics in Seventeenth-Century Britain* (Oxford: Oxford University Press, 2014) (Abbreviated hereafter as *WPP*).

apart in its evaluation of this work as a token of royalist culture, touching on many crucial points. Like Ezell, I believe this manuscript is of immense importance to understanding 'what' women's writing should look like in the period',[22] but, I also argue their work reveals much about the royalists facing the end of an era as it relays the story of acute ambition to preserve and maintain royalist literature, cultural heritage and identity through a traditionally aristocratic medium at such a precarious time. Moreover, in the absence of real reunion, their utilization of the manuscript tradition offers a virtual transmission of a common history and cultural identity, as well as reconnection and reunion with those of their creed. As Ezell notes, the manuscript functions as a 'social tool', the contents of which provide links between the fractured royalist community during the mid-1640s and that its 'general intent is to praise virtue and lament the conditions brought on by war'.[23] However, I read the manuscript as endowed with much more than a social function arguing that it has a flagrant political purpose to firmly assert allegiance to the crown and celebrate royal culture at a time when allegiance was continually questioned and all forms of royalist culture were being systematically banned and intentionally erased.[24] More recently, Sarah E. Ross has attended to this gap in scholarship as she undertakes the important work of exploring Jane Cavendish's poetry as far more than a social instrument. Acknowledging the important precedent set for Jane by her father's coterie—that of William Cavendish—Ross argues for a complexity in Jane's poetry which 'exploits the generic fluidity of the occasional verse to fuse the social, devotional and political moment, and to identify her father with the divine…in order to articulate her allegiance to the royalist cause'.[25] Ross's work elegantly draws out generic

[22] Ezell, Margaret, "'To Be Your Daughter in Your Pen': The Social Functions of Literature in the Writings of Lady Elizabeth Brackley and Lady Jane Cavendish.' *Huntington Library Quarterly* 51.4 (Autumn, 1988): 281–296.

[23] Ibid., 291, 251.

[24] Other scholars who have engaged with the sisters' work within the context of royalism and political defeat include Milling, Jane, 'Seige and Cipher: the Closet Drama of the Cavendish Sisters.' *Women's History Review* 6.3 (1997): 411–426; Stone Stanton, Kamille, 'The Domestication of Royalist Themes in *The Concealed Fancies* by Jane Cavendish and Elizabeth Brackley.' *Clio* 36.2 (2007): 177–197; Chedzgoy, Kate, *Women's Writing in the British Atlantic World* (Cambridge: Cambridge University Press, 2007); Hughes, Ann and Julie Sanders 'Disruptions and Evocations of the Family Among Royalist Exiles' in *Literatures of Exile in the English Revolution and its Aftermath 1640–1690*, Philip Major ed. (London: Ashgate, 2010), pp. 45–64.

[25] Ross, Sarah, E., *WPP*, 104.

precedents for Jane's occasional poetry, her networks and sources and the ways in which her writing operates within the pre-existing 'authority of the elite inter-familial coterie'.[26]

On 11 January 1642, under the King's command, William Cavendish, the Earl of Newcastle left Welbeck Abbey secretly at 'about twelve of the clock at night, hastened from his own house when his family were all at rest' and made his way to Hull.[27] This departure marked the beginning of a narrative that, two and a half years later, would see the Cavendish sisters suffer house arrest under parliamentarian control. Prior to 1644, the family had lived amidst the trammels of war, with Welbeck thirty miles north from the centre of Nottingham, where parliamentarians were garrisoned at Nottingham castle. The royalist garrison was at Newark, fifteen miles north-east of Nottingham and both of these locations 'were focal points of the opposing causes in the shire'.[28] Throughout the campaign the sisters' father, William Cavendish, and his army moved between York, Hull, Wakefield and Pontefract. During December 1643, Cavendish moved from York to Bolsover Castle and then to Welbeck, where he spent the winter months, and, as 'Christmas passed in a home he was not to see again for seventeen years, the offensive slipped from his hands and the attacker became the attacked'.[29] On 2 August 1644, Welbeck, the home of the Cavendish sisters, was taken over by parliamentarian forces. Within the month Bolsover was delivered up to the Earl of Manchester, and 'Welbeck, the Earl of Newcastle's house…was given to Colonel Tornhagh's command'.[30] Turberville writes that Welbeck remained an important garrison 'until the very end of the Civil war, one of the most important Royalist strongholds in Nottinghamshire, held in her father's absence by the courageous Lady Jane Cavendish'.[31] Indeed, when taken the garrison still held about 200 men. The Earl of Manchester later evacuated the stronghold and 'put a garrison of Nottinghamshire parliamentarians into

[26] Ibid., 111/112.

[27] Cavendish, Margaret, *The Life of William Cavendish, Duke of Newcastle: to which is added the True Relation of My Birth, Breeding and Life.* C.H. Firth ed. (New York: Scribner & Welford, 1886), 15.

[28] Wood, Alfred, *Nottinghamshire in the Civil War* (Oxford: Clarendon Press, (1937), 32.

[29] Wood, 62

[30] Hutchinson, Lucy, *Memoirs of the Life of Colonel Hutchinson: Charles I's Puritan Nemesis.* N.H. Keeble ed. (London: Phoenix Press, 2000), 173.

[31] Turberville, A.S. *A History of Welbeck Abbey and its Owners.* Volume I, 1539–1755 (London: Faber & Faber, 1938), 92.

it, so that it was held for a time against the King'.[32] At this point, Newcastle's daughters and other members of his family were also in the house, but 'Manchester promised to safeguard 'their quiet there' and to intercede with the Parliament for a complete maintenance for them'.[33] Thus, the Cavendish sisters lived within an enemy garrison, surrounded by soldiers and in close proximity to many Nottinghamshire skirmishes. Prior to house arrest, they may have been prevented from visiting friends and family by oppressive confinement acts discussed in Chap. 2, and, as their father was fighting for the King, they rarely saw him. This sense of isolation, as well as the experience of house arrest, is documented through the songs interspersed throughout the manuscript.

### *The Manuscript*

The Cavendish sisters' manuscript opens with a tribute to their father entitled "The Greate Example"[34] and continues with poems dedicated to immediate family such as Brother Charles, Henry and Uncle Charles as well as the King, the Queen, the Prince of Wales and a roll call of extended noble familial connections.[35] Thus, the volume represents a textual regrouping of both family and prominent royalist figures, thereby superseding acts and ordinances which ban meetings of any kind between royalists. Through groupings of poems—relating to numerous members of royalty, nobility and family—networks damaged by war and enforced dispersion are re-established in a medium which could not be interrupted by parliament. Moreover, by placing their father at the head of the manuscript and celebrating him throughout, the sisters acknowledge both his privileged position as the patriarch within royalist society and as the head of their household, thus reaffirming the royalist metaphor of the state concerning the patriarchal relationship between the nation and the King.[36] Inclusion of an intergenerational familial roll call further establishes links

[32] Ibid., 112, 113.

[33] Ibid., 113, cites from the *CSPD*, Earl of Manchester to the Committee of both Kingdoms, 6 August, 1644, 404–405.

[34] Lady Jane Cavendish and Lady Elizabeth Brackley. *Poems, Songs, a Pastoral and a play by the rt honble the Lady Jane Cavendish and Lady Elizabeth Brackley.* MS Rawl Poet. 16. 1r.

[35] MS Rawl Poet 16., 1v, 1v, 2r, 5r, 5r & 15v–18r, respectively.

[36] See de Groot, *Royalist Identities*, on discussion regarding the King as head of the hierarchically controlled space of the nation—both as the head of the body politic and as the head of the family, the latter metaphor 'emphasises the patriarchal authority of the father-King',

with peerage both past and present, and preserves within the pages of the manuscript their affiliation with royalty for posterity. This roll call is book-ended by dedications to the sisters' "Noble Grandfather" and their "Honourable Grandmother Elizabeth Countess of Shrewsbury".[37] Their grandfather was the youngest son of Bess of Hardwick, Countess of Shrewsbury, who amassed great fortune through her penchant for arranging marriages and alliances within both the nobility and royal circles.[38] Continuing in this project of arranged marriages, of her own children to those of her husband's from previous marriages, Bess brought about the amalgamation of the houses of Talbot and Cavendish.[39] The sisters' grandfather did not support his mother after the death of her husband, and remained 'on the closest terms' with Gilbert Talbot, his step-brother.[40] Turberville suggests that Charles's fortune 'owed more to' Gilbert and Mary than to his mother, as he acquired both Welbeck and Bolsover from Gilbert.[41] Henry Ogle[42] was a member of 'a collateral branch' of Charles's wife Katherine's family, herself the younger daughter and co-heiress of Cuthbert, Lord Ogle.[43] Other wider connections to nobility in the manuscript link the family to the Egerton's, and, by extension, we can surmise the sisters may have met Henry Lawes, musical tutor to Alice Egerton and member of Lord Brackely's household, when Elizabeth married John Egerton in 1641.[44] These networks and affiliations not only link the Cavendish sisters to royalty and nobility but by naming families and individuals also written about by Katherine Philips in Wales they also hint at the possibility of their mingling among clandestine royalist circles during

12. For contemporary theory see Filmer, Robert, *Patriarcha, or The Natural Power of Kings* (London: Walter Davis, 1680).

[37] MS Rawl poet 16., 15v, 18r.

[38] Bess came to Queen Elizabeth's attention when she arranged the marriage between her second daughter Elizabeth to Charles Stuart, descendant of Henry IIV, and uncle of Mary, Queen of Scots, who had possible claims to the English throne. The Queen was furious with Bess's meddling in royal alliances and consigned her to three months in the Tower of London. Turberville, 28.

[39] Turberville, 24, 25.

[40] See: "On Gilbert Earl of Shrewsbury", MS Rawl Poet 16., 17r.

[41] Turberville, 37/40. Charles obtained Welbeck through a lease Gilbert had 'obtained from the younger Richard Walley in Feb 1584', 37.

[42] "On my good and true friend Mr Henry Ogle", MS Rawl Poet 16., 17v.

[43] Turberville, 16.

[44] "An Answer to my Lady Alice Egerton's Song", 8v and "On the Lord Viscount Brackley", 10r. See Ross in *WPP* for more inter-familial details.

the war years and interregnum.[45] The emphasis on these networks points to the Cavendish sisters' ambition to memorialize both eminent personages and their own familial position in relation to these culturally elite circles, and argues for their cultural and political agency during the volatile mid to late 1640s.

In addition to emphasizing familial and royal connections, royalist victories, values and models of virtue are reinstated and upheld within the manuscript, in defiance of military defeat, as well as social and cultural oppression. Despite the ill fortune of the royalists, the occasional poem "On the 30th June to God" celebrates Newcastle's victory over Lord Fairfax at the battle of Aldwaton Moor.[46] Other poems which comment on their father's absence, such as "On a false reporte of your Lordships Landinge", or "Thankes Sir" (a poem which uses gifts received from her father to ease the grief brought on by separation) may be interpreted as personal lamentations yet may also be read as commentary on the wider royalist experience of loss due to war, enforced dispersion and exile.[47] Further, there is a cluster of what I term the 'ideal subject poems', "On a Noble Lady", and a group of poems all entitled "On an Aquaintance" which appear to be establishing royalist social values and models of virtue.[48] As Margaret Ezell argues, these poems 'are a public proclamation of patterns of behaviour' within which 'the virtues of the king and queen and Prince of Wales are applauded as well as those of Family members'.[49] Anglican feasts and traditions are also celebrated and poems such as "On Christmas day to God" and "On good Fryday" stand as an explicit rebuttal to puritan reforms of the church calendar.[50] In 1616 James I's speech before the Star Chamber called 'for the proper celebration of Christmas',[51] and within the 'great country houses, the keeping of a traditional Christmas involved collective feasting…merriment…dancing, dicing…and St George's plays performed by local villagers'.[52] Along with this, the celebra-

[45] See: Philips, "To the Right honourable Alice, Countess of Carbury, at her coming into Wales". The countess, Alice Egerton, was directly connected to the Cavendish sisters as sister-in-law to Jane Cavendish's married sister Elizabeth.

[46] MS Rawl Poet. 16., 19v. The year of this battle was 1643.

[47] MS Rawl Poet. 16., 4v, 8r

[48] MS Rawl Poet. 16., 9v and 9r respectively. Also see, "On a worthy Friend", 11v.

[49] Ezell, 285.

[50] MS Rawl Poet. 16., 19r.

[51] Marcus, *Politics of Mirth*, 77.

[52] Ibid., 77.

tion and preservation of royalist cultural heritage of drama are also embedded within the manuscript. Theatre and theatre-going, now banned, were replaced by play-reading or surreptitious and spontaneous play-acting on tennis courts or other enclosed areas.[53] However, for the Cavendish sisters under house arrest even play-reading might have been curtailed by fear of punishments and fines.[54] Thus, once again, the communal nature of the manuscript is utilized to commemorate cultural heritage dear to royalists. Both *A Pastorall* and *The Concealed Fancies* by virtue of their genre are subversive notwithstanding the themes and motifs of both plays.[55] Thus, the manuscript presents examples of cultural norms among royalists in a bid to preserve exemplary modes of behaviour; a socio-cultural blueprint for the next generation. Along with this diasporic drive to preserve common royalist cultural heritage in a variety of poems and through drama, there are numerous songs interspersed throughout the manuscript which further imply defiance in the face of parliamentarian restrictions.

### *The Songs*

Foregrounding a sort of paralysis mimetic of the limbo felt in exile, Robert Herrick's poem "To his Friend, on the [H] untuneable Times"[56] conflicts with many contemporary songs concerned with confinement or imprisonment. The title itself suggests that the times are 'untuneable', that there is no harmony to be found during these times, or, even in song itself. He writes:

> Play I co'd once; but (gentle friend) you see
> My Harp hung; here on the Willow tree.
> Sing I co'd; and bravely too enspire
> (With luscious Numbers) my melodious Lyre...
> Griefe (my deare friend) has first my Harp unstrung;
> Wither'd my hand, and palsie-struck my tongue.

[53] See an ordinance concerning stage-plays and order burning of the book of sports, 2 September 1642 & 22 October 1643 in Acts and Ordinances, Vol. I, 26.

[54] The sisters' lyric regarding house arrest at least implies that they were watched, possibly by women from the 'other side'. See: "A Songe", 16/7r.

[55] See footnote 69 below.

[56] Herrick, Robert, "To his Friend, on the [H] untuneable Times", *Hesperides, or, The works both humane & Divine*. 1648, p. 94. Henry E. Huntington Library and Art Gallery. Reel position: Wing/72:19a.

Herrick's poem expresses a different sentiment to the morale-boosting poetry of Lovelace's 'Stone Walls do not a Prison Make, &c' and 'To Lucasta. From Prison' (c1642), which '[c]aptured the mirthful spirit of stoicism buoyed by the love, friendship and loyalties expressed in its trinity of wine, women and royalism'.[57] Written some years later, within this poem the notion of playing or singing is consigned to the past—grief has undone the instrument of song and sucked dry the tongue's ability to sing. The long years of war and defeat have taken their toll on both those that sing and on song itself.

It is to this darker trend of song-writing or composition that the Cavendish sisters belong. As they are directly occupied by the circumstances of civil war and the absence of their father, their songs register the continual psychological battle between despair and hope through a linguistic dichotomy of melancholy and resilience. Further, the sisters' songs are particularly important to the understanding of later poetry of confinement as their work precedes that of Alexander Brome or Richard Fanshawe, and indeed, even that of Robert Herrick, mentioned above. Thus, as it predates writing of the mid-century, the Cavendish sisters' work should be read as a significant contribution to the understanding not only of women's war literature but also of royalist women's war literature more specifically. Philip Major argues that the systematic banishments, confinement acts and the general oppression of royalists in England during the 1650s contributed to a 'poetics of desolation which sets itself apart from other royalist verse'.[58] Writing during the early war years of the 1640s, the Cavendish sisters also wrote under these same conditions to produce a form of consolatory verse interspersed with metaphors of confinement. The sisters' writing was inevitably conditioned by their close proximity to the skirmishes in and around Nottinghamshire, by house arrest, as well as by the traumatic separation from their father, family and friends. Thus, during these repressive years, as it was later in the interregnum, the chief aim was to reconnect and stay connected with one another, and song was one way of accomplishing that aim at least in spirit if not in person.[59]

[57] See Anselment, 'Stone Wall's', 15. See also: 'The Liberty of the Imprisoned Royalist' (1647).

[58] Major, *Writings*, 127.

[59] For that and other means, see Potter. She suggests Wilkins (1641) found ways of concealing a message: shooting letters in arrows, writing in invisible ink; ways of communicating more quickly, that is, birds, speaking tubes, smoke trumpets and bells; separate languages like

Infused with melancholy, the Cavendish sisters' songs convey their frustration and fear regarding the absence of their father, however, they also offer subtle resistance to parliamentarian oppression. Lois Potter suggests that some writers of the time were 'self-confessed melancholics' and that melancholy was a trope commonly appropriated by royalists to describe their woes of perseverance in an uncongenial society.[60] Like their contemporaries, the Cavendish sisters looked to this literary trend to relay their experience of war in a manner recognizable to royalist allies within the diasporic group, and, most certainly, their songs are interspersed with the rhetoric of emotional turmoil. However, this negative language is juxtaposed with language conveying hope—a dichotomy which renders both the songs and, by extension, the sisters, in a sort of stasis, trapped between one reality and another, hoped for, reality. The opening lines of "A Songe" convey emotional bleakness and a desire for seclusion—a turning away from the world overcome by fear and grief:

> Our Eyes are fixed looking on thee
> Soe nothinge care wee for to see
> Our senses are turn'd all to feares
> And inward thoughts, Sighs turns to teares.[61]

The sisters' emotional connection to their father generates the need to know where he is, however, paradoxically, when they seek him out they find there is little that comforts them. Thus, their zombie-like obsession regarding information about their father comes up against the unwanted realities of war. Paralyzed, or 'fixed', by the twin emotions of desire and 'feares' their senses are completely overcome, 'all turn'd' or reduced to despair and even withdrawal into the self allows no reprieve. As the songs convey a paralysis brought on by fear for their father, the sisters themselves and their songs are similar to Lovelace's flies caught in webs or paralyzed toads, who was also writing within the royalist mode concerned with royalist woes. Their mournful lament is concerned not just with the absence of their father but also the more general royalist condition of inward movement—'inward thoughts' and 'fears' conjoined with melancholic 'sighs'. However, towards the close, the language of melancholy, and its

canting; visual codes, shorthand, hieroglyphics, emblems, even pictures and musical compositions, *Secret Rites, Secret Writing*, 38.

[60] Ibid., 134.

[61] MS. Rawl Poet. 16., 5v.

attendants 'feares' and 'teares', is exchanged for more motivational terms. The speaker states they 'pray', 'hope' and 'wish' to see their father 'againe in Welbeck' so that they may replace their 'sad' emotions with 'glad' ones. The final couplet crucially draws both the sisters and the wider royalist 'family' together:

> Then let us cry, our [King] obey
> Make hast I pray thee make our day.[62]

Playing on the unstable meaning of the word 'cry', the speaker transforms an individual and private emotional act into a communal action and statement intended to rouse spirits and defy their oppressors. In this manner, the song strikes an unconnected similarity with Lovelace's "To Althea" as it too endeavours to surmount royalist isolationism and asserts identity through defiant song.[63] The communal 'let us cry' becomes a powerful declaration of resilience for both the Cavendish sisters and royalists more generally, notwithstanding the double connotation of the word 'cry' within the genre of song itself. Thus, to 'cry' takes on a tripartite purpose, representing personal emotion, royalist sentiment and embedded within the song it consolidates both in a twist of defiance against the opposition.

While frustration and fears are surmounted through rhetorical manipulation, the sense of isolation and distance, not only from their father's absence but also from any news of him, is further exacerbated by immediate proximity to skirmishes and the experience of being under house arrest. This all-consuming environment manifests poetically through metaphors of confinement common to contemporary royalist poetry later in the century.[64] Lois Potter has written that much of the 'characteristic imagery' found in poetry of the period is that of 'confinement' leading to the 'royalist mode in the mid-century… increasingly characterised by this sense of darkness and confined spaces'.[65] Repetition of the image of graves throughout the Cavendish sisters' songs becomes a way to express the stifling impact of war, acts and ordinances by parliament and ensuing isola-

[62] MS. Rawl Poet. 16.

[63] Anselment, 'Stone Walls', 16.

[64] Potter argues that imprisonment can mean more like exile or a sense of restraint and writers 'may simply have felt themselves confined by an uncongenial society'. Also see: Major, *Writings of Exile*, 136. For the Cavendish sisters, imprisonment was a reality and internal exile a result of such restrictions.

[65] Ibid., 134.

tion felt in Welbeck during these early war years. For example, "A Songe" dolefully conflates wartime existence with death as the speaker laments that the 'eclipsed life wee have/That livinge may be called a grave'.[66] As life becomes a kind of internment, the speaker gestures to the darkness that has come with war—the dramatic change to life on the ground. Moreover, the sister's utilization of the emblem of political upheaval, the eclipse, underscores the unfolding political and military ruin of the royalists reaching its low point in the mid-1640s, while use of the collective pronoun 'wee' suggests the universal demise of the society and the culture they have known.

Elsewhere in the manuscript, other songs deploy the image of the grave to convey a space of isolation and mourning.[67] "The Songe", sang by the shepherdess Jnn in *A Pastorall*,[68] refers to the grave in its traditional sense:

> For sadness Earth I hate, should bee my grave
> But passions teares I'le swim, in to the wave
> Of happines…[69]

However, despite the apparent sadness and the inability to escape this woeful age, there is a transcendent quality to this couplet. The 'grave' is replaced by the 'wave' of the second line and 'passions' replace the 'sadness' of the first to effect a sort of resistance and recuperation. Major argues that some poetry of internal exile during the 1650s seeks to surpass the physical space by that of the contemplative effecting a physical dislocation and safety to be found there.[70] Indeed, this short lyric seems to not only suggest that within the grave they are free from corporeal anguish of their oppressors but that within their imagination they may 'swim' beyond their grasp into the realms of 'happiness'. Thus, an early form of what Major terms as the 'poetics of desolation' may be discerned, however,

[66] "A Songe", MS. Rawl Poet. 16.

[67] See also the song sang by the sad shepherds, MS Rawl Poet. 16., 40r.

[68] *A Pastorall* tells the story of three sisters who, during times of war and the loss of their loved friends, choose to isolate themselves from the world of men by becoming shepherdesses. Their friends, and more specifically their Lord, have been sent out of the country by the witches of the antemasque. The three shepherdesses vow to remain solemn until their friends are returned to them 'out of France' (MS Rawl Poet. 16., 26v-42v., 42r). Their father, William Cavendish was in Paris 1644–1647, before moving to Rotterdam and then Antwerp in 1648 with Margaret.

[69] "The Songe", MS. Rawl. Poet 16., 35r.

[70] Major, *Writings*, 120.

encoded within are forms of resistance and transcendence, much like Richard Lovelace's celebrated prison song, 'Stone walls do not a prison make' (c1641). As Lovelace deploys the nightingale and the linnet as motifs of freedom, the Cavendish sisters deploy the wave. However, while Lovelace redefines space and inspires prisoners 'to transform harsh reality and to transcend physical boundaries',[71] the Cavendish sisters struggle to maintain this positive transcendence which endeavours to place distance between them and their oppressors. Tears, like waves of reality, wash away this idealistic reverie as the shepherd Per responds, 'The sad countynuance of your Teares/All ready makes mee Seasick of my feares'. Thus, the loss of their freedom, the absence of their father, the reduction of their prestige and the sequestration of their home becomes too much to bear—the dissolution of all becomes a form of cultural demise, which can only be poeticized in terms of internment and death.

For the Cavendish sisters the battle between melancholy and defiance was continual. The struggle between their personal investment in, and proximity to, the wars in Nottinghamshire unfolds in their songs. However, they do achieve a stoical resolve common to cavalier poets. "Songs Anthome", penned by both Jane and Elizabeth and sung by three characters in *A Pastorall*, Chi, Jnn and Ver, is concerned with two pillars of royalist literary preserve—friendship and stoicism—and the overall plot of the play appears to be designed to demonstrate the triumph of royal virtue over the forces of disorder and dissent.[72] It is worth quoting in its entirety:

> Chi:
> When once the presence of a friend is gone
> Not knowing when hee'le come or stay how longe
> Then greife doth fill it selfe wth a reward
> That is when passion flows without regard.
> Jnn:
> His absence makes a Chaos sure of mee
> And when each one doth looking looke to see
> They speakeing say, That I'm not I
> Alas doe not name for I desire to dye
> Ver:
> And I your sister can not way goe lesse
> As by my face of paleness you may gesse

[71] Anselment, 'Stone Walls', 19.

[72] These speech prefixes are taken directly from the manuscript.

Then let us singe in chorus Anthome pray
To see our loved Friends, doth make our day.[73]

This melancholic opening resonates with a tone of uncertainty signifying the fear of the unknown future for royalists and the painful emptiness left behind as friends and family are internally exiled by dispersal within England, or are exiled to the continent. For cavalier poets 'who were so deeply conscious of their society… friendship provided a way to follow the pattern of the good life'.[74] More specifically, for royalists during the war and interregnum years, friendship signified unity, political affiliation or allegiance and provided metaphorical as well as psychological protection from the destructive and disorientating effects of the times. The trope of the 'friend' here, so popular among cavalier writers as a symbol of fellowship and as a morale booster, is removed, is 'gone', and in its place uncertainty and uncontrollable 'greife'. Once more, the language of melancholy conveys the effect of this absence as 'not knowing', while 'griefe' 'passion' and 'Chaos' combine to produce a mournful lament on the realization of immense loss. However, within the second half of the song, the language of resilience turns emotional desolation into stoic resolve, and unfettered grief is transformed into something altogether more positive. Paradoxically, within this unbound grief, freedom is to be found, indeed, the grief transforms into a source of resilience as together the sisters (shepherdesses) unite in their shared isolation. With all that they love now lost, they can sing 'without regard', they can resist those who 'looke to see' and those who say 'I am not I' as the loss of identity or anonymity paradoxically becomes a liberating and empowering experience. Ver exhorts unification in the final couplet, both for them as sisters and for the wider royalist 'family'. This couplet reads like a master refrain for all isolated, confined and separated royalists. To be sure, 'let us singe', 'chorus' and 'Anthome' are all powerfully suggestive of the patriotic concept to be found in this couplet and as well as calling for communal connectivity and action, the first line implores togetherness 'in chorus' while intimating a wider national inference by the term 'Anthome'. The return to the concept of the friend in the final line completes the form of the song, denoting self-sufficiency and insularity, as it draws on the emblematic circle, the symbol of

[73] "Songs Anthome", MS Rawl Poet 16., 39r.
[74] Miner, *Cavalier Mode*, 251.

fellowship so common to cavalier poetry.[75] Thus, once more the Cavendish sisters close their song with what can be described as both fanciful desire and resilient hope. This final couplet retrieves them from the depths of despair and endeavours to rouse royalist spirits both near and far. It shows strength of character and fortitude in the face of dire misfortune and provides a stern retort to attempted parliamentarian domination.

While the Cavendish sisters' songs may not have entirely managed to recreate 'a genuine summer' in a metaphorical winter, they do manage to transmit an air of positivity and defiance. As royalists were systematically controlled by parliament and many cultural forms were banned, many individuals turned to coded and clandestine modes of communication and commemoration. The Cavendish sister's manuscript is representative of part of a counter-public sphere necessitated by strict parliamentarian censure. All elements of the manuscript coalesce to produce a literary artefact intent on preservation and commemoration during times of great socio-political insecurity. Their songs poignantly portray the psychological trauma of living through war and the experience of house arrest and as such are a vital contribution to women's literature of the English civil wars and to the literature of the civil wars more generally. Recognition of their status as not just aristocratic women writers but as writers *of* internal exile, and their contribution to the trend of royalist prison poetry must not be underestimated. As discussed, their work provides earlier examples of literary metaphors and tropes commonly used by well-known royalist writers during the 1650s, an important precedence hitherto unacknowledged. Through the juxtaposition of despair and resilience, they aligned both the desolate present in which they existed with the desired future in which they wish to exist, conveying the very real temporal stasis experienced by subjects of the royalist diaspora as they faced a most uncertain future. Their motifs of confinement poignantly iterate the reality of the royalist condition during the early 1640s. The sister's unfortunate experience of living in a garrison, the loss of their father and the period of house arrest paradoxically produced one of the most important manuscripts of English women's extant writing known today, a manuscript which, in the absence of actual communal gatherings, performs as a site of reunion, details familial connections, affirms status, preserves threatened cultural forms and

[75] Jonson, Ben, "An Epistle to Master John Seldon"—'upon your centre/doe your circle fill'. Miner refers to the circle as 'an emblem of perfection', 70.

speaks of and to the wider royalist 'family' as they were dispersed throughout England and the continent during the 1640s.

## Spes Alunt Exsules: Clandestine Communications and the Verse Letters of Katherine Philips

Love is the Life of Friendship, Letters are
The Life of Love, the Loadstones that by rare
Attraction makes Souls meet…[76]

Writing to Lucasia, Katherine Philips asserts '[t]here's a Religion in our Love',[77] a point which echoes John Donne's similar admission that friendship is his 'second religion'. Donne chose to express his 'extasie' regarding his friendships in the form of verse epistles, and his collection of *Letters to Severall Persons of Honour* (1651) is 'rightly considered the first major achievement in that mode in English'.[78] Thus, when Katherine Philips chose to write to her friends in verse epistles on the subject of friendship, she was drawing on a previously established literary tradition in which an earlier generation of writers chose to celebrate their friendships, as well as complimenting her own contemporaries such as James Howell, Henry Vaughan and Alexander Brome, who deployed the mode to strengthen royalist resolve during the war years and the interregnum.[79]

We have seen the ways in which Philips's ideological and political life often complicated her domestic life, yet she continued, throughout the interregnum, to write to royalists and contribute to royalist publications. This section situates Philips's coterie and her verse epistles within the oppressive climate of parliamentarian surveillance of the early 1650s and

[76] Howell, James, "To the Knowing Reader. Familiar Letters". *Epistolae Ho-Eliane, familiar letters domestic and forren divided into sundry sections, partly historicall, politicall, philosophicall, vpon emergent occasions* (1650). http://eebo.chadwyck.com.elib.tcd.ie/search/full_rec?

[77] Philips, Katherine, "Friendships Mystery to my dearest Lucasia". NLW MS. 775B. 39r–40r.

[78] Pebworth, Ted-Larry and Claude J. Summers, "Thus Friends Absent Speake': The Exchange of Verse Letters between John Donne and Henry Wooton'. *Modern Philology*. 81.4 (May 1984): 361–377.

[79] Henry Vaughan, "To my Ingenious Friend, R.W."; Alexander Brome, *Songs and Poems* (Pub 1661). An entire section of this work is given over to verse epistles to friends.

drawing on evidence from a number of acts and ordinances designed to inhibit the movement and communications between royalists, it re-evaluates the very motives for the emergence of her coterie. Through the initiation of her coterie, or society of friendship, she managed to continue to write and, through the use of pseudonyms, shield her royalist friends from the much unwanted attention of both censors and parliament, while the use of verse letters invested with royalist themes provided a more secretive mode of communication.

In addition, as I consider the historical context of enforced dispersion, the regular purges of London, and other reproaches, such as "five mile tethering", acts of confinement and routine searches of royalist homes, I posit the coterie evolved into a counter-public sphere, in which disorientated and disbanded royalists could reunite, while at once both projecting and protecting their cultural and political identities. This they could do both metaphorically, through their poetic contributions and communications, and literally, as and when they may have met in secret, for example at Henry Lawes' concerts in London. Acting as a diaspora and under these oppressive conditions, royalists were made to operate outside the usual societal parameters and, as such, were forced into forming counter-public alternatives of communal gathering. In this instance, we find that the virtual counter-public space of the coterie has a tripartite function. First, it provides an alternate political forum for the voices of oppressed royalists. Second, it works as a site of cultural engagement and an important *locus* for the maintenance of cultural identity and heritage. Third, it provides the much-needed site of succour for the distressed subjects of this diaspora.

While epistolary verse is a well-recognized genre within literary studies, few scholars have argued for some of Philips's poems to be considered as verse epistles.[80] Within this section, I examine a small selection as potential verse epistles, Philips's use of pseudonyms necessitated by the contemporary context of surveillance, and I re-evaluate the thematic content in the context of internal exile as well as the unrest which unfolded in Cardiganshire in the early 1650s. By mapping the geographical locations of some of Philips's friends, we will see that communications were difficult

[80] The exception being Line Cottegnies's paper delivered at the Reading Early Modern Studies conference in July 2013 arguing for the interpretation of Philips's poem as verse epistles that could have been real letters. Philips's poems conceived as verse letters are mentioned by Hageman & Sununu in Hageman, Elizabeth and Andrea Sununu. 'New Manuscript Texts of Katherine Philips, The "Matchless Orinda"'. *English Manuscript Studies* 4 (1993): 174–219.

and that while her verse epistles serve both an ideological purpose and as tools of cultural resistance, they also provided Philips with a clandestine mode of connection. While the nature of the poems and the use of sobriquets offer some protection for both sender and recipient, both the themes and content serve to unite Philips and her friends across many hundreds of miles. Indeed, quite apart from its content, the verse epistle as a genre is inherently bound to the concept of friendship, the letter being in Miner's words the 'most appropriate form for representing intercourse between friends'.[81]

It has been well documented that for royalists at this time, friendship provided a pattern of goodness and virtue, and could symbolically represent political bonding and even royalism itself. Certainly, 'by affirming true friendship', royalists were 'affirming a true polity for the state, what was natural and just'.[82] While a substantial amount of scholarship on Philips's friendship poems has been published,[83] much of the work on her friendship poetry has focused on what is perceived as platonic friendships between women or veiled lesbianism within the friendship poems.[84] These readings obscure both Philips's worth as a female poet engaging as an

[81] Miner, *The Cavalier Mode*, 261.

[82] See, for example, Miner, *The Cavalier Mode,* pp. 250–305, 263; Chalmers, *RWW*, pp. 56–86; Evans, 'Paradox in Poetry', pp. 174–185.

[83] For examples, see: Brady, Andrea, 'The Platonic Poems of Katherine Philips.' *Seventeenth Century* 25.2 (Oct 2010): 300–322; Gray, Catherine, 'Katherine Philips and the Post-Courtly Coterie'. *English Literary Renaissance* 32 (2002): 426–451; Hageman, Elizabeth, 'The Matchless Orinda: Katherine Philips' in *Women Writers of the Renaissance and Reformation*. Katharina M. Wilson ed. (Athens: University of Georgia Press, 1987): 566–607; Limbert, Claudia, '"The Unison of Well Tun'd Hearts": Katherine Philips's Friendships with Male Writers.' *English Language Notes.* 29 (1991): 25–37; Post, Jonathon, *English Lyric Poetry: The Seventeenth Century* (London: Routledge, 1999); Strier, Richard, 'Lyric Poetry from Donne to Philips' in *Columbia History of British Poetry.* Carl Woodring and James Shapiro eds. (New York: Columbia University Press, 1994) pp. 229–253. Hero Chalmers traces the overlaps between Philips's conceptualizations of the philosophy of friendship and those of contemporary treatises by Francis Finch and Jeremy Taylor. *RWW*, pp. 59–72.

[84] Andreadis, Harriette, 'The Sapphic-Platonics of Katherine Philips, 1632–1664.' *Signs. Journal of Women in Culture and History* 15.1 (1989): 34–60; Faderman, Lillian, *Surpassing the Love of Men: Romantic Friendship and Love between Women from the Renaissance to the Presence* (London: Women's Press, 1981); Stiebel, Arlene, 'Not Since Sappho: The Erotic in the Poems of Katherine Philips and Aphra Behn', in *Homosexuality in Renaissance and Enlightenment England: Literary Representations in Historical Context.* Claude J. Summers ed., a special issue of the *Journal of Homosexuality* 23.1/2 (1992): 153–164.

equal with male writers of her time, as well as her significant contribution to royalist literary history and culture. Such readings also overlook factual information, outlined here, which places Philips at the centre of a unisex group who had encountered war, enforced dispersion, banishment from and within their own country. Departing from modern queer readings, this section offers a re-contextualization of Philips's coterie and is aligned with Catherine Gray's assertion that Philips's emergence was not as a '[r]estoration writer or poet of private homoerotic verse but as an interregnum writer of public-political commendation'.[85] Moreover, this section will build on, as well as provide new contextual aspects to Gray's important work concerning Philips's creation of her coterie as a royalist and elitist counter-public space. As Mark Llewellyn rightly notes, Philips was producing texts 'which formed not so much communications between individual women but rather "verse essays" on the nature of friendship itself'.[86] This more public and gender-neutral version of Philips's work on friendship is evidenced not only by her poems addressed to men with coterie sobriquets, but also by contemporary correspondence from men such as Jeremy Taylor and Francis Finch, as well as Edward Dering's letter to Lucasia, written several months after Philips's death:

> Orinda had conceived the most generous designe, that in my opinion ever entered into any breast, which was to unite all those of here acquaintance, which she found worthy, or desired to make it so... into one societie, and by the bands of friendship to make an alliance more firme then what nature, our country or equall education can produce...[87]

From 1648 to 1654 Katherine Philips's husband James was Commissioner on a number of parliamentary committees which involved him in the settling of the militia in Wales, in sequestering delinquents' estates in South Wales, overseeing the propagation of the Gospel, acting on the Committee for the Army, standing as a Treasurers at War and as a

[85] Gray, Catherine, 'Post-Courtly Coterie', 427, 438.

[86] Llewellyn, Mark, 'Katherine Philips: Friendship, Poetry and Neo-Platonic Thought in Seventeenth Century England.' *Philological Quarterly* 81.4. (2002): 441–68, 441.

[87] Dering, Sir Edward, 'Letterbook'. University of Cincinnati Library. Philips Ms 14392. f. 65. See also: the treatises on friendship addressed to Philips by both Taylor and Finch, dated 1657 & 1654, respectively.

Commissioner on the High Court of Justice.[88] Thus, James Philips was involved with the parliamentarian war effort politically, militarily, religiously and judicially. Under these conditions, Katherine's royalist sympathies would have had to have been tempered, and it is very unlikely that she would have had royalist visitors in her home. Patrick Thomas posits that the only writer to have visited Philips in Cardigan is the translator John Davies of Kidwelly, who met her during his 'almost two years of retirement in Wales'.[89] Davies was a Presbyterian and possibly the only one of her literary acquaintances in the years before the restoration who was politically acceptable to her husband. Indeed, Katherine's 'involvement with known royalists caused [James Philips] serious difficulties when it was used to undermine the security of his own position by the religious radicals Vavasor Powell and Jenkin Jones'.[90] Thomas suggests that as a

> man of moderate Cromwellian views and considerable local political influence, James Philips was an obvious target for the Fifth Monarchists and other radical opponents of Cromwell, who were led in Wales by Vavasor Powell and Jenkin Jones, Llandetty. Such men must have regarded the expression of monarchist sympathies by Orinda in her verses against Powell as a useful piece of evidence with which they could undermine her hus-

[88] See respectively: an ordinance for settling the Militia in several Counties, Cities and places within the Kingdom of England, Dominion of Wales and Towne of Barwick upon Tweed. 2 December 1648, Vol. I, 1233; an act concerning the Sequestration of South-Wales, and County of Monmouth. 23 Feb 1648–1649, Vol. II, pp. 14–16; act for the better Propagation and Preaching of the Gospel in Wales, and redress some Grievances. 22 Feb 1649/1650 Vol. II, 342–348; an act Appointing a Committee for the Army, and Treasurers at War. 1653, Vol. II, 703; an ordinance for establishing a High Court of Justice. 13 June 1654.Vol. II, 917. The propagation of the gospel was most likely a measure taken to speed up the progress of Puritanism in Wales. 'This faith, after all, had inspired opposition to Charles I, and Puritan fervour had been a potent force impelling the soldiers'. Soon the 'commissioners under the Propagation act soon discovered that it was much easier to destroy an old edifice than to erect a new one'. W.S.K. Thomas, *Stuart Wales* (Llandysul: Gomer Press, 1988), 57, 67. Another interesting clash between the Philipses given that Katherine's loyalties nonetheless 'increasingly inclined towards orthodox Anglicanism and the royalist cause'. Thomas, Patrick, Vol. I, 5.

[89] Thomas. Patrick. *The Poems.* Vol. I, 11.

[90] Thomas, Vol I, 5–6. This contentious issue is addressed by Philips in 'To (the truly competent Judge of Honour) Lucasia, upon a scandalous libel made by J. Jones' and 'To Antenor, on a paper of mine wch J.Jones threatens to publish to his prejudice'. The poems are dated after 1651 when Anne Owen had received the name of Lucasia and was adopted into Philips's society. See 'To the excellent Mrs A.O. upon receiving the name of Lucasia and adoption into our Society' dated 26 Dec. 1651. NLW MS 775b. 20r.

> band's position. They may have also uncovered Orinda's connections with "conspicuous royalist" John Jeffreys… and the Royalist polemicist John Berkenhead.[91]

Hence, Philips would have had to find more surreptitious means to communicate with her royalist friends.

Along with these domestic tensions, in early 1650 Philips's friends faced yet more reproaches from parliament. Royalists were not only ejected from London, but they also endured other impositions such as confinement within London should they not heed the banishment acts. Additionally, those who returned to their dwellings in the country were not to 'pass or remove above five miles from thence' and 'within twenty days of coming to any of the said places…notifie their coming hither…present themselves, and deliver their true names' to the minister and to the constable of the parish, and, in London licenses were required to move around, either *in to*, or *out of* the capital.[92] Furthermore, in July 1650 parliament issued another act upon which:

> Commissioners for the militia in the several counties and places of England and Wales… shall observe and put in execution… means to inform themselves, and from time to time to take from others Informations… of all Conspiracies, Designs, Practices, secret and suspitious Meetings of disaffected persons, whether expressed by *words* or *actions*, spoken, *printed*, preached, *written or published* wheresoever… by securing, dispersing or committing to prison the parties whom they finde to be especially active and dangerous.[93] [my emphasis]

Thus, at the outset of the interregnum, parliament had put in place numerous measures to track and control royalists as well as censure their written and spoken words not only in and around London but also in parishes countrywide.

With each of these acts, communications between and gatherings of Philips and her royalist friends may have been rendered next to impossible. Anne Owen (Lucasia) was in Angelsey. John Jeffreys (Philaster) is

[91] Thomas, Vol. I, 348.

[92] Firth and Rai, *Acts and Ordinances of the Interregnum*. Vol. II, 26 February 1649/1650, 349–354, 351, 352.

[93] Ibid., 'An Act for settling of the militia of the commonwealth of England'. Vol. II, 11 July, 1650, 398/399. James Philips was also commissioner of this committee.

mentioned as owing fines in Cardigan in late 1648/9[94] while he was living in Brecknock.[95] Later on, he contributes to Cartwright's posthumous volume published in 1651. In fact, this volume places many of Philips's coterie, such as John Berkenhead (Cratander), Francis Finch (Paelemon) and Henry Lawes in London around 1650–1651. Indeed, Henry Lawes was well known for holding secret concerts for many eminent royalists, and it is at these gatherings that Philips may have been able to slip copies of some poems or verse letters to other coterie members. Yet, for the most part, scattered as they were throughout north and south Wales, close to London and in London, Philips's establishment of her coterie provided the perfect solution to their geo-political challenges, and her utilization of the verse letter would provide less obvious means to realize their communication requirements.

Four poems by Philips are of particular interest in this period. They range in dates from 1651 to 1654, are addressed to friends using sobriquets—or pseudonyms—and centre on the royalist and politically charged topic of friendship, while proving the purpose of Philips's coterie. Both "To the excellent Mrs A.O. upon her receiving the name of Lucasia and adoption into our society" and "A Retir'd Friendship, to Ardelia" are situated immediately within this claustrophobic socio-political environment engendered by parliamentarian acts and ordinances. The first is dated 29 December 1651 and the second is dated 23 August 1651. The third poem, "To my excellent Lucasia on our friendship", dated 17 July 1653, focuses specifically on the friendship between Anne Lewis Owen and 'Orinda', while the fourth, "To the noble Palaemon on his incomparable discourse of friendship", must be written after 1654.[96] Focusing on the first two poems, referencing the other two as well, this section outlines characteristics these poems have in common with the genre of the verse letter. Further, Philips's utilization of sobriquets to address her friends during this tense period of political turmoil will be reconsidered in the context of such cultures of surveillance. Lastly, this section explores the notion of friendship as a unifying trope, which once in circulation among coterie members could provide both solace and generate political defiance. Brought together in these poems, it will be seen that these literary

[94]An act concerning the Sequestration of South-Wales, and County of Monmouth. 23 February 1648–1649, Vol II, pp. 14–16.

[95]Thomas, Vol. III, 182.

[96]Finch's treatise on Friendship is dated 1653/1654.

strategies and unifying themes, provided Philips and the coterie not only with a more clandestine means to communicate away from prying parliamentarians but also engendered a virtual site of reunion, strategically coded yet easily recognizable to royalists.

In James Howell's *Discourse betwixt Patricius and Peregrin, touching the Distractions of the Times, with the Causes of them*, the fictitious character 'Peregrin', who has been travelling throughout Europe, states that an 'intercourse of letters' is 'the best sort of fuell to warme affection and to keep life in that noble vertue friend|ship'.[97] During the uncertainty of the early war years, then, letters were seen as a comfort, and as a means to sustain friendships and offer stability despite long temporal and geographical separation. Moreover, letters were viewed as a form of sacred communication imbued with secrecy, or at least confidentiality among friends, as Peregrin remarks:

> hee who breaks open ones Letters, which are the Idea's of the minde, may bee said to rip up his brest, to plunder and rifle his very braine, and rob him of his most precious and secretest thoughts.[98]

Hence, the letter to a friend was invested with elevated notions of noble and trusted friendship, a *locus* in which true transactions of the heart and mind take place and any interception of such correspondence is militarized. However, Miner notes that 'friendship did present the poets with the problem of demonstrating the accepted virtues of friendship in usable poetic forms'.[99] Writing that Ben Jonson, for example, experimented with different poetic forms in a bid to find one which suited the topic, Miner states the verse epistle eventually became the 'one that dominated the field of poems for friendship'.[100] Ted-Larry Pebworth and Claude J Summers write that utilization of the verse letter is 'fundamentally referential and occasional... rooted in external reality. Hence, full appreciation of any verse letter requires knowledge of the contexts from which it arises'.[101] Operating

[97] Howell, James, *The trve informer who in the following discovrse or colloqvie discovereth unto the vvorld the chiefe causes of the sa[]d distempers in Great Britanny and Ireland/deduced from their originals; and also a letter writ by Serjeant-Major Kirle to a friend at VVinsor* (1643), 2.

[98] Ibid., 1.

[99] Miner, *The Cavalier Mode*, 260.

[100] Ibid., 261.

[101] Ted-Larry Pebworth and Claude J Summers, 'Thus Friends absent Speake', 361.

within the precarious conditions of parliamentary rule, Philips turned to the verse letter as a tool of discretion that could provide her with both the privacy of the letter form along with the literary codification of poetry.

"To the excellent Mrs A. O"[102] is set out in iambic tetrameter, rhyming couplets and verse paragraphs, characteristics most common to the Horatain epistle. As opposed to the 1667 edition of Philips's poems, this version uses initials rather than Anne Owen's full name in the title.[103] At a time when political tensions ran high, the choice of initials was common among many who wrote letters or verse letters to friends.[104] Moreover, the speaker not only addresses the secret subject but also opens up the initiation and the topic of friendship to the entire coterie by deploying the universal pronoun 'we':

> We are Compleat; and fate hath now
> No greater blessing to bestow
> Nay the dull world must now confess
> We have all worth; all happiness

Here, Philips celebrates the inclusion of her closest friend into her society, yet while she addresses the poem to Anne, it is the society which is 'compleat' with the blessing of this 'sacred' adoption. This arrival provides members with perspective as Philips admits 'we by thy relation are allow'd/ Lustre enough to be Lucasia's cloud'. Thus, the poem takes on a double address or a 'double enunciation',[105] as the speaker looks towards the addressee yet simultaneously beyond to address the rest of the coterie on this auspicious occasion. Similarly, 'To the Noble Palaemon'[106] utilizes the

[102] Philips, "To the excellent Mrs A. O. upon her receiving the name of Lucasia and adoption into our society, 29 Demb, 1651", NLW MS 775B, 20r. All citations are taken from this manuscript.

[103] The 1664 edition and the Rosania MS, composed after Philips's death all have Anne Owen's full name.

[104] See, for example, Alexander Brome, *Songs and Poems* (pub, 1661). There is a section devoted to epistles many of which are addressed with initials. Before taking the name Orinda, Philips herself used initials in William Cartwright's posthumous volume *Comedies, Tragicomedies, with Other Poems*, 1651.

[105] I thank Line Cottegnies for her insightful comments here. Line was kind enough to offer some insight regarding her thoughts on Philips's poems as verse letters. The phrase 'double enunciation' is directly attributed to Line.

[106] Philips, "To the Noble Palaemon on his incomparable Discourse of Friendship", NLW MS. 775B, 47–48r.

pronoun 'we' and focuses on the topic of friendship at the heart of Philips's coterie. This poem follows the alternative Horatian mode, while set out in rhyming couplets it differs in that they are pentameter couplets set in a verse essay form. These two poems may bookend the tumultuous early 1650s but they offer an aperçus into the beginnings and the development of Philips's enterprise, both on a personal level with close friends and on a wider, more societal level, with the coterie in general.

While "A Retrir'd friendship, to Ardelia, 23rd Aug. 1651"[107] is set out stanzically, a form uncommon to the verse epistle, the poem nevertheless has an addressee, and carries distinct characteristics of the verse epistle's form. The addressee, Ardelia, has not been identified but Philip Souers has suggested that it may be Lady Dering, wife of Philips's 'Silvander', Sir Edward Dering. The Dering's estate was at Surrenden House, Kent. However, a letter addressed to Edward from his mother, dated 11 June 1650, locates him at Lambeth, a long way from Cardigan and perilously close to the parliamentarian power base of London.[108] While stanzic form was uncommon in verse epistles, it was not completely absent. For instance, Alexander Brome writes an epistle 'To his Friend J.H', which is five stanzas long.[109] Philips's poem is set out in tetrameter quatrains, and focuses on the theme of friendship and its power to protect. Further, the date is significant in the context of internal exile and the contacting of distanced friends. A rebellion had broken out in Cardiganshire, a rebellion which Colonel James Philips was appointed to deal with in its aftermath.[110] John Kerrigan notes that this unrest and Philips's royalist sympathies 'quite possibly troubled her marriage.'[111] Thus, given the proximity of the rebellion, Philips's passion for her royalist friends, along with the fact that her husband was dispatched to deal with the rebels—a band of royalist gentry and their friends—it must have been a tense time.

These poems by Philips also adhere to the verse epistle tradition through their form of address. Earl Miner terms the genre of the verse epistle the 'poetry of address',[112] and Bill Overton insists that the verse epistle must

[107] Philips, NLW, MS 775B, 29–30r.

[108] Ninth Report of the Royal Commission on Historical Manuscripts, Part 1, Part 2 & 3, 441.

[109] Brome, 'Epistles', *Songs and Poems*, 1661, 105.

[110] *CSPD*, 1651, 266–267. Also see Kerrigan, *Archipelagic English: Literature, History and Politics 1603–1707* (Oxford & New York: Oxford University Press), 211–212.

[111] Kerrigan, 212.

[112] Miner, *Cavalier Mode*, 265.

have an addressee, that of either a friend or patron.[113] The four poems examined here are but a fraction of the poems pseudonymously addressed to members of the coterie. Previously, Philips's use of sobriquets has been linked to the popular cultural trend associated with the *precieux* of the Caroline court that drew its inspiration from romances and pastorals.[114] For example, one of the sources of Anne Owen's name comes from Leucasia in Cartwright's *The Seige*, a character who praises the loyalty of her friend and attendant. While the literary origins of the sobriquets are perhaps indisputable, the motive for their application has not been addressed.[115] Margaret Ezell points out that even the 'most well-known coterie circles during the renaissance do not appear to have adopted this practice', for example, The Sons of Ben.[116] Thus, this was a system of circulation, movement, address and response that was unique to Philips's coterie. As Ezell suggests, the unusual use of sobriquets in seventeenth-century coteries involved an 'active, on-going exchange between two or more individuals constituting a dynamic literary system rather than a static artefact'.[117]

Additionally, useful at times when lines of allegiance are in question, the sobriquets also acted as a neutralizing device which obscured exact

[113]Overton, Bill, 'Aphra Behn and the Verse Epistle. *Women's Writing.*' 16.3 (2009): 369–391, 370.

[114]See, for example, Bush, Douglas, *English Literature in the Earlier Seventeenth Century* (New York: Oxford University Press), 1945; Thomas, Patrick, *The Collected Works of Katherine Philips.* Vol. I. *The Poems.* Thomas points out that 'the Ideals of Queen Henrietta Maria's precieux culture were an important cohesive influence among defeated Cavaliers', 10; Bernikow, Lousie. *The World Split Open: Women Poets* 1552–1950 (London: Women's Press, 1974).

[115]For example, other pseudonyms include Francis finch (Palaemon)—a character associated with friendship in Chaucer's *The Knight's Tale*, Shakespeare's *Two Noble Kinsmen* and Spenser's *Fairie Queen.* Although Patrick Thomas suggests she took the name from 'Honore D'Urfe's *L'Astree* and a sea god named Palaemon is mentioned in Saint-Amant's "La Solitude", a poem which was translated by Philips' (Thomas, *The Poems*, 331); Philips's husband (Antenor)—the Trojan who tried to make peace between Troy and Greece; John Berkenhead (Cratander), named after the hero of William Cartwright's *Royal Slave.*

[116]Ezell, Margaret, 'Reading Pseudonyms in Seventeenth-Century English Coterie Literature'. http://web.archive.org/web/20040906084215/http://www.geocities.com/katacheson/philipsezell.html, 3. Ezell also reminds us that previous use of pseudonyms, for example in Sidney's sonnet sequence, did not require the object (Stella) to respond or to be interactive in the literary enterprise. 'Her role was to be written about, not to engage in an exchange of verse', 3.

[117]Ezell, 'Pseudonyms', 3.

identity and offered easy access to a group of like-minded individuals. As Ezell argues, pseudonyms 'acts not as a cloak or mask, but a password to single membership in an exclusive and much desired group'.[118] By deploying sobriquets, Philips could position all members of the coterie within a sanctified group which shared the same beliefs and wrote on common themes. The members of Philips's coterie were all staunch royalists, with William Cartwright as their ideal. His posthumous *Comedies*, to which many members of Philips's coterie contributed, lamented the loss of this royalist literary giant and committed royalist, and, as Catherine Gray points out, his text 'works to foreground a collection of displaced Oxford wits gathered to mourn the loss of the university as a royalist power base, thus Cartwright comes to stand as a synecdoche not only of this geopolitical space, but of its symbolic centre, Charles I'.[119]

Given what the coterie stood for, then, during the interregnum the sobriquets not only worked aesthetically but also had a logical and ideological purpose too in that they announced values such as honour, loyalty and the intrinsic belief in the goodness of friendship and all it symbolized. Catherine Gray has written that Philips furthered her intention to neutralize tensions through the construction of a 'series of interchangeable literary heroes, Royalists who show their commitment to the cause not through military exploits...but through the kind of poetic production she engages in to create them'.[120] Thus, through the use of sobriquets, Philips generates a collective group breaking down the barriers between writer and audience; each persona becomes equalized within a shared cultural space; each takes turns in her poems of commendation to stand as a model for royalist values yet no one person is predominant, thus leaving the values and principles of the group to be foregrounded. Hence, Philips's 'assumption of another identity was not to disguise the true nature or intent of the person but to enhance and to announce the values and characteristics upheld by the group',[121] as well as 'function to protect the iden-

[118] Ibid., 4.

[119] Gray, 'Post Courtly Coterie', 433.

[120] Gray posits that Philips creates a series of identities in her poetry of commendation; by her pastoral sobriquets, she inscribes the notion of a shared cultural investment with each individual bearing the hallmarks of the ideal characters from Royalist plays and romances. 'The repetitions of tropes and romantic/heroic personae constructs a community through identification' distilling each person and verse into a 'homogenous politico-aesthetic value', 'Post Courtly Coterie', 441.

[121] Ezell, 'Pseudonyms, 5.

tity of a group rather than only an individual'.[122] Hence, Philips's sobriquets not only transcended the awkwardness between individuals during a time when one's allegiance was continually called into question, but could also, if required by difficult conditions, allow the coterie to deny its own existence. Ultimately, Philips and her royalist friends had to be sure that their 'words or actions, spoken, printed…written or published' could not be traced directly to them and adopting sobriquets was one way to mask their identity should letters or poems be intercepted.

The content of Philips's poems and the ways in which that content is shared among the coterie also conforms to the standard verse epistle convention. Earl Miner asserts that the author of a verse epistle 'addresses himself in a double sense, that is, both to person and a topic…the poet makes his topic important not only between the speaking poet (or 'persona') and his addressee but also between the poet and his readers'.[123] Returning to Cottegnies' term 'double enunciation', it is clear Philips utilized such a strategy to speak about friendship on both a personal and group level.[124] Within these poems, Philips deployed the notion of platonic friendship in her verse letter as a universal and unifying force amongst royalists, as well as valorizing the strength within refined spirits of those who do choose to retire. She offered friendship itself as a site of refuge and outlined the integrity that is to be found in partaking in such faithful endeavours, as discussed above. During the war years, friends and societies were vital to the cavaliers,[125] and it is well documented that friendship was a common theme in cavalier literature throughout the period, with the notion of friendship by the fireside encouraging royalists to persevere. By drawing on Platonicism and neo-stoicism, Philips not only was able to construct 'a discourse of honour, truth and beauty which could be fulfilled privately'[126] but also espouse the benefits of retirement, advocate reason above passion and urge acceptance of fortune. Philips recreated these themes by adopting a moralistic tone, as she

[122] Ibid., 4.

[123] Miner, *The Cavalier Mode*, 265.

[124] Hero Chalmers offers in-depth analysis of the codifying of friendship between royalists in general, and the overlaps between Philips's discourse on friendship and those of Francis Finch and Jeremy Taylor, *RWW*, 70.

[125] Miner, *The Cavalier Mode*, 6.

[126] Brady, Angela, 'The Platonic Poems of Katherine Philips', 301. Brady posits that Philips frequently draws on Plato's model of friendship as that which 'composes the chain of human Society; and the central motif of her friendship poems is the belief that, as Cicero's *De Amicitia* has it, 'versus amicus est tamquam alter idem': the real friend is… another self', 305.

crafted friendship as a barrier against the moral and physical perils of the age. Her verse epistles show a demonstration of a community consciousness with a strong interest in fellowship and goodness, as well as offering an option for weathering out the cavalier winter of the interregnum.

"A Retir'd Friendship, To Ardelia" clearly outlines a moral manifesto for those who may doubt the power of retired communal virtue to withstand the rigours of the interregnum.[127] Having set up the image of this age being ruled by 'serious follies,'[128] Philips suggests that the shelter to be found in the valleys in Wales, discussed above, can just as easily be found within amity among companions. Friendship itself is hailed as a space in which there is 'no quarrelling for Crowns', 'Nor any slavery of State'. Indeed, within the realm of friendship there is no 'disguise or treachery' and 'From Blood and Plots this place is free'. Building on this sense of safety to be found within companionship the speaker states, it is 'remov'd from noise of Wars'/in one anothers hearts' it 'lives', thus at once placing distance between oneself and the trauma of war whilst indicating the originary source of such strong bonds. Each stanza within this verse epistle compounds the sense of security and order to be experienced by withdrawing to a communal refuge, or, in this case, a diasporic counter-community. Friendship is deemed to be virtuous and, as a result, impenetrable as the speaker states:

> We wear about us such a charm,
> No horrour can be our offence,
> For mischiefs self can do no harm
> To Friendship or innocence.

Thus, friendship acted as a safeguard against the 'mischiefs' of the age and one could commit no offence once blessed by its grace. Hence, as with Ben Jonson, Philips's poetry is characteristic in its moral integrity and this places her work and her intentions squarely within the sphere of cavalier poetry. Earl Miner has noted that this integrity 'marks the firm center of his [Jonson's] poetic compass'[129] and there is no doubt that Philips appears to be following this ethical track. "A Retir'd Friendship" endeavours to remove all disguise to invoke honesty and virtue. Friendship, impervious

[127] "To the Noble Palaemon" is also didactic in content, another characteristic of the Horatian epistle.

[128] Philips, "A retir'd Friendship".

[129] Miner, *The Cavalier Mode*, 57.

to the strife of the age, can provide a safe haven, and it is a means by which the speaker asserts 'we'[130] are elevated. It is a state through which:

> we (of one anothers mind
> assur'd) the boisterous World disdain;
> With quiet Souls and unconfin'd
> Enjoy what Princes wish in vain.

Philips here not only offers friendship as a space of solace but also suggests it is a place within which they may be free from ideological constraint and even overcome socio-political divides wrought by civil war—friendship is endowed with qualities powerful enough to transcend human folly or greed. Philips's poem appears to insist that friendship, like retirement to the country, can act as a shield against not only physical battles but moral warfare also. In building on this moral stance through the addition of each stanza, Philips's emphasis on innocence and virtue to be found in friendship stands defiantly against the moralistic 'treachery' of the interregnum years. Placing such emphasis on friendship, fraternity and bonds between souls, Philips draws on the distinct royalist tropes which separate and elevate them from the parliamentarians. In Philips's poetry, the trope of friendship which stands for goodness, virtuousness and even royalism itself assumes new meaning—it becomes not just a trope for political or fraternal bonding but it becomes space in which that bonding and uniting can occur.

The failure to fully consider the historical context of Philips's verse letters has resulted in criticism that presents a false image of Philip's purpose and her persona in these and other verse letters, as well as the conditions which shaped the initiation of her coterie. In many cases, assessment of her work seems to have been considered in a historical vacuum, with little attention given over to the events and difficulties which had beset the royalist community as they struggled to negotiate parliamentarian climates of surveillance during the early 1650s. Cast into internal exile and separated from one another not just by hundreds of miles but also by acts and ordinances, which sought to control or monitor royalists movement, their correspondence and censure their written word, royalists had to find means to stay connected to each other. Many turned to letters and verse letters, others reiterated bonds through manuscript circulation such as the Cavendish sisters discussed above. Philips, in west Wales, utilized her

[130] Philips, "A retir'd Friendship".

coterie to maintain connection and strengthen bonds between her and her childhood friends, as well as those she later collaborated with on various royalist publications. Taxed with navigating a *via media* between her domestic and literary life, she chose to initiate a counter-public within and through which friends joined together and similar ideals were shared in the absence of physical presence. Through her coterie, subtly codified verse letters and occasionally at royalist gatherings in London, Philips and her friends could remain connected and preserve ideals and mores important to the King's supporters throughout the very uncertain years of the interregnum.

## Counter-Public Entertainments at the Courts of Queen Elizabeth of Bohemia and Mary of Orange

> there is little mischief brought forth, but it is hatched at the Hage, which is a nest of malignant vypers. The princess royall's and the queen of Bohemia's Court nourishes those creatures…[131]

Though political in nature, this quotation from a letter of intelligence can also be applied to the climate of cultural resistance at play in The Hague during the 1650s. The Hague had become a royalist satellite city during the interregnum, where exiles from England gathered in great numbers. From here royalists looked back at their homeland and planned both political and monarchical restoration. From England, Cromwell sought to both spread Protestantism across Europe and reduce the Dutch state to complete reliance on England.[132] Home to Charles I's sister Elizabeth and to his daughter Mary Stuart both of whom were targeted by parliamentarian spies and information gatherers, the political environment at The Hague was volatile. However, both women crucially encouraged and maintained the royalist community during the years of the interregnum through a potent form of cultural resistance. By staging royalist entertainments, an activity that was banned in England at the time, these women offered exiled royalists in and around The Hague a point of contact, not

[131] Letter of Intelligence from Holland. 12, June 1654. Collection of State Papers John Thurloe, Vol II., 344. http://sources.tannerritchie.com.elib.tcd.ie/browser.php?bookid=215.

[132] Rait, Robert S., *Five Stuart Princesses* (Westminster: A. Constable & Co., 1902), 186.

only with each other as a diasporic group but also with Mary as a living symbol of the link to the English throne.

While the Cavendish sisters and Katherine Philips formed diasporic counter-publics through textual and virtual forms in response to parliamentarian oppression in England, the entertainments at the courts of Queen Elizabeth of Bohemia and Mary of Orange also generated a counter-public space of reunion for dispersed royalists on the continent. This section argues that their cultural contributions stand in opposition to the systematic suppression of theatre and stage-plays, and are part of a wider network of royalist cultural work designed to preserve a distinctive royalist cultural heritage. Situating previously examined entertainments in the context of the royalist diaspora, this section argues that the cultural output of these two women is not just concerned with assertion of their own identity in peripheral life, but is crucial for thinking about the wider network of the royalist diaspora on the continent and how this group consciously endeavoured to preserve royalist cultural heritage and identity at a critical point in their history. To these ends, I recontextualize three of many characteristically royalist entertainments staged by these two Stuart women at The Hague. I argue that *A King and No King*, *La Carmesse*, and *The Enchanted Lovers* can be considered as both virtual and real *fora* for reunion, and that Elizabeth and Mary's choice enabled a group consciousness which worked to preserve royalist cultural forms through transmission, thereby creating a transnational counter-public. For royalists cut off from their homeland, these examples of expressly royalist forms recreated the coherence of a common history which had been shattered by enforced dispersion, diaspora and exile.

On 2 September 1642, parliament issued its first ordinance against stage-plays which outlined that due to 'the distracted estate of England, threatened with a cloud of blood by civil war', all 'public Stage-Plays shall cease, and bee forborne'.[133] A later ordinance in 1647/8 declared that plays be 'co.demned', that stage-players be declared as 'rouges…punishable within the statutes' and 'liable unto pains and penalties'.[134] Play houses were systematically demolished or pulled down to ensure that no surreptitious playing could take place. The Globe was demolished in 1644; on

[133] Order for Stage-Plays to cease. 2 September 1642. *Acts and Ordinances*. Vol. I., 26–27.

[134] An Ordinance for the 'utter suppression and abolishing of all Stage-Plays and interludes within the penalties to be inflicted on the actors and spectators therein expressed'. 11 February 1647/1648. *Acts and Ordinances*. Vol. I., 1070.

16 July 1645, the Commons ordered that 'the boarded Masque House at Whitehall, the Masque House at St. James', and the Courts of the Guard, be forthwith pulled down, and sold away'.[135] In March 1649 Salisbury Court, Phoenix theatre and the Fortune were also dismantled, and Bear Gardens were closed in 1650.[136] Thus, in England, between 1642 and 1660, the extant 'records of dramatic activity ... show only sporadic and usually hasty play-acting in an extremely hostile environment'.[137]

In England, theatre was viewed by puritans as immoral and idolatrous. Edward Phillips notes that the ordinances vary to reveal a burgeoning religious agenda, and comparing an ordinance from 1642 with one dated 1647, he argues that the latter act is different in moral tone from that of 1642. The 1642 order, he writes, 'has indeed moral objections to the levity and lasciviousness of plays, but its justification of action is that frivolous entertainment is inappropriate at a time of war'.[138] This seems perhaps a reasonable concern. However, Phillips asserts that the ordinance of 1647 is 'really a Puritan tract' which argued that 'stage plays are not to be tolerated among professors of the Christian religion'.[139] Therefore, as conflict increased in the 1640s, the opposition utilized the banning of theatre not only to 'avert the wrath of God' but also to antagonize the monarchy and its supporters.[140] Yet, it is important to consider that before the war there were objections on both sides regarding the propriety of theatre and Lois Potter has observed that some 'admired classical drama but not the modern stage; some liked plays but not the expensive and exclusive court masques; some objected not to plays but to the rowdy spectators who attended them; some wished only for the banning of performances on Sundays'.[141] However, after 1642, material that had potential partisan

[135] Journal of the House of Commons, IV. Cited in Hoston, Leslie. *Commonwealth and the Restoration Stage* (Cambridge: Harvard University Press, 1928), 14.

[136] Nigel Smith notes that Folger Lib Ms V b 275 shows survey of London c 1658 in 'Public Fora' in *Literature and Revolution in England 1640–1660* (New Haven, Connecticut: Yale University Press, 1994), 71.

[137] Bentley, Gerald Eades, 'The Period 1642–1660'. *The Revels History of Drama in English IV 1613–1660.* Edwards et al. eds. (London: Methuen & Co. Ltd, 1981), 69–125, p. 121.

[138] Phillips, Edward, 'Society and the Theatre: the Closing of the Theatre in *The Revels History of Drama in English IV 1613–1660.* Edwards et al. eds. (London: Methuen & Co. Ltd, 1981), 1–67, p. 62.

[139] Ibid., 62.

[140] Order for Stage-Plays to Cease, 27.

[141] Potter, Lois, 'The Plays and Playwrights 1642–1660', *Revels History*, in *The Revels History of Drama in English IV 1613–1660.* Edwards et al. eds. (London: Methuen & Co. Ltd, 1981), 264.

implication became politically charged, and this was particularly true of the two forms that had been most in fashion at court—the masque and the romance.[142]

Meanwhile, George W. Brant notes that the 'reformation and condemnation of the theatre went hand in hand' and that 'nowhere was the opposition so strong and enduring as in Holland'.[143] Performance, rather than drama, was the key problem with enactment of sacred subjects completely off-limits. In 1643 Gysterbus Voetius, a clergyman and professor of theology at Utrecht, wrote a 'Disputatio' concerning stage plays. The treatise outlined what kind of performances should be permitted by a Christian magistrate, issuing one specific proviso concerning productions that would only be allowed if 'disguisings, women mixing with men, men posing as women, abuse of God's name, mockeries or old plays, follies, improper jests, dancing, and all that goes with it' were banned.[144] However, the divide of opinion regarding theatre in England was evident in Holland also. The nobles at The Hague paid little heed to irate Calvinists with courtiers at the court of Frederick Henry and Amalia indulging in their own love of (French) theatre, for instance.[145] To be sure, the Stadholder's court at The Hague continuously employed French companies, and William II, in particular, 'spent enormous sums on jewelry for French actresses'.[146] It is also worth noting that both Elizabeth and Mary were continually reproved by the Calvinists for their extravagant entertainments. As early as 1624 Elizabeth was 'openly reprimanded from the pulpit…suggesting a casual relationship between late-night dancing at her

[142] Ibid., 267.

[143] Brant, George W., *Theatre in Europe: A Documentary History. German and Dutch Theatre 1600–1848* (Cambridge, New York & Melbourne: Cambridge University Press, 1993), 398.

[144] Voetius, Geysterbus, Disputatio de Comoedies, Dat is, Twist-redening van Schouspellen. Gehouden en voorgestelt in the Hooge-school van Uitrecht. Uit de Latijnsche in de Neerduitsche taal veraalt door B.S. (Gybertus Voetius, D.D, C., Being a Critical Argument on Theatrical Performances). Given and proposed in the illustrious school of Utrecht. Trans. from Latin into the Dutch language by B.S. (Amsterdam, Jasper Adamsz Star, 1650), 37–38 cited in Brant.

[145] Keblusek, Marika, 'Books at the Stadholder's Court' in *Princely Display, The Court of Frederick of Orange and Amalia Solms in The Hague*. Keblusek and Jori Zilmans eds. Trans. John Rudge (The Historical Museum, The Hague: Waanders Publishers, Zwolle, 2012), 143–152, p. 147.

[146] Brant, *Theatre in Europe*, 381–382.

court, and the break of a dyke elsewhere in Holland'.[147] Much later still, their entertainments remained under attack. In 1655 Elizabeth wrote to Charles II that after two nights masquing 'a little French preacher Carre saide in his sermon wee had committed a greate sinne as that of Sodome and Gomora, which set all the church laughing'.[148] Thus, conflict between Calvinist ethics and royalist expressions of identity and cultural heritage caused much consternation and discord between the religious community and that of the courts at The Hague.

## Royalist Community

It was not only Elizabeth's and Mary's entertainments which irked the Calvinists. Both royals formed courts that welcomed royalists, carried on Anglican traditions and, in Mary's case, provided much financial support for Charles II and his court. Elizabeth was well established at The Hague since she and her husband Frederick had arrived as exiles from Bohemia in 1621. Mary 'held a contested and ambiguous role in the tangled affairs not only of the House of Stuart but also the House of Orange and the United Provinces'.[149] Daughter of Charles I and wife of Prince William of Orange, Mary's actions were watched and studied carefully. On 4 January 1653, Sir Edward Hyde wrote 'It is a great misfortune that the Princess Royall will not take counsel from persons of honour and interest, but subjects herself solely to Henfleet and his lady [Katherine Stanhope]'.[150]

[147] Keblusek, Marika, 'Entertainment in Exile' in *Triumphs of the Defeated: Early Modern Festivals and Messages of Legitimacy*. J. Beppler, P. Davidson eds. (Wiesbaden/Wolfenbüttel, 2007), pp. 173–190, p. 180.

[148] Letter from Elizabeth of Bohemia to Charles II, from The Hague, 13 December 1655. *Collection of State Papers John Thurloe*, Vol. I, 672. http://sources.tannerritchie.com.elib.tcd.ie/browser.php?bookid=214.

[149] Hughes and Sanders, 'The Hague Courts', 3.

[150] Hyde to Nicholas, *Calendar of the Clarendon State Papers*, Vol. II, 169. http://sources.tannerritchie.com.elib.tcd.ie/browser.php?bookid=768. Sir Edward Hyde was a politician, historian, lawyer and prominent royalist exile. Henfleet was a Dutch diplomat Jehan ban der Kerckhoven, an advocate of the Stuart—Orange match between Mary and Frederick. Kerckhoven was married to Katherine, Lady Stanhope, governess to Mary since 1641. Mary, including Hyde and Nicholas, were concerned about the influence of Stanhope and her husband over Mary. See Hughes and Sanders, 'Gender, Geography and Exile: Royalists and the Low Countires in the 1650s' in McElligott and Smith, *Royalists and Royalism during the Interregnum*.

However, Mary was at all times loyal to her family, and constantly endeavoured to further her brother's cause. As Marika Keblusek notes:

> the Princesse Royal's household in particular, numbered a great many British courtiers and servants. Admittedly, not all of them were exiles, although of course they had strong royalist sympathies, some acting as intermediaries or agents for the Stuart cause. Also, royalist refugees whose family members already resided at Mary's court, consequently came to The Hague or Breda.[151]

Hughes and Sanders have also written that 'Mary, and to a lesser extent Elizabeth, did provide places in their courts for many exiled royalists'.[152] These eminent royalists sought roles and offices in court, positions which simply ceased to exist at home as the court was displaced and then dispersed in exile. For example, Sir Charles Cotterell, courtier, translator and later close friend of Katherine Philips, accompanied William Aylesbury and the Duke of Buckingham into exile. Initially, in Antwerp, Cotterell managed the Duke's affairs, however, in 1652 he had moved to The Hague to become steward and financial advisor to Elizabeth. Nicholas Oudart, a government official, and handler of royal correspondence fled into exile in 1648 and he is recorded as being secretary to Mary by 1649, while later lending his services to Charles II. Others include, Sir Alexander Hume, Mary's Chamberlain, Thomas Howard and Nicholas Armorer. It also appeared that Mary wished to surround her son with English, rather than French courtiers. National archives at The Hague reveal numerous appointments by Mary: Sarah Story, plate cleaner; Anna Dove, Laundry woman; Thomas Davids, Cook; Mrs Howard, governess; Charles Henry, Baron Wooton, First Groom of the bedchamber, for example.[153]

In addition to welcoming royalists to The Hague, 'by the 1650s, Mary's court—as well as that of Elizabeth of Bohemia—had become one of the

[151] Hume cited in Keblusek, 'Mary's Court'. I am indebted to Professor Marika Keblusek for allowing me to read her chapter on Mary's court from her forthcoming book. Citations from this chapter will be henceforth referred to as 'Mary's Court'.

[152] Hughes, Ann and Sanders, Julie, 'Gender, Exile and The Hague Courts of Elizabeth, Queen of Bohemia and Mary, Princess of Orange in the 1650s' in *Monarchy and Exile: the Politics of Legitimacy from Marie de Medicis to William II*. Philip Mansel and Torsten Riotte eds. (Hampshire: Palgrave Macmillan, 2011), 52.

[153] *National Archives*, The Hague, Nassause Domeinraad, inv. 564. Cited in Keblusek, 'Mary's Court', 13.

few places where Anglican services were still being read'.[154] These women maintained their religious identity despite being distanced from their homeland by employing their own chaplains and ministers. Elizabeth usually employed conformist Anglicans, especially after 1649 when she dismissed the Puritan William Cooper for his connection to her brother's trial. After this, William Stampe and George Morely, and then George Beaumont in 1656 presided over sermons. Morely had fled England in 1648/9 to reside first at Queen Henrietta Maria's court in Paris. Later he moved on to Antwerp where he lived with Hyde's family, read sermons to royalists such as William and Margaret Cavendish, preaching in both English and French, while also privately administering to dying royalists and baptizing children at home.[155] In Mary's court, from 1651 Anglicans performed ceremonies under the ministry of Thomas Browne.[156] Browne persuaded Anglican exiles to enter Mary's service as chaplains, engaging these royalist refugees to preach for them from time to time and also led a private service at the 1651 commemoration of Charles I's death due to the original gathering having been disrupted and royalists dispersed by Dutch authorities.[157] Both Elizabeth and Mary 'sometimes worshipped in the French Church, which served as the Orange court chapel, and in the English Church, which was situated very close by their town palaces'.[158] Thus, as Hughes and Sanders and Keblusek have indeed found, a 'relatively large number of exiled Anglicans in the Dutch Republic can be linked to the presence of Elizabeth of Bohemia's and Mary's courts'.[159]

[154] Bosher, *Restoration Settlement*: brief over view Paris, Antwerp etc. cited in Keblusek, 'Mary's Court', 7.

[155] Keblusek, 'Mary's Court', 10.

[156] Hughes and Sanders, 'Gender, Geography and Exile', 136.

[157] Keblusek, 'Mary's Court,' 9–11.

[158] Hughes and Sanders, 'Gender, Geography and Exile', 136. This church would have been initially Calvinist but later in the 1640s English politics divided émigré communities, and royalists became involved in church affairs. Samuel Banford, strongly puritan, became unpopular and was replaced in 1650. See also Sprunger, Keith, *Dutch Puritanism: A History of English and Scottish churches of the Netherlands of the Sixteenth and Seventeenth Centuries* (Leiden, 1982), 152–153.

[159] Keblusek, 'Mary's Court'. Keblusek has identified these exiled Anglicans as George Morley, Thomas Browne, John Bramhal and Henry Leslie. Hughes and Sanders have noted that 'Mary, and to a lesser extent Elizabeth did provide places for exiled royalists' such as Sir Charles Cotterell, Nicholas Oudart, Sir Alexander Hume, Thomas Howard, Nicholas Armorer.

However, the sudden death of the Prince of Orange in November 1650 signalled misfortune for exiled royalists, for 'now all hope for (financial) support was invested in the Princess Royal, who had become entangled in complicated legal procedures concerning her baby son'.[160] The following year, in 1651 an alliance was sought by Cromwell between England and the United Provinces. This complicated Mary's position even further. In March, England dispatched a 'solemn embassy to The Hague with instructions to effect a close association between the two Republics'.[161] Loyal to her family, Mary could not stand idly by, and neither could royalist residents at The Hague. From the day of arrival the English envoys were welcomed 'with hoots and threats…by defenders of the young Princess of Orange', and, to make matters worse, Mary's 'pages reportedly distributed money and incited the populace to heap abuse on the envoys'.[162] Further, according to Robert Rait, Mary 'did all she could to stir up strife' and:

> [e]veryday the Princess Royal and her brother, the Duke of York, rode slowly past the ambassador's residence with ostentatious pomp and an imposing suite, staring at the house from top to bottom, in a manner to encourage the rabble, which her procession gathered up in its way, to commit insult.[163]

Mary's certain involvement in the riots in 1651, her protection of royalist rioters and her behaviour to parliamentarian envoys would have been seen by royalists in The Hague as a 'rallying call'.[164] However, that was not all that Mary did to cause friction between her court and opposing factions in her host country. In addition to employing royalists as chaplains and ministers, and providing appointments for royalists within her household, funding royalist campaigns to take back the throne, as well as inciting riots

160 *Mercurius Politicus* 38 (20/27-2-1651), 616 (letter of intelligence, The Hague, 24-2-1651): 'this great disbanding of the English is to be attributed to the death of the Prince of Orange, whose onely study and indeavor was to win the hearts of the strangers wholly to himself' cited in Keblusek, 'Mary's Court'.

161 Geyl, Pieter, *Orange and Stuart 1641–1672* (London: Weidenfeld and Nicholson, 1939), 82.

162 Ibid., 84 cites Cf. Aitzema, VII, p. 482 for corroboration by English royalist witnesses, see especially Carte's Ormonde Papers, Vol. II.

163 Rait, 206, cites Geddes Administration of John de Witt, Vol. I, 178.

164 Geyl, 83–85; See also, Rait, *Five Stuart Princesses*, 205–206 on Mary's involvement in the riots.

Mary refused to assimilate—she recognized only the English king as head of her house, and obeyed only his commands. She also refused to learn Dutch, speaking French if needs be. As the years went on, she 'nurtured a growing hatred of her son's country and people'.[165] Through her actions and linguistic defiance, Mary stood her ground as a royalist, maintained her English identity and formed a resistant community for royalists, a community which utilized entertainments as diasporic counter-public spaces within which they could reconnect with their lost home, their culture and each other; ironically, a royalist counter-culture created in a republic.[166]

Thus, The Hague, a hub of intellectual and cultural activity,[167] provided a favourable *locus* for royalists, who found protection, support and employment at the courts of Elizabeth and Mary.[168] However, it was the live entertainments as recognizable cultural forms reminiscent of their lost home and its culture which offered royalists in The Hague a much-needed site of reunion. Marika Keblusek has documented a series of entertainments in Elizabeth's and Mary's courts which 'serve to emphasise their "royalist" identity, and can thus be perceived as political statements'.[169] Noting that in the 1650s these widowed women oversaw 'strongly English orientated courts,' she argues that Mary and Elizabeth's theatre culture was 'concerned…with the notion of identity' and that through their

[165] Ibid., 77.

[166] There is an appropriate irony in the royalists seeking refuge from a republican regime in the Dutch republic. See: Helmers, Helmer, J. H., *The Royalist Republic: Literature, Politics, and Religion in the Anglo—Dutch Republic Sphere, 1639–1660* (Cambridge: Cambridge University Press, 2015).

[167] See Hughes and Sanders, 'Gender, Exile and The Hague Courts', 45–65. Hughes and Sanders explore 'the impact of existing courts in The Hague on the experience of the newly-arrived English and Scottish royalist exiles in the 1650s, and discuss what difference it made that women headed these courts', 45. See also: Pal, Carol, *The Republic of Women: Rethinking the Republic of Letters in the Seventeenth Century* (Cambridge: Cambridge University Press, 2012) for an engaging appraisal of women's involvement in, and significant contribution to, the republic of letters on the continent. For more on the social, political and religious contexts within which these entertainments were presented, see for example, Keblusek, M., 'The Bohemian Court at The Hague' in *A Princely Display*. For exploration of forms of display, baptisms, garter ceremonies and political demonstrations, see Hughes and Sanders, 'Gender, Geography and Exile' in *Royalists and Royalism during the Interregnum*, 136,134,141.

[168] Professor Keblusek details the funding, the employment of Anglican ministers, and the great many royalist courtiers that accumulated at Mary's court in 'Mary's Court'.

[169] Keblusek, 'Entertainment in Exile', 179.

conflicts with the Calvinists, for instance, they consolidated royalist identity.[170] While there is little information on the entertainments at The Hague, early staged entertainments are listed as including *The Joys of Human Life* (March 1635), *Balet de Marriage* (November 1642) and *Acteonisation de Grand Veneur d'Hollande* (1643). After the regicide, entertainments ceased as both women refused to attend performance. Then, in the mid-1650s, theatricals were resumed and Stuart heritage 'intensified'.[171] Later entertainments included *A King or No King* (April 1654), *Ballet de la Carmesse* (December 1655) and *The Enchanted Lovers* (1658). Keblusek argues that these performances 'reveal a set of shifting identities, overlapping and interacting', and that 'it is mostly through conflicts and side-taking that the building of these identities is realized'.[172] While Keblusek argues that royalist cultural identity is affirmed through the conflict surrounding the entertainments, I argue that it was also maintained through the entertainments themselves. Meanwhile, Ann Hughes and Julie Sanders also explore exiled royalist communities on the continent, and, focusing on The Hague, assert that Elizabeth and Mary brought with them 'elements of the courtly culture they had known…in England and adapting them to their surroundings'.[173] While they argue that the 'Stuart cultural heritage interacts and hybridizes with that of host culture of the Netherlands', they fail to show how it does so.[174] However, Sanders and Hughes do trace a particular female agency and a form of resistance within the courts of Elizabeth and Mary by examining the context surrounding entertainments such as *A King and No King* and *The Enchanted Lovers.* Moreover, they correctly argue that theatrical and ceremonial cultures should be considered 'within a wider campaign of royalist allegiance and resistance'.[175] Reading these productions as a product of the royalist diaspora, I build on this observation to argue that the satellite locales of

[170] Ibid., 179, 185, 186.

[171] Ibid., 184.

[172] Ibid., 185.

[173] Hughes, Ann and Julie Sanders, 'The Hague Courts of Elizabeth of Bohemia and Mary Stuart: Theatrical and Ceremonial Cultures'. *Early Modern Literary Studies Special Issue* 15.3 (August, 2007): 1–234

[174] Ibid., 4.

[175] Ibid., 1.

The Hague or Antwerp were part of a much wider trans-channel network focused on widespread group cultural preservation.[176]

While these scholars provide more of an overview of the entertainments put on by Elizabeth and Mary at The Hague, Nadine Akkerman and Paul R. Sellin's reading and investigation into the Stuart masque *La Carmesse de la Haye* (1655) offers an important intervention regarding where and how these performances were conducted.[177] They acknowledge local forms of royal entertainments such as the tradition of masque balls at the court of the martial Stadholder Prince Maurice of Orange or the Burgundian displays of civic pageantry; however, they take the arrival of the Winter King and Queen as the event which 'transformed social life in The Hague'.[178] They argue that key to understanding the masque is 'the occasion behind the production…the social and political needs and contexts…and to what extent did they shape its contexts and organization'.[179] Through analysis of the programme, the audience, the performers and the space in which the performance took place, they provide a fascinating reconstruction of all elements of the production of *La Carmesse* and invite comparison with productions at home in England. These contributions are invaluable to the study of cultural negotiation at these courts during a pivotal time in royalist history on the continent. However, this section further argues that the entertainments at these courts stand as counter-public expressions of community within the diasporic environment on the continent, and, as such, are part of the push to preserve royalist heritage and flag Stuart allegiance. Moreover, it will be seen that these entertainments become sites of reunion for royalists, spaces within which they can address each other and their political concerns, while enjoying familiar modes of representation. While scholars such as Hughes and Sanders have provided a basis for further discussion of networks and communities of royalists exiled on the continent brought together by these

[176] In 'Entertainment in Exile' Marika Keblusek examines the entertainments of William and Margaret Cavendish in Antwerp alongside that of Elizabeth of Bohemia and Mary Stuart. Her analysis asserts that Newcastle's notions of continuity in his entertainments bear 'strong political connotations' similar to that of the entertainments of Elizabeth and Mary at The Hague; that both circles are working to preserve identity through cultural manifestations, 178.

[177] Akkerman, Nadine and Paul R. Sellin. 'A Stuart Masque in Holland: *Ballet de La Carmesse de La Haye* (1655)'. *The Ben Jonson Journal.* 11 (2004): 207–258, 208/209.

[178] Ibid., 208/209.

[179] Ibid., 232.

entertainments, the value of these entertainments as counter-publics of reunion to the dispersed group has not been addressed within the context of the diasporic environment and its impulse to transmit a strong ethnic group consciousness. As we have seen, protection and projection of cultural heritage are vital for preservation of identity within a diasporic environment. Groups within the diaspora turn to their common history as a means to overcome the rupture of dispersion from the homeland and from each other—one way to overcome the rupture is through the maintenance of recognizable and communal cultural forms.

## Royalist Entertainments as Counter-Publics: Tragi-Comedy, Stuart Masque and a Pastoral Romance

> The gentlemen and maids of honour to the Princess Royal are preparing to act a play in French and English before Whitsuntide, the very name of which seems to please many in her Court, more than the play itself, it being so judicious and discreetly chosen, viz. *A King and No King*.[180]

For royalists the genres of tragi-comedy, romance and pastoral became highly politicized during the war years and interregnum.[181] These genres could and did represent symbolic counter-publics for the diasporic group. Genre could be utilized as a space within which alternative political opinion could be aired. Moreover, as a symbolic entity, genre stood as a site of cultural engagement in an increasingly hostile environment and its endurance represented the very survival of royalist cultural forms under threat in England during these turbulent years. Masques were also symbolic of the old order, recalled past gaieties and were encoded with political messages. Martin Butler offers a way to think about these entertainments as alternative *loci* to the power base of London. Writing about private drama in the great aristocratic houses and palaces during the reigns of James I and Charles I, he suggests that the private theatrical provided space for experimentation or could be more politically adventurous, and that for a disconcerted and disillusioned aristocrat, provincial theatricals might be a way of

[180] Nicholas, Edward, *Calendar of the Clarendon Papers*, 23, April 1654, Vol. II, 339. http://sources.tannerritchie.com.elib.tcd.ie/browser.php?bookid=768.

[181] For example, see Potter, *Secret Rites Secret Writing*.

establishing one's alternative to an unfavourable world.[182] At The Hague Elizabeth and Mary endeavoured to create their own alternative to the socio-political melting pot they inhabited. More than that, as part of the diasporic community, they capitalized on tragi-comedy, masques and pastoral romances as a way of articulating an alternative cultural and political sphere.

This production of Beaumont and Fletcher's *A King and No King* in 1654, was probably the most famous entertainment hosted by Elizabeth and Mary.[183] The play, 'a characteristically English tragi-comedy... had proved enduringly popular in the public and private theatres since its initial performance in 1611'.[184] It had been put on clandestinely in Salisbury court after the ban on theatre and had been subsequently published by Humphrey Moseley in 1647 in England, yet another subversive act of resilience 'and a gesture of royalist solidarity by the Cavalier poets who contributed its enormous number of commendatory verses'.[185] The staging of the play in or around Whitsuntide further suggests that Elizabeth and Mary chose to maintain seasonal Anglican traditions with regard to plays and festivities.

By choosing this play Elizabeth and Mary also gestured to their lineage, its history and asserted their own cultural validity, while also raising fraught contemporary topics surrounding legitimacy and the future of the monarchy. Lee Bliss asserts that *A King and No King* is Janus-faced, and it would appear that Elizabeth of Bohemia and Mary of Orange exploited this double aspect of the play, partaking in both the nostalgia associated with its genre and the emphasis on human agency and ambition.[186] The play's stage history emphasizes the intergenerational links between Mary, Elizabeth, the court of Charles I and Henrietta Maria, and the court of James I, while also gesturing towards Elizabeth I's reign, a time also fraught with decisions surrounding the future legitimacy of the crown. While Bliss notes that Beaumont and Fletcher 'express, as well as play to,

[182] Butler, Martin, 'Private and Occasional Drama' in *The Cambridge Companion to English Renaissance Drama*, A.R. Bruanmuller and Michael Hattaway eds. (Cambridge: Cambridge University Press, 2003), 127–160, 160.

[183] *A King and No King. Beaumont and Fletcher*. Lee Bliss ed. (Manchester & New York: Manchester University Press, 2004), 5. *A King and No King* was 'not entered for publication in the Stationer's Register until 1618' but it was acted in 1611 and performed at court on 26 December 1611 during Christmas revels season and again during the winter season 1612–1613.

[184] Hughes and Sanders, 'Gender, Exile and The Hague Courts', 58.

[185] Bliss, *A King and No King*, 33.

[186] Ibid., 28.

the crisis of authority' manifest in their own times, they also 'pose the question, 'Where does authority lie?'[187] Certainly, the play's topicality, dealing with issues surrounding the legitimacy of authority, the balance of order versus disorder and questions of identity and separation would have resonated strongly with royalists both at The Hague and at home.

In *A King and No King* the stateless, crownless and captured Tigranes, the true King of the play, is held captive for the duration of the entertainment by Arcebes, King of Iberia. Eventually, as it is revealed by Gobrius, Lord Protector of Iberia and father of Arcebes that his (Arcebes') kingship is illegitimate due to his genealogy, Tigranes allowed to 'go so home' (5. 4. 315). This would have greatly appealed to royalist desire for restoration of their own peripatetic and stateless monarch, Charles II, and the manner in which Tigranes is restored can be read as a clear message to parliamentarians back in England. As soon as Arcebes learns he is 'found no king!' (5.4.267), he graciously and willingly steps down. Not only does he step down but he offers his self in repentance as he says:

> O, my Tigranes, pardon me!
> Tread on my neck; I freely offer it
> And if thou beest so given, take revenge,
> For I have injured thee. (5.4.340-5)

Perhaps, this is the aspect of the play which appealed most to royalists at this time, as they wished not only to see their legitimate king restored and visualized a return to hierarchical and monarchical order, but also imagined revenge on their enemies. Further, the play foregrounds the highly resonant theme of order versus disorder. For royalists, Cromwell had transgressed all boundaries of order and plunged England into chaos. In *A King and No King* dissent into chaos is represented by incest, sexual desire and the resulting transgression of social, political, familial and sexual boundaries. This discord is resolved through the emergence of genealogical truth and the restoration of the true King—a conclusion which may be read as a truly royalist ending in which crisis is supplanted by the rule of the father/king. The two central characters represent this struggle between order and disorder. Arcebes has no self-control, is passionate and

[187] Ibid., 16.

self-absorbed—all characteristics of a tyrant.[188] He finds himself engulfed by his weaknesses 'left as far without a bound/As the wild ocean that obeys the winds', his 'sudden passion throws' him, 'overwhelms' him, he is lustful towards his sister and admits his heart is set on 'wickedness' (4.4.68–72). Arcebes's tyrannical kingship is figured through his irrationality and ripening madness, as rejects his sister, accepts his sister, then imprisons her (3.1.315), eventually declaring that 'incest is' in him (3.1.344), a monstrous and 'ungodly sickness' (3.1.197). Tigranes, in contrast, is constant and consistent, and appears to be full of humanist ideals.[189] At the denouement of the play Tigranes chooses to 'forgive' (5.4.344) Arcebes, and rejoices more that Arcebes has 'found repentance' than he his 'liberty' (5.4.345), once again urging the importance of realizing one's mistakes. This broad thematic inference would have struck a cord with royalists in The Hague as they looked back at England in turmoil and considered Cromwell as the tyrant who caused such chaos. While personal loss of identity is figured through genealogical confusion (3.1.81/4.4.64-6), and cultural loss of identity explored through the disintegration of the sovereign systems of order (5.4.1-3), separation is another theme which royalists could readily associate with. Separated by war, Panthea lives for news of her big brother, however, upon their meeting Arcebes does not recognize his sister and pronounces 'she is no kin to me' (3.1.168). Indeed, in this scene Panthea, so disorientated, declares herself a 'stranger' and 'a lost thing' (3.1.22/24). These are all themes which would have held particular resonance for royalists separated from loved ones by the hardships of war and enforced dispersion.

The genre of tragi-comedy was not the only category of entertainment hosted by Elizabeth and Mary in the mid-1650s. By staging the Stuart masque *Ballet de La Carmess de La Haye*, Elizabeth and Mary looked back to a long history of royal entertainment which utilized this genre as a political tool. Royal revelry was first systematically promoted by Henry VIII, desiring to compete publicly with the powerful and high-profile monarchies of Francis I and Charles V.[190] In Queen Henrietta Maria's time, masquing and 'ostentatious display was intricately bound up with political expression and she promoted social fashion that drew on her

[188] Bliss uses Plato and Aristotle to determine that a 'tyrant' is 'one who gives in to excessive desire, thus dethroning the proper sovereignty of reason', 16.

[189] Ibid., 23.

[190] Butler, 'Private', 141.

French heritage and religion'.[191] By selecting to host two performances of *La Carmesse* in 1655, Elizabeth and Mary drew on their cultural heritage at a contentious time which involved uncertainty about the future Stadholder, disputes about William III's upbringing, and the end of the first Anglo-Dutch war, which meant support in the Dutch republic for the Stuarts was tentative.[192] As Akkerman and Sellin note, the 'ostentatious entertainment...constituted a vivid re-assertion of dynastic claims to political power and rightful place in both the Dutch republic and Great Britain',[193] not dissimilar to the themes evoked in *A King and No King*. Akkerman and Sellin have found that the number attending the ballet 'was not small or intimate',[194] it is thought there were no masks worn, that Queen Elizabeth of Bohemia's dress sense caused outrage among local clergy and that Mary 'participated vigorously in the revels.'[195] All of this point to the utilization of masquing as a means to resist local, and, I would argue, parliamentarian restriction through the transmission of royalist cultural heritage. The fact that the entertainment was not private opened it up to the wider royalist community and Mary's unmasked and energetic involvement was both an undisguised celebration of her cultural heritage and tantamount to a tribal remonstrance of defiance.

In their decision to stage the pastoral romance, *The Enchanted Lovers* (1658), Elizabeth and Mary drew not only on cultural heritage that defined England as a *locus* of harmonious governance but they also took advantage of the ambiguous nature of the pastoral and its ability to encode political messages. The pastoral, or pastoral romance, for instance, had been utilized in the 1620s and 1630s by some government critics to imagine an alternative social order or question aspects of government policy.[196]

191 Britland, Karen, *Drama at the Courts of Queen Henrietta Maria* (Cambridge: Cambridge University Press, 2006), 2.

192 Akkerman and Sellin, 'Stuart Masque', 232.

193 Ibid., 234.

194 Alexander Hume noted: 'there was a great croud in the place with confusion enough, which could hardly be auoyded at such an occasion where there was no chief to command the rest' cited in Akkerman and Sellin, 227.

195 Akkerman and Sellin, 238. Elizabeth of Bohemia is recorded as writing: 'my deare Neece recouers her health and good looks extremlie by her excersice the twice dauncing <with> the maskers': Letter from Elizabeth of Bohemia to Charles II, from The Hague, 13 December 1655 (Lambeth Palace Library, London, MS 645/82) cited in Akkerman and Sellin, 229.

196 Knowles, James, 'We've Lost, Should we Lose too our Harmless Mirth? : Cavendish's Antwerp Entertainments' in *Royalist Refugees: William and Margaret Cavendish in the Rubens House 1648–1660*, 72.

Queen Henrietta Maria utilized the pastoral to reinforce images of harmony and union that were put forth at the time of her marriage.[197] In particular, during the 1630s it had been used as a vehicle for royalist vision of an edenic England, a shepherd nation ruled over by a pastoral king and queen, dedicated to the order of the realm.[198] However, the pastoral could also simply function as an aristocratic mode celebrating pleasure and leisure, its 'chief motive' being 'a desire to escape from the complexity of city life with its vices and follies, and to refresh themselves [aristocrats] with the simplicity and freedom of the golden age'.[199] *The Enchanted Lovers*, written by William Lower, is a pastoral written by an exile, in exile, about exile and for other exiles at the court of Mary of Orange.[200] Lower, a Lieutenant-Colonel for the King's forces, had arrived in The Hague in October 1655[201] after being 'discharged from imprisonment, and permitted to go beyond the Seas: and that he gave Security not to act anything against the Parliament'.[202] While in exile Lower translated many works and wrote *The Enchanted Lovers* which Marika Keblusek asserts must have certainly been staged at the Princess Royal's court 'and warmly received by its royalist audience'.[203]

The topical themes of separation, exile and reunion would have resonated poignantly for royalists who were separated from family, home and country during the interregnum. The plot 'is that of the romance adventure with shipwrecks, separations and reunions after many years'.[204] The characters are all nobles living on the island of Erithrea, a colony that is

[197] Britland, *Drama at the Courts of Queen Henrietta Maria*, 37.

[198] Ibid., 72.

[199] Smith, Homer, 'Pastoral Influence in the English Drama.' *PMLA* 12.3 (1897): 355–460, 356.

[200] Philip Major asserts Lower is 'one of the most neglected figures among the English royalist exile community' and his work should be recognized as a 'rich resource' for exploring the 'writing' of the royalist exile. See: Major, Philip, 'Sir William Lower at The Hague.' *English Studies* 92.5 (2011): 508–522.

[201] Sir Edward Nicholas wrote 'Sir Wm. Lower is now in towne…'.*The Nicholas Papers, Correspondence of Edward Nicholas, Secretary of State.* George F Warner ed, 4 Vols. Camden Society Publications, 1886–1920, III, 83 cited in Gates, William Bryan, *The Dramatic Works and Translations of Sir William Lower, with a Reprint of The Enchanted Lovers.* PhD thesis, University of Pennsylvania, 1932, 15.

[202] Journal of the House of Commons, V, 48 cited in Gates, *The Dramatic Works and Translations of Sir William Lower, with a Reprint of The Enchanted Lovers*, 14.

[203] Keblusek, 'Entertainment in Exile', 185.

[204] Gates, *Dramatic Works*, 70.

repeatedly figured in the text as a site of 'sanctuary', 'repose', or 'quiet region' a 'quiet island', and a 'happy island' throughout the text.[205] This fantasy locale, a common mode of representation to exilic writing, provides much succour and relief for the characters of the text as well as conjuring up for members of the audience idyllic images and memories of pre-war England. Meanwhile, the experience of the cavalier and his lover separated by controlling parents refers indirectly to the misfortunes of royalists separated by politics and tyrants at home in England.

While the themes in the tragi-comedy, the masque and the pastoral romance were meaningful for royalists, we cannot say whether these plays evolved, as Hughes and Sanders claim. There is little evidence of how the entertainments were staged. In the case of *A King and no King* we have no way of knowing whether it was a direct replica of the English production or whether for the sake of projecting cultural identity at a tenuous time, Elizabeth and Mary accentuated elements of the play. For example, the restoration of Tigranes, while only glimpsed at through a few lines (5.4.317-22), could have been exaggerated to reinforce royalist cultural expressions of monarchical reinstatement, glory and power. We do know that the play was staged in both English and French, a choice which intentionally included royalists who may not have spoken French. The same letter above intimates that there were vast numbers of royalists gathering in The Hague, if not already there, for the performance. It mentions Lord Wentworth (leaving for Flanders in a few days' time), Lord Culpepper (staying only ten days) and Sir Charles Cotterell (who came from Breda). Thus, a picture of a vibrant English-speaking royalist community emerges, a community which is tuned to the inherent symbolic cultural and political meaning of genre, as well as the themes of uncertainty and crisis of political and regal authority that *A King and No King* brings to the fore. Thanks to Akkerman and Sellin, *La Carmesse* has been retrieved from such obscurity. We know more about the audience, where they sat, the costumes, who was there, the performers, and the location of the ballet.[206] Most interestingly, we know from a letter from Sir Alexander Hume to Sir Edward Nicholas that the space in which the entertainment was held was 'purpose fitted for it' and a 'great crowd' was in attendance,[207] thus an

[205] Lower, William, *The Enchanted Lovers, a Pastoral* (Hage: Adrian Vlack, 1658), 6, 22, 14, 21, respectively.

[206] Akkerman and Sellin, 'Stuart Masque', 236–242.

[207] Letter from Sir Alexander Hume to Sir Edward Nicholas, The Hague, 9 December 1655, repr. in *The Nicholas Papers: Correspondence of Sir Edward Nicholas, Secretary of State.*

environment, along with a political message, constitutive of a diasporic counter-public sphere was generated. The connections between *La Carmesse* and *The Enchanted Lovers* are also of interest in terms of generating a wider counter-public network, both across the continent and within England. *La Carmesse* was a royalist production and publication. The organizers of the ballet chose to publish with a well-known royalist sympathizer, printer Adriaan Vlaq. The title page badge resembles the Tudor rose and confirms Vlaq as one of the 'royal' printers working in the Netherlands to further the King's cause during the 1650s.[208] *The Enchanted Lovers* was also printed by Vlaq, at The Hague in June 1658. However, more significantly, *The Enchanted Lovers* was published almost simultaneously in London by Herringman the following year, 1659. This points to a cultural counter-public that includes authors, performers, audiences, readers, publishers and printers, working against parliamentarian oppression to continue to transmit royalist cultural forms and the political messages within these works. Further to this, the letter which heads this section additionally notes that *A King and No King* will 'be shortly in the English prints'. These 'prints' Nicholas refers to are 'printed newsletters which often originated in Holland and which supplied the English market for continental news and … had also been the place of publication of seditious or critical material'.[209] Indeed, *A King and No King* was printed in England in 1655 by William Leak, following up on its performance at The Hague in 1654. Thus, the printing of *A King and No King*, and its dissemination across the continent, was specifically intended to reach English readers, allowing them access to the subversive political and cultural sphere, thus widening the reach of the diasporic counter-public which was now established at The Hague.

Despite being castigated by Cromwell's spies for nourishing fellow royalists, or that 'nest of vypers', Elizabeth of Bohemia and Mary of Orange went to great lengths to provide a *locus* of social, religious and cultural continuity, as well as providing morale-boosting entertainments at a time of great trepidation while on foreign soil. The 'remobilisation'[210] of a *King and No King*, *Ballet de La Carmessee de La Haye* and the addition of an exilic pastoral romance *The Enchanted Lovers* bound royalists together in a counter-public

Ed George F, Warner, 4 vols. (1886–1920; repr. New York: Johnson Reprint, 1965), 3: 191. Cited in Akkerman and Sellin, 'Stuart Masque', 227.

[208] Akkerman and Sellin, 'Stuart Masque', 226.

[209] Knowles, 'We've Lost our Mirth', 75.

[210] Hughes and Sanders, 'The Hague Courts', 6.

sphere concerned with the maintenance of cultural identity, heritage and political allegiance, as well as providing a space within which royalists may feel that they were temporarily 'home', or at the very least, not so distanced from home. As Keblusek notes, the performances functioned to maintain 'an almost masque-like allusion of continuity; a staged continuation of aristocratic life in Caroline England'.[211] Moreover, the genre of tragi-comedy, pastoral romance and the royalist masque were 'also another motivating factor' in the choice of entertainments put on in The Hague by these royalist women.[212] A contemporary English audience would have been familiar with the flexibility of these particular genres at this time and understand that the very use of such a genre could express political allegiance. The entertainments addressed topical and painful themes specific to royalists, and as such they gestured towards solidarity in the face of opposition. Through these entertainments, Elizabeth and Mary provided sites of virtual as well as real reunion for disbanded royalists at a time when their future was most uncertain. In doing so, they fostered connective cultural *fora* for royalists similar to that of the Cavendish sisters' 'family' manuscript or Katherine Philips's coterie. As Elizabeth and Mary transmitted their common cultural and religious heritage, an alternate public sphere was articulated and a community consciousness was generated which enabled a process of cultural re-orientation and a site of reunion for royalists exiled on the continent during the long and disorientating years of the interregnum despite geographical location or immediate political climate.

## Works Cited

### Manuscripts

Cavendish, Lady Jane and Lady Elizabeth Brackley. Bodleian Library, Oxford, Bodl. MS. Rawl Poet. 16.

Dering, Sir Edward, 'Letterbook'. University of Cincinnati Library. Philips Ms 14392.

Philips, Katherine, NLW MS. 775B.

[211] Keblusek, 'Entertainment in Exile', 186.

[212] Hughes and Sanders, 'The Hague Courts', 5.

## Books and Poems


Alexander Brome, *Songs and Poems* (1661).

[Beaumont and Fletcher], *A King and No King. Beaumont and Fletcher.* Lee Bliss ed. (Manchester & New York: Manchester University Press, 2004).

[Cavendish, Margaret], *The Life of William Cavendish, Duke of Newcastle: To Which Is Added the True Relation of My Birth, Breeding and Life.* C.H. Firth ed. (1886).

[Filmer, Robert], *Patriarcha, or The Natural Power of Kings* (London: Walter Davis, 1680).

Herrick, Robert, *Hesperides, or, The Works Both Humane & Divine* (1648).

Howell, James, *The trve informer who in the following discovrse or colloqvie discovereth unto the vvorld the chiefe causes of the sa[]d distempers in Great Britanny and Ireland/deduced from their originals; and also a letter writ by Serjeant-Major Kirle to a friend at VVinsor* (1643).

______. "To the Knowing Reader. Familiar Letters". *Epistolae Ho-Eliane, familiar letters domestic and forren divided into sundry sections, partly historicall, politicall, philosophicall, vpon emergent occasions* (1650).

[Hutchinson, Lucy], *Memoirs of the Life of Colonel Hutchinson: Charles I's Puritan Nemesis.* N.H. Keeble, ed. (London: Phoenix Press, 2000).

William Lower, *The Enchanted Lovers, a Pastoral* (Hage: Adrian Vlack, 1658).

Voetius, Geysterbus, Disputatio de Comoedies, Dat is, Twist-redening van Schouspellen. Gehouden en voorgestelt in the Hooge-school van Uitrecht. Uit de Latijnsche in de Neerduitsche taal veraalt door B.S. (Gybertus Voetius, D.D, C., Being a Critical Argument on Theatrical Performances. Given and proposed in the illustrious school of Utrecht. Trans. from Latin into the Dutch language by B.S. (Amsterdam, Jasper Adamsz Star, 1650).


## Catalogues, Calendars and Papers


*Calendar of State Papers, Domestic* (1651), Mary Anne Everett Green ed. (London, 1877).

*Calendar of the Clarendon State Papers*, Vol. II. http://sources.tannerritchie.com.elib.tcd.ie/browser.php?bookid=768.

*Collection of State Papers of John Thurloe*, Vol II. (1654) Thomas Birch ed. (London, 1742). http://sources.tannerritchie.com.elib.tcd.ie/browser.php?bookid=215.

*The Nicholas Papers: Correspondence of Sir Edward Nicholas, Secretary of State.* Ed George F, Warner, 4 vols. (1886–1920; repr. New York: Johnson Reprint, 1965).

*Ninth Report of the Royal Commission on Historical Manuscripts*, Part 1, Part 2 & 3. Printed by Eyre and Spottiswoode for H.M.S.O. (London, 1883).

## Secondary Sources

Akkerman, Nadine and Paul R. Sellin, 'A Stuart Masque in Holland: *Ballet de La Carmesse de La Haye* (1655).' *The Ben Jonson Journal* 11 (2004): 207–258.

Andreadis, Harriette, 'The Sapphic-Platonics of Katherine Philips, 1632–1664.' *Signs Journal of Women in Culture and History*. 15.1 (1989): 34–60.

Anselment, Raymond A., "Stone Walls' and 'I'ron Bars': Richard Lovelace and the Conventions of Seventeenth-Century Prison Literature.' *Renaissance and Reformation* 29 (1993): 15–34.

Bentley, Gerald Eades, 'The Period 1642–1660'. *The Revels History of Drama in English IV 1613–1660*. Edwards et al eds. (London: Methuen & Co. Ltd, 1981).

Bennet, Alexandra, "Now Let my Language Speake': The Authorship, Rewriting, and Audience(s) of Jane Cavendish and Elizabeth Brackley.' *Early Modern Literary Studies* 11.2 (September 2005): 1–13.

Bernikow, Lousie, *The World Split Open: Women Poets 1552–1950* (London: Women's Press, 1974).

Brady, Andrea, 'The Platonic Poems of Katherine Philips' *Seventeenth Century* 25.2 (Oct 2010): 300–322.

Bosher, Robert S., *The Making of the Restoration Settlement: the Influence of the Laudians 1649–1662* (London: Dacre Press, 1951).

Brant, George W., *Theatre in Europe: A Documentary History. German and Dutch Theatre 1600–1848* (Cambridge, New York & Melbourne: Cambridge University Press, 1993).

Britland, Karen, *Drama at the Courts of Queen Henrietta Maria* (Cambridge: Cambridge University Press, 2006).

Burroughs, Catherine, 'Hymen's Monkey Love': The Concealed Fancies and Female Sexual Initiation'. *Theatre Journal*. 51 (1999): 21–31.

Bush, Douglas, *English Literature in the Earlier Seventeenth Century* (New York: Oxford University Press, 1945).

Butler, Martin, 'Private and Occasional Drama' in *The Cambridge Companion to English Renaissance Drama*, A.R., Bruanmuller and Michael Hattaway, eds. (Cambridge: Cambridge University Press, 2003), pp. 127–160.

Chalmers, Hero, *Royalist Women Writers 1640–1689* (Oxford: Oxford University Press, 2004).

Chedzgoy, Kate, *Women's Writing in the British Atlantic World* (Cambridge: Cambridge University Press, 2007).

Clifford, James, 'Diasporas' in *Migration, Diasporas and Transnationalism*. Robin Cohen and Stephen Vertovec, eds. (Cheltenham, Glos., & MA: Edward Elgar Publishing Limited, 1999).

Cohen, Robin, *Global Diasporas* (London: Routledge, 2008).

Coolahan, Marie Louise, 'Presentation Volume of Jane Cavendish's Poetry. Yale University, Beinecke Library Osborn Ms b. 233', in *Early Modern Women's*

*Manuscript Poetry*. Jill Seal Millman and Gillian Wright, eds. (Manchester & New York: Manchester University Press, 2005).

Comfort Starr, Nathan, 'The Concealed Fancies: A Play by Lady Jane Cavendish and Lady Elizabeth Brackley'. *Publications of the Modern Language Association.* 46 (1931): 802–838.

de Groot, Jerome, *Royalist Identities* (Hampshire & New York: Palgrave Macmillan, 2004).

Ezell, Margaret, "To Be Your Daughter in Your pen': The Social Functions of Literature in the Writings of Lady Elizabeth Brackley and Lady Jane Cavendish.' *Huntington Library Quarterly* 51.4 (Autumn, 1988): 281–296.

______. 'Reading Pseudonyms in Seventeenth-Century English Coterie Literature.' *Essays in Literature* 21.1 (Spring 1994): 14–26.

Faderman, Lillian, *Surpassing the Love of Men: Romantic Friendship and Love between Women from the Renaissance to the Presence* (London: Women's Press, 1981).

Findlay, Alison, 'She Gave you the civility of the House': Household Performance in the Concealed Fancies' in *Readings in Renaissance Women's Drama: Criticism, History and Performance 1594–1998.* S.P Cerasano and Marion Wynne Davis, eds. (London, NY: Routledge, 1998).

______. 'Playing the Scene-Self: Jane Cavendish and Elizabeth Brackley's The Concealed Fancies' in *Enacting Gender on the Renaissance Stage.* Viviana Comensoli and Anne Russell, eds. (Urbana & Chicago: University of Illinois Press, 1999).

Fraser, Nancy, 'Rethinking the Public Sphere: A Contribution to the Critique of Actually Existing Democracy' in *Habermas and the Public Sphere.* Craig Calhoun, ed. (Cambridge MA: MIT Press, 1992).

Geyl, Pieter, *Orange and Stuart 1641–1672* (London: Weidenfeld and Nicholson, 1939).

Gates, William Bryan, *The Dramatic Works and Translations of Sir William Lower, with a Reprint of The Enchanted Lovers.* PhD thesis, University of Pensylvania, 1932.

Gray, Catherine, 'Katherine Philips and the Post-Courtly Coterie.' *English Literary Renaissance* 32 (2002): 426–451.

Gilroy, Paul, 'Diaspora' in *Migration, Diasporas and Transnationalism.* Robin Cohen and Stephen Vertovec, eds. (Cheltenham, Glos., & MA: Edward Elgar Publishing Limited, 1999).

Habermas, Jürgen, *English Translation, The Structural Transformation of the Public Sphere: An Inquiry into a Category of Bourgeois Society*, Thomas Burger, ed. (Cambridge Massachusetts: The MIT Press, 1989).

Hageman, Elizabeth and Andrea Sununu. 'New Manuscript Texts of Katherine Philips, The "Matchless Orinda".' *English Manuscript Studies* 4 (1993): 174–219.

Hageman, Elizabeth, 'The Matchless Orinda: Katherine Philips' in *Women Writers of the Renaissance and Reformation.* Katharina M. Wilson ed. (Athens: University of Georgia Press, 1987), pp. 566–607.

Helmers, Helmer, J.H., *The Royalist Republic: Literature, Politics, and Religion in the Anglo—Dutch Republic Sphere, 1639–1660* (Cambridge: Cambridge University Press, 2015).

Hoston, Leslie, *Commonwealth and the Restoration Stage* (Cambridge: Harvard University Press, 1928).

Hughes, Ann and Julie Sanders, 'The Hague Courts of Elizabeth of Bohemia and Mary Stuart: Theatrical and Ceremonial Cultures.' *Early Modern Literary Studies Special Issue* 15.3 (August 2007): 1–23.

______. 'Disruptions and Evocations of the Family Among Royalist Exiles' in *Literatures of Exile in the English Revolution and its Aftermath,* Philip Major ed. (London: Ashgate, 2010).

______. 'Gender, Exile and The Hague Courts of Elizabeth, Queen of Bohemia and Mary, Princess of Orange in the 1650s' in *Monarchy and Exile: the Politics of Legitimacy from Marie de Medicis to William II.* Philip Mansel and Torsten Riotte eds. (Hampshire: Palgrave Macmillan, 2011).

Kebluesk, Marika, 'Wine for Comfort: Drinking and the Royalist Exile Experience, 1642–1660' in *A Pleasing Sinne: Drink and Conviviality in Seventeenth Century England.* Adam Smyth ed. (Cambridge: D.S. Brewer, 2004).

______. 'Entertainment in Exile' in *Triumphs of the Defeated: Early Modern Festivals and Messages of Legitimacy.* J. Beppler and P. Davidson, eds. (Wiesbaden/Wolfenbüttelm, 2007), pp. 173–190.

______. 'Books at the Stadholder's Court' in *Princely Display, The court of Frederick of Orange and Amalia Solms in The Hague.* Keblusek and Jori Zilmans eds. Trans. John Rudge (The Historical Museum, The Hague: Waanders Publishers, Zwolle, 2012a), pp. 143–152.

______. 'The Bohemian Court at The Hague' in *A Princely Display, The Court of Frederick of Orange and Amalia Solms in The Hague.* Keblusek and Jori Zilmans eds. (The Historical Musue, The Hague: Waanders Publishers, Zwolle, 2012b).

Kerrigan, John, *Archipelagic English: Literature, History, and Politcs 1603–1707* (Oxford & New York: Oxford University Press, 2008).

Knowles, James, 'We've Lost, Should We Lose Our Mirth Too?: Cavendish's Antwerp Entertainments' in *Royalist Refugees: William and Margaret Cavendish at the Rubens House 1648–1660* (Antwerp: BAI, Rubeianum, 2006).

Limbert, Claudia, '"The Unison of Well Tun'd Hearts": Katherine Philips's Friendships with Male Writers' *English Language Notes.* 29 (1991): 25–37.

Llewellyn, Mark, 'Katherine Philips: Friendship, Poetry and Neo-Platonic Thought in Seventeenth Century England.' *Philological Quarterly* 81.4. (2002): 441–468.

Major, Philip, *Writings of Exile in the English Revolution and Restoration* (Surrey & Burlington: Ashgate, 2013).

Marcus, Leah, *Politics of Mirth: Jonson, Herrick, Milton, Marvel and the Defense of Old Holiday Pastimes* (Chicago and London: University of Chicago Press, 1986).

Marotti, Arthur, *Manuscript, Print and the English Renaissance Lyric* (New York: Cornwall University Press, 1995).

Milling, Jane, 'Seige and Cipher: The Closet Drama of the Cavendish Sisters.' *Women's History Review* 6.3 (1997): 411–426.

Miner, Earl, *The Cavalier Mode from Jonson to Cotton* (Princeton: Princeton University Press, 1971).

Norbrook, David, 'Women, the Republic of Letters, and the Public Sphere in the Mid-Seventeenth Century.' *Criticism* 46.2 (Detroit: Spring): 223–241.

Overton, Bill, 'Aphra Behn and the Verse Epistle.' *Women's Writing* 16.3 (2009): 369–391.

Pal, Carol, *The Republic of Women: Rethinking the Republic of Letters in the Seventeenth Century* (Cambridge: Cambridge University Press, 2012).

Pebworth, Ted-Larry and Claude J. Summers, "'Thus Friends Absent Speake': The Exchange of Verse Letters between John Donne and Henry Wooton'. *Modern Philology.* 81.4 (May 1984): 361–377.

Phillips, Edward, 'Society and the Theatre: The Closing of the Theatre in *The Revels History of Drama in English IV 1613–1660.* Edwards et al. eds. (London: Methuen & Co. Ltd, 1981), pp. 1–67.

Post, Jonathon, *English Lyric Poetry: The Seventeenth Century* (London: Routledge, 1999).

Potter, Lois, 'The Plays and Playwrights 1642–1660', *Revels History*, in *The Revels History of Drama in English IV 1613–1660.* Edwards et al. eds. (London: Methuen & Co. Ltd, 1981).

______. *Secret Rites, Secret Writing: Royalist Literature 1641–1660* (Cambridge: Cambridge University Press, 1989).

Rait, Robert S., *Five Stuart Princesses* (Westminster: A. Constable & Co., 1902).

Ross, Sarah E., *Women, Poetry and Politics in Seventeenth-Century Britain* (Oxford: Oxford University Press, 2014).

Smith, Nigel, 'Public Fora' in *Literature and Revolution in England 1640–1660* (New Haven, CT: Yale University Press, 1994).

Spink, Ian, *Henry Lawes: Cavalier Songwriter* (New York & Oxford: Oxford University Press, 2000).

Sprunger, Keith, *Dutch Puritanism: A History of English and Scottish Churches of the Netherlands of the Sixteenth and Seventeenth Centuries* (Leiden, 1982).

Stone Stanton, Kamille, 'The Domestication of Royalist Themes in *The Concealed Fancies* by Jane Cavendish and Elizabeth Brackley. *Clio.* 36.2 (2007): 177–197.

Steer, Richard, 'Lyric Poetry from Donne to Philips' in *Columbia History of British Poetry*. Carl Woodring and James Shapiro eds. (New York: Columbia University Press, 1994), pp. 229–253.

Stiebel, Arlene, 'Not Since Sappho: The Erotic in the Poems of Katherine Philips and Aphra Behn' in *Homosexuality in Renaissance and Enlightenment England: literary Representations in Historical Context*. Claude J. Summers ed., a special issue of the *Journal of Homosexuality*. 23.1/2 (1992): 153–164.

Thomas, Patrick, *The Collected Works of Katherine Philips*, The Matchless Orinda. *The Poems*. Patrick Thomas, ed. (Brentford: Stump Cross Books, 1990).

Turberville, A.S., *A History of Welbeck Abbey and Its Owners*. Volume I, 1539–1755 (London: Faber & Faber, 1938).

Thomas, W.S.K., *Stuart Wales* (Llandysul: Gomer Press, 1988).

Warren, Robin, 'A Partial Liberty: Gender and Class in Jane Cavendish and Elizabeth Brackely's the Concealed Fancies' in *Renaissance Papers*. T.H. Howard-Hill and Philip Rollinson eds. (Rochester, NY: Camden House, 2000).

Wood, Alfred, *Nottinghamshire in the Civil War* (Oxford: Clarendon Press, 1937).

CHAPTER 4

# This Triple Identity: Sites of Self-fashioning in Diasporic Environments

> we are not made Citizens of the Commonwealth, we hold no Offices, nor bear we any Authority therein; we are accounted neither Useful in Peace, nor Serviceable in War; and if we be not Citizens in the Commonwealth, I know no reason we should be Subjects to the Commonwealth: And truth is, we are no Subjects.[1]

As we have seen, then, during the 1640s and 1650s, royalists endured a homeland decimated by war, regicide and the enforced dispersal of at least 40,000 people which led to diaspora, disorientation and a crisis of identity for many of the King's supporters.[2] Charles I and his 'loyal cohorts' had stood as 'a thin red line preserving the physical fabric of the nation from the destruction by the forces of disorder [the parliamentarians]'.[3] More than that, for royalists, Charles was 'the guarantee of stability, the validation of security…the centre'.[4] Destabilization of this centre due to wars and regicide led to an unmeaning and a decentring of belonging, and, within contemporary literature the loss of the monarch 'was represented

[1] Cavendish, Margaret, *Sociable Letters* (London, 1664), 27. Cavendish speaking on women's exclusion as subjects in the nation state.

[2] This figure comes from Geoffrey Smith's *Cavaliers in Exile.*

[3] de Groot, *Royalist Identities*, 5.

[4] Ibid., 5.



S. Cronin, *Women, Royalisms and Exiles 1640–1669*,
https://doi.org/10.1007/978-3-030-89609-6_4

as the disruption of normality, the rupturing of order'.[5] While this event was indeed catastrophic for the state of royalist identity, this chapter posits that marginalized royalist female writers responded to this unravelling of identity as they experimented with and formed new identities within their work. Thus, as the previous chapters have shown that royalist women sought to elide the fracture in the royalist narrative through a variety of cultural forms, this chapter will show how ongoing destabilization of notions of royalist identities within the diasporic environment paradoxically proved to be an emancipatory environment for women writers.

After the devastating event of the regicide, the new socio-political landscape acquired a new dimension for royalist women. Now, those women who supported the King and the monarchy were not only 'ex*patria*ted in patria'[6] but also part of a collective group subjected to displacement and diaspora. Their already marginalized identity, as women and as women writers, was further complicated by national fragmentation, disorientation and deterritorialization which placed strains on royalist women's sense of home, sense of culture and most profoundly, their sense of selves. Inextricably bound to events, places and people linked invariably to a painful past, Azade Seyhan has suggested that through narrative subjects of displacement may 'redress forcibly forgotten experiences, allow silences of history to come to word and imagine alternate scripts of the past'.[7] She insists on locating texts in context—understanding of the present is invariably predicated on actual or imagined links to, or ruptures from, a recalled past. Moreover, narratives that originate at border crossing take on new forms and a textual fluidity unavailable to those writing from within the nation state.[8] This chapter will show that the experience of displacement and 'exile' became a transformative arena of negotiation and redefinition for Margaret Cavendish and Katherine Philips who strove to simultane-

[5] Ibid., 6.

[6] Shari Benstock deploys this phrase to show how women are exiled, outside or peripheral in their home country. She expands by saying that the opposite to patria is *matria*, 'that which is repressed, rejected, colonized, written over, subjected, erased, silenced' by forces of patriarchy. Thus, '*matria* need not leave home to be exiled and expatriated; indeed the effects of this outsidership within the definitional confines are most painfully felt at home'. These theorizations echo Cavendish's declaration in the quotation that opens this chapter. Benstock, Shari, 'Expatriate Modernism: Writing on the Cultural Rim' in *Women's Writing in Exile*. Mary Lyn Broe and Angela Ingram eds. (Chapel Hill & London: University of North Carolina Press, 1989), pp. 19–40, 24/25.

[7] Seyhan, Azade, *Writing Outside Nation*, 4.

[8] Ibid., 4.

ously maintain an identity and develop their voice as royalist women writers as they explored this new-found autonomy.

## Identity Undone

The formation of royalist identity has been determined by scholars as a categorization which until the wars did not exist. As Robert Wilcher stresses, 'the term "royalist", in fact, was not needed until the governing class polarised into parties engaged in an ideological and military contest over the locus of supreme power in the state'.[9] Jerome de Groot has further written that the term 'royalist' was coined by William Prynne (anti-monarchist) 'as a term of abuse by polemicists'.[10] The designation, or naming, of the King's supporters not only defined them in opposition to parliamentarians but gave anti-monarchists like Prynne a subject, or entity, against which derogatory allegations could be levied. Prynne declared that these royalists were 'ignorant' 'malignants' and 'parasites' who were 'unjust and unlawful' and as a caution wrote that:

> If Kings may lawfully take up arms against their subjects, as all royalists plead, after they reject their power, and become open Rebels or Traitors...they cease to be subjects any longer.[11]

Polemical it may be, yet this statement points to the fragmentation of English identity already underway by 1643.[12] It also points to the positioning of royalists as 'other' within their own nation state, their identity now fashioned by others for them. While the royalist/roundhead binary allowed each group to define itself in opposition to their enemy, parliamentarians felt the more important part of the binary, enlarging their end as the wars continued, as they urged a move from top-down hegemonic

[9] Wilcher, *The Writing of Royalism*, 5.

[10] de Groot, *Royalist Identities*, 1.

[11] Prynne, William, *The Third Part of the Soveraigne Power of Parliaments and Kingdomes* (1643), 10. http://eebo.chadwyck.com.elib.tcd.ie.

[12] Jerome de Groot provides excellent insight into the construction of royalist identity in opposition to the roundheads and the struggle to maintain an identity through writing as the wars increased. With the bifurcation of the body politic, the removal of the King to Oxford and then the exile of the queen models of identity were disrupted. I argue their displacement, and the event of diaspora further complicated this fragmentation of identity pushing them further into unknown territory both psychologically and physically.

ideologies to parliamentarian bottom-up ideologies. The impact of this agitation and eventual shift of power was immense for royalists as they could no longer take for granted notions of identity. Moreover, now occupying a precarious liminal status as non-subjects in their own homeland, the general position for royalist supporters as 'subjects' now came to resemble that which women specifically experienced during this period.

Second to this disorientating rupture of identity during the war years and interregnum, royalist women's ideas concerning both their private and public selves in seventeenth-century England were also profoundly altered within the environment of diaspora. Before the wars, traditional seventeenth-century binaries reinforced oppositions between men and women, thereby subordinating women, which locked women into ways of thinking, acting and reacting.[13] However, 'contemporary discourses of gender were not static, seamless wholes…they changed shape as they interacted with other determinants of identity, like class, religion and politics', indeed, 'flagrant internal contradictions' allowed women to 'question how they could simultaneously be subjects on the grounds of their common humanity and non-subjects on the grounds of their gender'.[14] During the interregnum, a period in which the normative structure of society was disrupted, I argue women were enabled by the absence of the

[13] On the subject of women's expected conduct and contemporary attitudes to women writing, see: Chalmers, *Royalist Women Writers 1650–1689*; Goreau, Angeline, *The Whole Duty of a Woman: Female Writers in Seventeenth-Century England* (Garden City, New York: Doubleday & Company Inc., 1985); Harvey, Elizabeth D., *Body Narratives: Writing the Nation and Fashioning the Subject in Early Modern England*; Hobby, Elaine, 'A Discourse so Unsavoury' in *Women, Writing History 1640–1740*; Purkiss, Diane, *Literature, Gender and Politics during the English Civil War* (Cambridge, Cambridge University Press, 2005); Mihoko, Suzuki, *Subordinate Subjects: Gender, the Political Nation, and Literary Form in England, 1588–1688* (Hampshire & Burlington: Ashgate, 2003); Wilcox, Helen, *Women and Literature in Britain 1500–1700* (Cambridge: Cambridge University Press, 1996); Ezell, Margaret, *The Patriarch's Wife* (Chapel Hill & London: University of North Carolina Press, 1987); Hobby, *Virtue of Necessity: English Women's Writing 1649–1688;* Beilin, *"Redeeming Eve": Women Writers of the English Renaissance;* For another perspective see Jennifer Summit, *Lost Property: The Woman Writer and English Literary History1380–1589* (Chicago & London: University of Chicago Press, 2000). Summit argues that women and women's writing was central to the construction of the English canon: that women were essential to canonical figures such as Chaucer and Puttenham in their construction of a distinguished vernacular which English literature could claim as their own, quite apart from the classical framework.

[14] Pacheco, *Early Modern Women Writers 1600–1720,* Anita Pacheco, ed. (London & New York: Routledge, 1998), 13.

centre or patriarchal fulcrum and they experienced even more autonomy which challenged 'the dominant social construction of the female self as 'chaste, silent and obedient'.[15] Moreover, as royalists were dispersed they were exposed to dichotomous forces which allowed for new modalities of being. While diaspora exposes the subject to displacement, fragmentation and discontinuity, it also opens up new ways of seeing that enable the subject to move beyond the static models of national identity. This emancipation comes from within the diaspora and as the diaspora crosses boundaries of nation state. Hence, despite being born of a moment of loss and disorientation, and exacerbated with feelings devoid of the rightful claims to belong, this crisis of identity 'opens up the chance to explore alternative modes of belonging'[16] and transforms the negative experience of displacement into more positive re-inscriptions of identity.

This chapter, then, argues that identity for Philips and Cavendish is profoundly altered through the experience of enforced dispersion and diaspora, and that the dynamic environment of diaspora offered opportunity for these women as writers. This chapter posits that a synthesis of their relationship with royalism, their aspirations as writers and the event of diaspora made possible the emergence of self-fashioned and hybridized selves breaking with traditionally static model of gendered and cultural homogeneous identity. It will be seen that their individual relationships with royalism tie them to the network of cultural resistance which sought to protect ideals and mores concomitant with the monarchy discussed in Chap. 2 and 3, however, this relationship also rendered them as marginal during the wars and for the period of the interregnum. This chapter argues that this marginalization—geographical, cultural and political—paradoxically generated an environment from within which these writers would find space to begin to write unrestricted by societal constraints 'that tolerated women writing but was deeply suspicious of women publishing'.[17] As this chapter re-contextualizes royalist women's cultural production of the period, it draws on James Clifford's assertion that 'diaspora and exile may reinforce or loosen gender subordination within patriarchal systems' and insists that on one hand:

[15] Mcgrath, Lynette, *Subjectivity and Women's Poetry in Early Modern England* (Aldershot & Burlington: Ashgate, 2002), 11.

[16] McLeod, John, *Beginning Postcolonialism*, 249. Hereafter cited as *BP*.

[17] Fitzmaurice, James, 'Fancy and the Family: Self Characterizations of Margaret Cavendish.' *The Huntington Library Quarterly* 53. 3 (Summer 1990): 198–209, 207.

> maintaining connections to homelands, with kinship, and with religious and cultural traditions may renew patriarchal structures. On the other, new spaces are opened up by diaspora interactions.[18]

Hence, I posit, that as these writers were re-located to marginal spaces through displacement and exile, they found their predicaments 'conducive to a positive re-negotiation of gender relations'[19] and that the space afforded through this movement allowed for a greater chance of participation within the literary, and by extension, public sphere. Thus, their work offers a unique aperçus into the heterogeneous nature of royalist identity, the personal identity of these writers and their endeavours to fashion and project an authorial identity while maintaining allegiance during a period of immense change in England.

Finally, this chapter argues for thinking about these women's work on a transnational level as it shows how their work addresses issues faced by their de-territorialized culture and speaks for communities which transnational scholar Azade Seyhan has termed 'para-national communities and alliances'.[20] Moreover, much like Bhabha, Seyhan notes that 'narratives that originate at border crossings cannot be bound by national borders, languages and critical traditions'.[21] This chapter asserts that reading Cavendish's and Philips's work in the light of established views, which are concerned with traditional modes of representation through traditional generic models, can be reductive and may obscure value to the study of royalist literary production in the context of exile and diaspora. Recently, Philip Major has brought attention to the issue of 'residual Anglo-centrism' concerning seventeenth-century literature, stating that 'scholarship on seventeenth century Britain has *ipso facto* tended to discourage the engagement with exilic literary material' with the result being 'that it has circumscribed our understanding' of 'the exiles themselves' and the 'host communities in which they lived' and he adds that this unexplored area of literature, 'rich in social, political and cultural potential…has all but been

[18] Clifford, *Diasporas,* 314/315.

[19] Ibid., 314.

[20] Seyhan, *Writing Outside Nation*, 'Transnational literature' is defined by Seyhan as a genre operating outside the nation canon…addressing issues raised by deterritorialized or displaced peoples', and 'paranational communities' is defined as 'communities that are within national borders, alongside citizens of host countries but remain culturally or linguistically distanced or estranged', 10.

[21] Ibid., 4.

ignored'.[22] The unwillingness to consider diaspora and exile as a very real event or experience for royalists during the civil war and interregnum not only limits, but shuts down, any possibility of reading and understanding their work within an exciting and enriching context. Additionally, and perhaps most crucially, it also restricts our readings to deep-rooted traditional parameters and denies an important part of not only English history or the history of the British Isles but also the history of those who experienced alternative cultures as they were dispersed from England to multiple locations across Europe, the Middle East and the British Atlantic during these years.

## Diasporic Identities

For many scholars of diaspora, identity is discursive and every diaspora is shaped by the conditions from which it emerged. Avtar Brah argues that 'all diasporas are differentiated, heterogeneous, contested spaces even as they are implicated in the construction of the common "we"; differences of race, class, religion and language make diaspora spaces dynamic and shifting, open to repeated construction and reconstruction'.[23] Further, although a diaspora crosses multiple geographies, inherent within its concept is the notion of border. Borders are arbitrary dividing lines at once social, cultural, ideological and psychic—they are more like 'territories to be patrolled against those whom they construct as outsiders, aliens, the Others'.[24] However, as discussed in Chap. 1, the border is also a place of possibility—it is a 'place where conventional patterns of thought are disturbed and can be disrupted by the possibility of crossing'.[25]

Stuart Hall asserts that identity is 'a "production" that is never complete...always in process, and always constituted within, not outside,

[22] Major, Philip, *Writings of Exile in the English Revolution and Restoration* (Surrey & Burlington VT: Ashgate, 2013), 4/5.

[23] Brah, Avtar, *Cartographies of Diaspora: Contesting Identities* (London & New York: Routledge, 1996), 18.

[24] Ibid., 198. As a border is an arbitrary line, the area surrounding it is more realistically a territory, each side of the 'line' making up the space of the border territory. Borderlands 'are distinct in that they presuppose a territory defined by a geo-political line: two sides arbitrarily separated and policed, but also joined by legal and illegal practices of crossing and communication'. Clifford, 'Diasporas', 217.

[25] McLeod, *BP*, 252.

representation'...problematizing the 'very authority and authenticity to which the term 'cultural identity' lays claim'.[26] Thus, writing from a place in time, a culture and history which are specific we write in context and are 'positioned'. Hall, further suggests that there are two ways of thinking about cultural identity. Firstly, that cultural identity is part of a shared culture, a 'sort of collective "one true self", hiding inside the many other, more superficial or artificially imposed "selves", which people with a shared history and ancestry hold in common'. Within this definition, cultural identities 'reflect the common historical experiences and shared cultural codes...which provide us, as "one people", with stable, unchanging and continuous frames of reference and meaning, beneath the shifting divisions and vicissitudes of our actual history'.[27] Secondly, that as well as the many points of similarity, there are 'also critical points of deep and significant difference which constitute "what we really are"; or rather—since history has intervened—'what we have become'. 'Cultural identity' is thus 'a matter of 'becoming' as well as of 'being'.[28] 'It belongs to the future as much as the past'. 'Cultural identities come from somewhere...[b]ut...they undergo constant transformation' as they are subject to the continuous play of history, culture and power. Ultimately, 'identities are the names we give to the different ways we are positioned by, and position ourselves within, the narratives of the past'.[29] Hence, due to border crossing, within the space of the diaspora, it is possible for identity to be remade and remodelled in new and innovative ways. Moreover, as one crosses the border between nation state and contrary/alternate lands inherited knowledge 'can be re-inscribed and given new unexpected meanings by becoming cross-hatched with cultural resources from other locations and sources, other times and places'.[30] For royalist women, political, cultural, ideological and geographical border crossing allowed a move away from oppressive, restrictive prescriptions placed upon them and engage in what Bhabha terms as 'a restaging of the past'.[31] These royalist women were no longer reliant on fixed notions of home and identity to

[26] Hall, Stuart, 'Cultural Identity and Diaspora' in *Colonial Discourse and Post-colonial Theory: A Reader*, Patrick Williams and Laura Chrisman, eds. (Columbia University Press, 1994), 392.

[27] Ibid., 393.

[28] Ibid., 394

[29] Ibid., 394.

[30] McLeod, *BP*, 253.

[31] See Chap. 1 above.

anchor them to a singular sense of self. Hence, their identity paradigm—one which is governed by collective traditions of royalism and gendered subordination—is open to being remade through a process of hybridity, multiplicity and most significantly possibility.

Examining one instance of internal exile and one external exile, this chapter traces the heterogeneous identities of these writers as they renegotiate, reconstruct their identities and shape themselves as royalist women writers from multiple locations. Mindful of the fluctuating sense of identity formation inherent in a diaspora setting, it pays close attention to women's projection and protection of their identities as they navigate exilic transitions in their lives. I explore how they blur the arbitrary societal boundaries that seek to restrict them as women writers and posit that the genre they appropriate serves to enhance their stratagem to negotiate (re)integration into their respective societies. In particular, by exploring the 'intersection of genre and personal identity',[32] I examine the ways in which genre may be a malleable tool for these writers as they experience predicaments which led to positive re-negotiation of gender relations within the environment of diaspora. The genre chosen by each writer reflects their identity in flux and yet is commensurate with the author's navigation of a tumultuous period in their lives, their relationship and identification with royalism and their marginal position as women writers. While the prior three chapters seek commonalities in, and connections between, royalist women's cultural production affected by diaspora, this chapter brings into sharp relief the heterogeneity of these women's experiences and cautions us to avoid reductive taxonomy in relation to royalism and exile. Through their differences this chapter solidifies the comparative element of this book, foregrounding individual experiences of types of exiles within the diasporic environment and examining the ways in which this existence is reflected through textual manifestations. Thus, while the women examined may share the paradigms of royalism, authorship and exile, the synthesis of these paradigms produce very different results in each case.

Examining Cavendish's prose fiction *Assaulted and Pursued Chastity*, included in the volume *Nature's Pictures* (1656), I trace a period of relocation and transition from one culture and indeed, nation, to another and a search for personal belonging. It will be seen the trajectory of this

[32] Dowd, Michelle, M., *Genre and Women's life Writing in Early Modern England* (Hampshire & Burlington: Ashgate, 2007), 1.

allegorical narrative traces an arc which reflects Cavendish's own experience of displacement from England,[33] dislocation from a culture she knows and a state of exile transformed by integration into her host country and the initiation of autonomous agency as a woman. Through the prose fiction, Cavendish re-inscribes a traumatic experience of exile, displacement and disorientation to render a poignant reworking of that moment of dislocation and border crossing which rearticulates the typical diasporic tension of loss and hope into that of transformation and triumph.

Katherine Philips's ascension to triumph was markedly different to that of Cavendish's. Through her private correspondence with eminent royalist Sir Charles Cotterell during the very early restoration years, not only can we read her growth and carefully controlled emergence as a royalist woman writer, but most crucially, through the letters, her previously fractured identity becomes whole and all the threads of her life discussed in Chap. 2 and 3 combine to provide us with a more unified picture of Philips's complex identity as a royalist woman writer. While on the one hand, we see that the contentious relationship between her domestic position, passion for the royalist cause and her coterie of royalist friends are brought together in the letters to suit Philips's strategy for emergence, on the other hand, the experience of cultural, personal and political marginalization after the restoration is seen to trouble Philips deeply and the letters thus reveal a tension between writer, her sense and experience of place as well as her psychological state, hitherto unexplored in this context. The letters here are analysed to provide insight into Philips's psychological state as she was intermittently detached and isolated from hubs (Dublin and London) of literary inspiration and political importance at a key moment of personal and historical transition. It must be noted, however, that this study of the letters does not suggest these writings as a work of political opposition, in fact, these letters were designed as anything but oppositional for Philips in the early 1660s as she strove to reintegrate and curry favour for herself and

[33] Cavendish served as maid of honour for Queen Henrietta Maria in Oxford at the outbreak of trouble in 1643 and wrote in her autobiography that 'after the Queen went from Oxford, and so out of England, I was parted from them' (her sisters who lived near Oxford), the impact of which she writes was akin to having 'no foundation to stand, or guide to direct me, which made me afraid', *True Relation*, 286/287. Residing for a time in the court in Paris, Margaret met and married William Cavendish, Lord Newcastle, in 1645. Margaret further writes that 'after being married some two or three years, my Lord travelled out of France…to a town called Rotterdam' where they remained for six months until they finally settled in Antwerp, *True Relation*, 296.

husband in relation to the newly restored court. Thus, the letters represent a chronicle of Philips's experience as a diasporic subject at all times navigating and negotiating her way back to London, her 'native place',[34] and that as she does so she creates cross-kingdom alliances that benefit both sides of the cultural and political divide.

## 'Not Anchored Nor Ballasted': Relocation & Transition in Margaret Cavendish's Assaulted and Pursued Chastity

> I would rather live as I do, in a Peaceable Banishment with my Husband although Accompanied with Pinching Poverty, than to be Possess'd With Fears in my own Native Country.[35]

This statement by Margaret Cavendish not only points to the gravity of the situation for royalists back in London during the war years but also iterates the sense of safety found through distance from her own nation state. It tells of Cavendish's willingness to sacrifice all she knows, her home, her family, her culture and her language to live a safer and more peaceful life in a country which is alien to her in a variety of ways. Moreover, it suggests that rather than be 'Possess'd With Fears' there is something to be gained by residing outside her 'own Native Country', that this 'banishment' is preferred to that of life at home, a declaration which positions Cavendish as central to her own world rather than peripheral. This positive view of her own alterity influenced Cavendish to devise fictional alternatives to her real life or alternative 'elsewheres' within which she could reign as 'Margaret the First'.[36]

In 1643 Margaret Cavendish (née Lucas) joined Queen Henrietta in Oxford as maid of honour after she had 'wooed and won' her mother over.[37] This act of persuasion was perhaps Margaret's initiation of her agency as a woman, however, it also points to her activism in capitalizing on networks which could enable realization of her ambitions. This was to

[34] Philips, Katherine, *The Letters*, Letter XXXVI in Patrick Thomas.

[35] Cavendish, Margaret, *Sociable Letters*. #185. James Fitzmaurice ed. (Ontario; Broadview Press, 2004), 251. Sociable Letters was published in 1664, however, composition dates are unknown.

[36] "To All Noble and Worthy Ladies", *The Description of a New World, Called the Blazing World* (1668).

[37] Cavendish, *True Relation*, CH Firth ed. 1886, 286

be her first experience of separation from her family. On 17 April 1644, as the war intensified, the Queen's court removed itself to Exeter and from there to Paris on 30 June. It was in Paris in 1645 that Margaret first saw her future husband, William Cavendish, Earl of Newcastle. However, before their marriage took place, Margaret lived for nearly two years within the testing environment of Queen Henrietta's court.

Since Queen Elizabeth's reign, the court of the Stuart queens had changed dramatically. Rather than being centred on an absolute model, the figure of the Virgin Queen, the courts were now multi-focused, with Henrietta Maria taking a serious role in patronage of the arts, just as her mother-in-law Queen Anna of Denmark had done. Through their sponsorship of courtly culture, patronage, commissioning of art, performance and literature, these queens fashioned their own courts. Clare McManus has written that reading early modern women's 'cultural production through the prism of the queen's court also allows a reading of the identities which such an institution conferred on its female members, whether royal or aristocratic, courtiers or court servants'.[38] Identities within the courts privileged class over gender, and both the Queen and her maids were free to fashion their identities by appropriation of masculine forms of identity 'to form a particular kind of institutional self-hood unique to these courts'.[39] This slippage embedded within the 'nature of court membership' allowed 'women of the queen's court to act like male courtiers and their queen to act like a prince'.[40] This blurring of gender roles and this status as part of the court could then be utilized by female courtiers wishing to enter into any sphere usually designated as the domain of men. The queen's court was thus an enabling place for women both personally and culturally.

While Cavendish's time here exposed her to such blurring of boundaries between men and women's domains, she was also exposed to the competitive nature of court patronage.[41] In her autobiography, Cavendish

[38] McManus, Clare, *Women and Culture at the Courts of the Stuart Queens*. Clare McManus ed. (Basingstoke & New York: Palgrave Macmillan, 2003), 2.

[39] Ibid., 2.

[40] Ibid., 7.

[41] Sarah Poynting provides useful insights to life at court for the maids of honour, the expectations placed upon them and the competition for patronage that shaped the 'extent to which they managed their own affairs or competed for court posts in order to improve their economic and social status'. While young women at court enjoyed a way of life that 'was highly privileged and protected'... 'a way of life which allowed them to begin to assert them-

works to distance herself from the less than orthodox manner in which women had to comport themselves at court when she writes she 'neither heeded what was said or practiced, but just what belonged to my loyal duty'.[42] She also reveals the financial pressure which led women to seek patronage at the court when she writes that courtiers never have money 'being always necessitated by reason of great expenses the courts put them to'.[43] In a letter to William Cavendish during their courtship, Margaret is at pains to point out that she takes no part in court frivolity or scandal when she writes 'pray doe not think I am inquisitive after such frivolus talk, for I avoid company to avoid ther discourse'.[44] Thus, Cavendish fought to remain dutiful and honourable during her appointment as maid of honour. However, conversely, she took advantage of courtly traditions as she set out to defend herself and her writing later on in the early 1650s.[45]

Having left the court of Queen Henrietta Maria, the Cavendishes first settled in Paris from early 1646–1648, their house serving for intellectual gatherings of French and English *libertin erudits*. William had arrived in Paris after Marston Moor (1644) and having impoverished himself, he offered his services to the Queen. He was a soldier, courtier and patron of poets (Ben Jonson), Humanists (Thomas Hobbes), and friends with Pierre Gassendi, Marin Mersenne and Rene Descartes. Mersenne was the 'hub of an important circle of intellectual friendship in Paris' during this time,[46] which included Hobbes and Gassendi and this group could be described as the intellectual centre of Europe. Marsenne carried on correspondence with many scientists and intellectuals including Hugo Grotius, Descartes and Galileo and is also recorded as dining with the Cavendishes, along

selves as individuals' assume roles and modes of expression usually the prerogative of men and learn that they could act and think independently, they also had to navigate an altogether more sinister side to living at court crucial to their very survival as maids of honour. Poynting, Sarah, 'In the Name of all the sisters': Hentrietta Maria's Notorious Whores' in *Women and Culture at the Courts of the Stuart Queens*. Clare McManus, ed. (Basingstoke & New York: Palgrave Macmillan, 2003): 163–185, 175, 180.

[42] Cavendish, *True Relation*. C.H. Firth ed., 1886, 287.

[43] Ibid., 288.

[44] Cavendish, in Battigelli, *Exiles of the Mind*. Appendix B, 121.

[45] Raber, Karen, *Dramatic Difference: Gender, Class, and Genre in the Early Modern Closet Drama* (Newark: University of Delaware Press; London: Associated University Presses, 2001), 466. See also Chalmers, *RWW*, 36.

[46] Smith, Charles Kay, 'French Philosophy and English Politics in Interregnum Poetry' in *The Stuart Court in Europe*. Malcom Smuts, ed. (New York & Melbourne: Cambridge University Press, 1996), 190.

with Descartes, Hobbes, Gassendi and Edmund Waller.[47] The many philosophies and scientific theories which circulated among these great minds of the century included beginnings of modern concepts of rationalism and atomist theories. Surrounded by these intellectuals, both English and French, Cavendish absorbed and applied these new cultural discourses to her own work. Indeed, the couple's move to Rotterdam in 1648 and then six months later to Antwerp would also have profound impact on Cavendish and her work.

A highly cosmopolitan place, its printing and publishing press still thriving, Antwerp not only was a suitable strategic location for Newcastle but was also a hub of artistic creativity in which the royalists were free to be themselves away from the oppression of parliamentarian acts, ordinances and proclamations which rendered life difficult throughout the war years and interregnum. Margaret writes that the city of Antwerp was a 'place of great resort for strangers and travellers',[48] the city 'being a passage or thoroughfare to many parts causeth many times persons of great quality to be here, though not as inhabitants'.[49] Thus, noting Antwerp's transient community Cavendish witnessed the movement of people of various nationalities and class commingling and travelling, while also being exposed to a culture within which women participated actively. She writes that she saw on stage 'Women Actors…indeed the Best Female actor I ever saw; and for Acting the Man's Part, she did it so Naturally as if she had been of that sex'.[50] She further writes that she did 'take delight in the customs thereof which most cities of note in Europe, for all I can hear, hath such like recreations for the effeminate sex' and that appearing abroad she would find 'several objects do bring materials for [her] thoughts and fancies to build upon'.[51] Thus, Cavendish's imagination was directly influenced by the vast swathes of travellers, expatriates or exiles which passed through the city, by the culture of Antwerp and she was inspired by these female actors who engaged in masculine professions.

[47] Jones, Kathleen, *A Glorious Fame: the Life of Margaret Cavendish, Duchess of Newcastle, 1623–1673* (London, 1988), 56.

[48] Cavendish, *The Life*. C. H. Firth ed. 1886, 115.

[49] Cavendish, *True Relation*, 309.

[50] Cavendish, *Sociable Letters*, letter 195, p. 261.

[51] Cavendish, *True Relation*, 309.

Friends and visitors to the Cavendish circle in Antwerp included Queen Christina of Sweden,[52] a keen scholar, patron of music and the arts who headhunted scholars and artists throughout Europe including the great intellectual Anna Maria van Schurman.[53] David Norbrook states that it is 'inconceivable that she [Cavendish] was unaware' of not only van Schurman's existence but also other leading women intellectuals such as Marie de Gournay for example.[54] Another frequent visitor and friend of Margaret's was Constantine Huygens, wealthy aristocrat, distinguished diplomat and statesman and secretary to the Prince of Orange at The Hague. He was also an admired poet who wrote in Latin, French, Italian and Spanish as well as Dutch and spoke English well. He was a friend of Descartes, an adherent to the new philosophy and shared his interest in music, poetry and literature with wide circle of intellectual female friends, of which Anna van Schurmann, Utricia Swann and the Duchess of Lorraine were included. Katie Whitaker has disclosed his mentioning both Margaret and van Schurman in a letter which further attests to Norbrook's theory.[55] Despite Cavendish's linguistic limitations she nevertheless took a keen interest in the issues that circulated within her husband's little academy[56] and has no doubt implemented some of the new theories and philosophies into her work.[57] Indeed, Norbrook has suggested that the reason she, or

[52] Katie Whitaker, *Mad Madge*, 176/177.

[53] Van Schurman played a pivotal role in a small European network of learned women, and corresponded, for instance, with Bir-gitte Thott (in Denmark), Christina Queen of Sweden, Marie le Jars du Gournay (in France), Bathsua Makin (in England) and Dorothea Moore (in Ireland), among others. Van Schurman's erudition may only be understood against the background of the humanistic Republic of Letters—a fraternity of scholars in Europe, who transcended the normal barriers of social class, faith, language and nationality. The language medium in this Republic of Letters was Latin. Peta van Beek. *The First Female University Student: Anna Maria van Schurman (1636)*. (Utrecht: Igitur Utrect Publishing and Archiving Services, 2010), 7/8.

[54] Norbrook, David, 'Women, the Republic of Letters, and the Public Sphere in the Mid-Seventeenth Century. *Criticism*. 46.2 (Detroit, Spring): 223–241, 4. http://lionchadwyck.co.uk [4/November, 2013].

[55] De Brifwisseling van Constantijn Huygens (1608–1687), ed J.A. Worp, 6 vols. (The Hague: Martinus Nijhoff, 1911–1917), 5: 186–187; van Schurman, Opuscula. Cited by Katie Whitaker, *Mad Madge*, 121.

[56] Norbrook, 'Women', 5. For further insights into William Cavendish's circle, see special edition of *The Seventeenth Century* 9.2 (1994).

[57] For examples of Cavendish's work in relation to new contemporary theory see: Price, Bronwin. 'Feminine Modes of Knowing and Scientific Enquiry: Margaret Cavendish's Poetry as case study in *Women and Literature in Britain 1500–1700*. Helen Wilcox ed.

her publications were not well received in England had little to do with her as a woman encroaching on male prerogatives or challenging the ideals of patriarchy, and more to do with the content of her work, or perhaps more precisely the lack of certain English trends and cultural expectations in her work, as well as 'her synthesis of profiles of Continental, and especially French, intellectual women for projection into the very different conditions of Puritan England'.[58]

However, despite this seemingly comfortable transition and a life spent in vibrant Continental countries, the collapse of all she and other royalists had previously known as well as the upheaval of exile placed particular pressure on royalist supporters to re-orientate themselves during the interregnum. From the margins in Antwerp, Cavendish not only responded to this fracturing of the royalist narrative but also went further to create an imaginary realm within which she would experiment with, and form, new identities to deal with such a difficult transition. Her theorizations regarding women's exclusion from political subject-hood, such as the quotation which heads this chapter, attest to her view of women as residing outside the state apparatus, which rendered them non-subjects, or as expatriated, in the nation state. We will see that subversive view was further complicated by the experience of exile and as she agitated the concept of the subject within her work to produce a hybrid persona capable of fluid subjectivity. For Cavendish, the experience of exile thus became an evolution of women's expatriation in patria and added an extra dimension to the ongoing process of negotiation, definition or redefinition of self-hood.

As mentioned in Chap. 2, previous scholarship has concentrated heavily on Cavendish's drama, scientific and philosophical writings and less so on her poetry. Her prose fiction also remains an area of her oeuvre which is relatively understudied, with what has been examined focusing mainly on her utopian imaginary voyage *The Blazing World* (1666).[59] Arguing

(Cambridge: Cambridge University Press, 1996), pp. 117–139; Charles Kay Smith, Charles Kay, 'French Philosophy and English Politics in Interregnum Poetry' in *The Stuart Court in Europe.* Malcom Smuts, ed. (New York & Melbourne: Cambridge University Press, 1996), pp. 176–209; Ankers, Neil, 'Paradigms and Politics: Hobbes and Cavendish Contrasted' in *A Princely Brave Woman: Essays on Margaret Cavendish, Duchess of Newcastle.* Stephen Clucas, ed. (Aldershot, Hampshire: Ashgate, 2003), pp. 242–253.

58 Norbrook, 'Women', 7.

59 See, for example, Lilley, Kate, 'Blazing Worlds: Seventeenth Century Women's Utopian Writing' in *Women, Texts and Histories 1575–1760.* Clare Brant and Diane Purkiss, eds. (London: Routledge, 1992); Salzman, Paul, *English Prose Fiction 1558–1700* (Oxford:

against commentary which criticizes Cavendish's work as formally flawed, chaotic or old-fashioned,[60] my treatment of *Assaulted and Pursued Chastity* (1656) differs in terms of its genesis and its potential as a cathartic tool for Cavendish as she herself comes to terms with the transition from one nation state to another. On one hand, I agree with Emma Rees that the text is perched on the threshold as a 'quite deliberate composite of genres emerges',[61] however, on the other hand, I disagree that the text occupies 'a generic position between epic and romance'.[62] In *Assaulted and Pursued Chastity* Cavendish blends both elements of the picaresque in that the narrative is episodic and focuses on a wandering character but it also draws on the movement and momentum of the travel narrative or imaginary voyage. As Paul Salzman has written, 'travel literature and travel itself were both extremely popular throughout the century'[63] and I argue it is through this blending of genres Cavendish negotiates her sense of displacement and fragmented identity by simultaneously reinventing that which was lost as she renders an imaginative allegorical present within which the disruptions of exile and deterritorialization could be overridden. This section thus aligns itself with Kate Lilley's suggestion that Cavendish's prose fictions 'resist categorisation',[64] yet I push further to argue that the fluidity, dynamic experimentation of form and cross-fertilization of genres which materialize within this narrative are a result of the experience of exile, border crossing and the lived tension of the double consciousness which result in a blurring of generic boundaries, as well as those associated with her position as a royalist woman writer in exile.

This section, then, explores *Assaulted and Pursued Chastity* specifically as a product of negotiation of deterritorialization through examination of what Michael Seidel theorizes as the 'double-ness implicit in exilic

Clarendon Press, 1985); Iyengar, Sujata. 'Royalist, Romanticist, Racialist: Rank and Gender, and Race in the Science Fiction of Margaret Cavendish. *ELH*. 69.3 (Fall, 2002): 649–672; Trubowitz, Rachel, 'The Reenchanment of Utopia and the Female Monarchical Self: Margaret Cavendish's Blazing World'. *Tulsa Studies in Women's Literature*. 11.2 (Autumn, 1992): 229–245.

[60] See respectively: Battigelli, *Exiles of the Mind*; Bowerbank, Sylvia & Sara Mendelson, *Paper Bodies: A Margaret Cavendish Reader* (Calgary: Broadview Press, 1999), 197–201. Mendelson, Sara, *The Mental World of Stuart Women*, 38.

[61] Rees, *Gender, Genre and Exile*, 113.

[62] Ibid., 112.

[63] Salzman, *English Prose Fiction*, 218.

[64] Lilley, Kate, *Margaret Cavendish: The Blazing World and Other Writings*. 3rd ed. (London: Penguin Group, 2004), Xi.

positioning'.[65] Further, this section examines the ways in which Cavendish narrates the experience of exile and disorientation through what he calls an 'alien voicing—the word "allegory" meaning—al-"other"/goria "voicing"'.[66] I argue that Cavendish's imagination creates solutions to 'exilic anguish' through the blending of multiple allegorical threads in an effort to create a necessary elsewhere within which to imaginatively negotiate such a momentous personal and historical transition. Through the double-ness of the form Cavendish blends both the experience of proximity concerning new surroundings and memories of her lost patria in an effort to re-suture the rupture caused by displacement. Moreover, through the imaginative creation of an archipelagic territory strewn with many kingdoms, Cavendish sets up an arena within which she negotiates her own personal transition from England to the continent. More than this, enabled by the distance from the nation state and the opportunity this presents, she devises this demesne as the locale within which she challenges woman's stasis as a subject trapped within the system of patriarchy and questions royalist notions of normative gender roles. For Cavendish, and for the heroine of this narrative, autonomy is only achieved by leaving the nation state, despite being rendered an exile. However, exile is not granted permanence and is replaced by the more positive notion of travelling. Indeed, the content of the narrative is not reduced to the simple or all-consuming presentation of banishment in the basic plot of the narrative. Rather, we find that exile is replaced with travelling, identity is re-inscribed and the ill-fated become agents, who despite being compromised by loss, displace dislocation itself, replacing it with relocation and recuperation; through movement, travel and distance from the oppressive homeland, her protagonist resists commodification and fetishization, and begins a transformation of the self which concludes with integration into the host country and the initiation of autonomous agency.

Utilizing the maritime metaphor both in its negative and positive guises, Cavendish renders a sea-borne odyssey which transports her protagonist—a symbolic figure of loss which figures both personal and royalist loss as one which is shaped by dislocation—from island to island. Douglas Bush notes that early in the century 'the spirit of travel and maritime discovery continued to affect every kind of imaginative and reflective

[65] Seidel, *Exile and the Narrative Imagination*, 13.
[66] Ibid.

literature'.[67] Initially compromised by this disorientation and loss 'steered by a storm' to 'a place and people strange unto her', the heroine was nonetheless 'sent' out of her homeland for 'safety' (55/6).[68] However, this apparent trauma and emphasis on loss at the outset of the narrative is negotiated and eventually displaced through a series of alternate locales which, for this disorientated protagonist, transform exile into travelling. This kingdom is just one of multiple locales, or microcosms, which dot the panorama of this archipelagic narrative and each time the maritime metaphor is deployed we are transported further away from the *locus* of the trauma, the homeland. In the early modern period, an island was an 'experimental place where opposing forces' might be 'brought together in dramatic confrontation',[69] like a theatre within the larger environment of the city. However, for the heroine of this imaginary voyage, this island is simply another space of entrapment and escape must be accomplished in order to resume travelling. Hence, she comes to the seaside and a 'ship just going off' (60) bound 'for new discoveries towards the south' (61). After sailing for months, 'a gust of wind drove them on a rock that split the ship' (62) but at last they 'espied' land (63). From this land she 'went in the same boat' as she came, (80) yet, this time seized by pirates she is thrust upon an 'unpeopled' (82) island. However, the maritime metaphor is deployed once more as the heroine 'being put out to sea' (86) moves ever onward and is relieved of her island prison. Here, parallels may be drawn from Hugo Grotius's *Mare Liberum* (1609), in which he provides an interesting precedent for thinking about the seas as a medium which connects rather than divides nations. Cavendish appears to be suggesting a similar philosophy as the maritime metaphor is deployed more often to enable rather than to hinder the action of the narrative and the individual growth of the protagonist. Indeed, numerous attempts to go home fail and the heroine continually moves forward, thus transforming her exile into travelling. Moreover, the multiple locales and the momentum of the fluid narrative remind us of Bhabha's moment of transit due to travelling

[67] Bush, Douglas, *English literature in the Earlier Seventeenth Century*, rev, edn (Oxford: Oxford University Press, 1962), 190.

[68] Cavendish, Margaret, *Assaulted and Pursued Chastity* in Lilley, *Margaret Cavendish: The Blazing World and Other Writings*, 48. All citations will be cited parenthetically within the text.

[69] Bate, Jonathon, 'Shakespeare's Islands' in *Shakespeare and the Mediterranean, The Selected Proceedings of the International Shakespeare Association*, World Congress, Valencia, 2001. Tom Clayton et al., eds. (Newark: University of Delaware Press, 2004), 290.

or leaving; this heroine is constantly in transit, encountering strange and exotic lands full of promise and possibility.

As exile is displaced with travelling and the heroine moves across alien lands, her subjectivity is dramatically altered and her identity re-inscribed. Once in transit her identity is constantly in a state of flux. In the first geographical displacement within the narrative, certain gender inequalities in royalist culture are represented through the protagonist's sense of disorientation, entrapment, commodification and loss. Arrival in the 'Kingdom of Sensuality' the protagonist is beset 'with treachery' (48) and abandonment as 'those she entrusted left her' (48). Next she is sold to an old bawd who 'trafficked' her to the 'land of youth' then sold as 'a rich prize' to a foreign prince (50). Thus, the protagonist is commodified, dehumanized and objectified. Despite women's elevated position within royalist culture, which drew on renaissance worship of the aristocratic woman, Sarah Poynting notes that women were 'unavoidably involved in the material culture of the court' as 'objects of male scrutiny' and subjects of judgement from both inside and outside the court.[70] Here, Cavendish renders her distaste for these sexist courtly traditions textually and as the Prince ventures to placate his charge with 'all kinds of Persian silks, and tissues, fine linen and laces', (58) the female protagonist begins to assume agency as she refuses the gifts, and since he 'could fasten no gifts on her', (58) she refuses his fetishization and will not be bought. In this manner, the nameless protagonist subverts traditional gender assignments as she refuses the allocations that patriarchy has placed upon her, and, despite her status as exile, she initiates control of her own subjectivity.

The names assigned to Cavendish's protagonist further indicate this flux in her identity. The exiled character is nameless at the opening of the narrative, a designation which intimates the universal experience all women endure as non-subjects in the nation state reflected in the quotation that heads this section. We are told this lost figure of woman was so disorientated that she knew not 'how to dispose of herself' (48). Such was this traumatic experience of being wrenched from her homeland, her family and culture that she expected 'nothing less than death' (54) for herself. Moreover, this nomad or no one, or every woman figure, is later fixed with the name 'Miseria' as her ill-fated destiny unfolds. By deploying the negative aspect of the maritime metaphor as an analogy for her inner turmoil, Miseria's 'troubled, and rough thoughts' 'drove her from one end of the

[70] Poynting, 'In the Name of all the Sisters', 181.

room to the other', and are described as being 'like a ship at sea, that is not anchored nor ballasted' (51). Thus, her naming assigns meaning to her very being—Miseria is displaced, she has no control and knows not how to 'avoid the shipwreck' (51) she anticipates in this, her unmoored existence. As the narrative unfolds, this feminized and subordinate allocation is dissolved and the heroine is ascribed with the more gender-neutral name of 'Travellia'. This transformation takes place at a crucial point in the narrative as she undertakes to escape from the prince and signifies the heroine's final shift concerning naming.

Voice and linguistic prowess are also signs by which we can trace the heroine's subjective transformation and negotiation of this strange land. For the exile, his or her language is at once a constant reminder of one's foreign-ness and an index of tradition and cultural identity.[71] Within this text, we find that Miseria cannot understand the local language at first, yet eventually, as Travellia, she masters the foreign language 'so well' that we are told she got 'in that twelve month their language' (70) and later she capitalizes on this asset to escape one of the islands. Additionally, as Travellia moves further away from her homeland, her mother tongue is slowly replaced by the 'other' tongue proving once more that for her distance from the nation state is not debilitating but engenders growth within the diasporic environment. Eventually, this heroine becomes a great orator and restores order through eloquent speeches which not only inspire the natives but also hint at the acceptance and level of integration Travellia finds in the significantly named 'Kingdom of Amity'. During her initial encounter with the people of this foreign locale, we are told she spoke with such 'smooth, civil and pleasing words' and 'begot such love in the hearts of the people that their 'mouths rang out with praises' (92). Later, Travellia rouses her army with eloquent speeches engendering unity and solidarity, an act which effects full cooperation from them and sees them proclaim her 'general' (95). Appropriating martial rhetoric usually the preserve of men, she invokes the Greek gods to encourage her army as she declares 'may Apollo' shoot 'his darts, dazzling your enemies eyes; may Mars the god of war direct you, in your fight; may Fortune give you aid, and Pallas give you victory' (987). This speech act generates inspiration and loyalty, transformed into action by her army who would rather choose to 'die or conquer' (99). Consequently, as Travellia masters foreign languages and the masculine art of rhetoric, she proves that 'access to

[71] D'Addario, *Exile and Journey*, 5.

language and access to self-hood are symbiotic'.[72] She enters a symbolic usurpation and appropriation of the male organ of speech (tongue) which transforms her from a passive agent to an active agent, who achieves integration. Moreover, she emerges triumphant from the counter-public sphere to the public sphere—her words of national import and explicitly public. Thus, Cavendish comments on the importance of women's voices within the public sphere and scripts a gendered narrative of wish fulfilment for both herself and all women. Through the figure of Travellia, Cavendish not only initiates linguistic agency but she also provides royalist readers with a linguistic register and recognizable cultural contours, the preservation of which is heightened within the diasporic environment.

The final stage of Travellia's transformation takes place as her gendered identity is revealed and then fully accepted. As the subjectivity of this heroine is slowly transformed, multiple disguises become partial disclosure and then full disclosure. Travellia's initiation of nomadic status coincides with her escape from the prince and her alteration to her outward appearance. As she 'stripped herself of her own clothes' (60) and cut off her hair, she enters an evolution of a complex figure of identity through which the arbitrary materialities expected of femininity are dissolved. This identity is threatened by a partial disclosure on the battlefield, then later as the prince reveals Travellia's identity to the King on the opposing side (110) and later still as the prince reveals to the Queen that Travellia is a woman dressed in a man's clothes. However, full disclosure unfolds as Travellia herself chooses to make public her true identity to the people of the 'Kingdom of Amity'. At this point, Travellia's identity hangs in the balance. Not knowing how the people will respond, Travellia assumes agency and publicly reveals her *real* self to which the people respond 'Heaven bless you, of what sex soever you be' (115). Thus, through naming, linguistic integration and multiple disguises, which free the self and then reveal the true self, identity is created or recreated. In this manner, Cavendish successfully overrides the disruptions of exile and fashions a hybridized identity made up of past and present—Travellia's identity becomes a composite of her past and present selves, composed of 'variable sources' yet forever changed by the experience of border crossing.

This re-inscription of identity as means to negotiate enforced relocation and transition is further amplified as Cavendish crafts the figure of an empowered heroine who integrates fully with her new surroundings.

[72] Myers, Mitzi, 'Fictions of the Self'. *Women's Review of Books.* 8.4 (1991):20–22.

Having already proved that she is an individual capable of agency as she escaped the foreign prince through disguise and then the natives of the island Kingdom by virtue of her linguistic abilities, upon reaching the Kingdom of Amity, Travellia is received into the family of the Queen and becomes 'counsel' to the Queen (91). More than this, Travellia is presented as an empowered military strategist and an inspiring leader, a figure which resonates with the figure of the femme fort, a distinctly royalist aristocratic icon.[73] The Queen of the 'Kingdom of Amity', being at war with the King of the 'Kingdom of Amour', turns to Travellia, who with confidence, orders the Kingdom and the army in preparation for war. 'Settling the Kingdom in a devout and orderly posture' (96), we are told Travellia confidently 'took a view of her arms and ammunition' (95) and set her army to re-take 'towns, forts and castles lost, beating the enemy out of every place' (96). She then 'drew up her forces', 'commanded' every captain, 'ordered' lieutenants and organized the 'squadrons' (96). Commanding the 'army to march in such a slow pace, as to not break or loosen their ranks' (97), Travellia and her army intimidated the opposing side and ultimately became 'masters of the field' (98). Moreover, Travellia's final transformation from army general to 'Viceregency' (116), at the people's request, seals her acceptance and integration. This empowerment as an effective military strategist, along with inspiring the collective army through rhetorical speeches, transforms Travellia from an agent capable of negotiating her new surroundings to a transnational agent capable of full integration as she adapts to those surroundings and is accepted by her host country.

Ultimately, the imaginary locale of 'The Kingdom of Amity' respresents a composite of both past and present. Despite the distance between her and her homeland Cavendish cannot fully escape her history, her culture and her sense of self which is bound to that. Within the narrative, Cavendish inserts a hierarchical system of governance, royal armies, a King and Queen and Travellia fights for this very system and is rewarded with position of vice regency. Thus, she undertakes to transport positive elements of the homeland and its top-down ideologies into her imaginative

[73]this image appeared from the 1630s on in court masques and Cavendish would be exposed to this from 1642/1643 onwards serving as maid of honour. The Queen continued to adopt this martial persona in her styling of herself calling herself 'her-she generalisima' in a letter to Charles I, 27 June 1643 in Green, Mary Anne Everett, *Letters of Queen Henrietta Maria* (London, 1857), 222. This particular letter described the march south in 1643 at the head of the army as they made their way to Oxford.

outland. As Seidel notes, for the exilic writer the 'territory beyond borders is appropriated and familiarized via the imaginative process' and endeavours to re-suture the rupture caused by the event of exile and find solution to exilic anguish find consolation by exporting 'just enough of the homeland to the outland; to metonymically purify it'.[74] In this Kingdom, there is much pageantry in the form of 'masques, plays, balls' and 'festivals' (117). 'Tiltings, running at the ring, fencing, wrestling, vaulting' and 'baiting of beasts' are also remnants of courtly entertainments that Cavendish has transplanted into this imaginary Kingdom. These resonances of royalist culture remind us of Bhabha's beyond as representing 'neither a new horizon, nor a leaving behind of the past'. It is through this process of hybridity that Cavendish manages to overcome the disjunction between her lost home and her new surroundings.

While the momentum of the narrative represents a freedom from the restraint of nation state, removal from the nation state has already loosened up gender restrictions both for Travellia and Cavendish as an author and the 'place of possibility' has become the narrative itself. As Philip Major notes, during this uncertain period for royalists the 'erasure of identity' generated a sort of 'assertion of identity' to compensate.[75] This unmoored, unballasted identity is forcefully re-inscribed through linguistic aptitude, a point of contention for Cavendish herself, neutralization of gender roles and a full disclosure of the real self positively transformed by the experience of exile.[76] Thus, through the identity of Travellia, Cavendish also blurs boundaries concerning women as visible, linguistically and rhetorically capable subjects in the public sphere, effecting an emergence from the counter-sphere to public sphere.[77] Further, Cavendish's notions of self-hood/subject-hood are manifest most clearly within *Assaulted and Pursued Chastity* as she blurs boundaries concerning the royalist system of governance and women's inclusion as political subjects. Here we find that Cavendish reorders the notion of *patria* to unearth the *matria* which Shari Benstock terms as 'an "internal exclusion" within the entire conceptual and definitional framework, the "other" by and through which patria

[74] Seidel, *Exile and the Narrative Imagination*, 4, 10.

[75] Major, *Writings*, 8.

[76] Cavendish appended a Latin index in her presentation of books to the Leiden library as she spoke no foreign languages herself.

[77] See Mihoko & Fraser on the public sphere vs. the counter-public sphere and women's access to.

is defined'.[78] As Travellia is separated not only from her family but also from the family of the nation state—the patriarchal embrace of her society—she achieves autonomy on many levels and it would appear that the narrative thus attests to Clifford's assertion that exile may 'loosen gender subordination within the patriarchal system'.[79]

However, while Travellia finds autonomy on her travels she nevertheless upholds royalist identity models. Jerome de Groot reminds us that during the war women who stepped beyond standard gender roles figure in royalist narratives as 'victims or martyrs, separated from their menfolk by the strictures of war'.[80] At the denouement of the narrative, the nature of female identity within the royalist system is complicated when Travellia is granted acceptance as military leader and vice-regent regardless of her sex. This position complicates royalist models of femininity and plays with the deep anxiety that existed within royalist culture regarding women, an ambivalence 'provoked by the trauma of war and the destabilizing of normality and meaning'.[81] Travellia's power, however, is nevertheless granted within the recognizable limits of a royalist cultural and ideological domain. Her movement from the queen's kingdom to the king's kingdom does not place her outside royalism but places her between the patriarch (or *patria*) and the idolized Queen (the matriarch or *matria*) the idealized notion of dutiful femininity. Thus, Travellia bridges the gap between the two realms as she blurs the arbitrary societal boundaries which excluded women. Moreover, while Cavendish's commitment to a royalist hierarchical structure is evident, she questions women's position within that framework. Travellia resists ownership and definition and moves beyond

[78] Benstock, *Expatriate Modernism*, 25/26. While Benstock's ideas relate to the modern world her theorizations regarding the *matria* as 'the implicit negative element of patria without which *patria* cannot be defined', is helpful when considering early modern women's identity, its suppression and denial. In this narrative, Cavendish seeks to uncover this potent identity as she reconfigures the power of the patria through the figure of Travellia who blurs the distinctions between what women can and cannot do.

[79] Clifford, 'Diasporas', 314.

[80] de Groot, *Royalist Identities*. de Groot gives this reference in *Mercurius Aulicus* as an example: The Countess of Derby represented martial femininity and duty to the royal cause: 'her refusal to yield her ancestral home became something of a symbol of aristocratic political defiance'. 'The Countess is forced to act in a masculine role by the absence of her husband', her courage is celebrated and the reader is never allowed to forget that 'she steps out of her traditional gender roles in order to defend them; she is not interrogating, but sustaining loyalist identity models', 128.

[81] Ibid., 129.

traditional means by which women could wield power—their grace and beauty. The character of Travellia agitates 'the perceived stability of gender and social roles, suggesting a fluidity of identity'[82] that was both challenging and distressing for contemporary readers, however, all this she is able to do within the confines of a royalist system of governance. As Travellia leaves behind the shadow of the homeland and inserts herself into her new surroundings she integrates on linguistic, cultural and political levels, and assumes a hybridized identity. Hence, Cavendish offers up a new sort of identity for royalist women. Moreover, she crucially effects a textual restaging of the past concerning the devastation of war, royalist defeat and her peripheral existence as a non-subject in the homeland.

For Cavendish, imagination not only provided solace but also fueled and sustained her literature of exile, through conceptualized locales, characters and events that were irrevocably resonant of the homeland, patria or country of origin. Through the power of imagination and with the help of memory of the homeland, she created an imaginary realm containing many Kingdoms. Devising alternative spaces as a means to negotiate her relocation to the continent and fashioning a heroine invested with fluid subjectivity superseded the seemingly disempowering effects of exile. The narrative both denies all manner of binary patterns which bind the female subject and enables a 'restaging' of a painful past. Through the reconceptualization of the diasporic movement from homeland to outland, negative connotations of exile become travel imbued with positivity and her subject of exile becomes an autonomous agent. Thus, *Assaulted and Pursued Chastity* transforms the tundra of marginality into a progressive space and within this imaginary realm of possibility, what was once a fragmented identity becomes a potent and hybridized identity. By providing an arena within which identity could be performed and re-inscribed, Cavendish enabled her own negotiation of this transitionary period in her life—a time during which she herself was a cultural and political nomad cut off from her own homeland.

[82] Ibid., 132.

## A Self Reunited: Archipelagic Identities in the Letters of Katherine Philips

As we have seen, Katherine Philips's relationship with royalism was a complicated one. In his book entitled *The Matchless Orinda* (1931), Philip Webster Souers observes that throughout 'the period of the commonwealth Katherine led a life beset with difficulties. She was in the unfortunate position of one whose desires and sentiments were in continual conflict with interest and duty'.[83] He goes on to note that her family and friends were two different parts of her life—they represented two irreconcilable points of view, and, what is even worse, two political parties. He is of course referring to her puritan background allied against her many royalist friends and her strong royalist sympathies. Most certainly, Philips did navigate, as Souers notes, a *via media* between her domestic duty and her royalist inclinations, a position he argues she was 'forced into'.[84] This section builds upon this navigation between the two worlds, discussed in Chaps. 2 and 3 above. Tracing Philips's nomadic movement across the British Isles, we will see that her letters were a crucial medium through which she fostered and maintained connections between new friends, patrons and allies, as well as with the restoration court in London while she was in Dublin and later on in Cardigan. However, and perhaps most crucially for Philips, the letters show that support from key figures in Dublin and London enabled the resolution of the socio-political balancing act that so characterized her life, and now, during the politically uncertain years of the early 1660s, she could also set about carefully reconstructing hers and her parliamentarian husband's precarious position in relation to the newly restored court.

Weaving together the complicated strands of Philips's life by examining her letters written to Sir Charles Cotterell in the final four years of her life, this section outlines the ways in which the maintenance of her wifely self, the cautious construction of her public authorial self and her unabashed passion for her royalist friends coalesce to reveal Philips's complex identity within the post-diasporic environment. While the social functions of the letters include networking, both on behalf of her husband, herself as an emergent author and her ambition to curry favour with the restoration

[83] Souers, Philip Webster, *The Matchless Orinda* (Cambridge: Harvard University Press, 1931), 79.

[84] Ibid., 80.

court, they most importantly stand as a medium by which she overcame the distance between her and her friends, and the distance between her and the cultural milieu she so dearly desired to be part of, her native place of London. In 'The Letters'[85] I examine the initial letters written to Poliarchus from Acton (letters I & II); Landshipping (letters VIII, IX, X, XLVI); Prysaeddfedd, the Lewis estate in Angelsey (letters XI); the 'Irish letters': Rostrevor (letters XII); Dublin (letters XIII-XXXV) and the letters written from Cardigan in the last year of her life (letters XXXVI-XLVII). Rather than deal with the letters under these more geographical divisions, I reconfigure them into three alternative categories. I explore Philips's 'royalisms' by concentrating on letters which reflect a strong sense of networking between herself, her husband and Charles Cotterell and figures at court, such as the Duchess of York and the King himself. Next, I examine Philips's authorial aspirations, her capitalization on Irish literati circles, her exploitation of Cotterell and her careful crafting of her authorial identity through manipulations of coterie critical practices as she emerges into the public literary sphere for the first time. Finally, I focus on her 'cultural exile' in Cardigan in the last nine months of her life, a period spent negotiating the distance from her friends and the literary circles she now, as a public author, wished to be part of. In these final letters, Katherine's sense of utter isolation is most evident and it is through these letters that the authorial self works to the benefit of the royalist and marginalized self. Ultimately, I argue that Philips's multiple selves (wife, poet, writer, translator, coterie member) commingle and are fully developed, and merge, in the letters to provide a more unified picture of her fragmented and ruptured life.

For many scholars, and contemporaries, the letter in the seventeenth century, or the epistolary genre, was a prose form that naturally suited women's expression in writing. Elizabeth Goldsmith asserts that the form 'seemed particularly well suited to the female voice'[86] and she goes on to note 'the editor of a 1666 collection of letters by the Comtesse de Bregy writes that, along with occasional poetry, epistolary prose is a form at which ladies have proven their skill'.[87] The epistolary genre was one in which women could excel as they did not have to concern themselves with

[85] Patrick Thomas's edition will be referenced throughout. Thomas, Patrick. *The Collected Works of Katherine Philips, The Matchless Orinda. Vol. II. The Letters* (Essex: Stump Cross Books, 1992).

[86] Goldsmsith, Elizabeth C., *Writing the Female Voice: Essays on Epistolary Literature.* (London: Printer Publishers, 1989), vii.

[87] Ibid., 47.

'scholastic rhetoric' or particular form. Letters were 'increasingly valued for their "natural", "authentic", and purportedly inimitable qualities'.[88] The history of the genre stretches back to Cicero (his epistles to Atticus considered an established model of the genre) and Seneca. Earlier in the period, renaissance letters 'with their conventionality of form, their rhetorical schemes and figures clung to a pseudo-classical ideal suggested rather by the oratorical precepts of the ancients than by their epistolary practice'.[89] However, by the middle of the seventeenth century, letters 'in the collected works of Balzac and Voiture' were used as models, incurring the 'French emphasis on exquisite sentiment and its inflated expression'.[90] For women of Philips's era, Du Bosque's *Secretary of Ladies* (1638) provided the template for letter writing[91] and as James Daybell notes 'letter writing was a quotidian activity connected to the rhythms of women's everyday lives'.[92] However, the insecurity of the epistolary medium 'promoted a degree of self-censorship among writers distrustful of letters going astray and falling into the wrong hands'.[93] Certainly, this was a concern for Philips as she plotted to get to London in what was to be the final year of her life—a concern which promoted her to insist that Cotterell write to her in Italian so as to ensure their secrecy. Moreover, as Daybell points out, women 'were well aware of the politically freighted nature of language; codes of deference and social courtesy were intricately utilized in communications', while 'negative gender assumptions were manipulated for strategic effect'.[94] We will see that all of these strategies, and more, were employed by Philips as she wove her assemblage of alliances together throughout her correspondence with Cotterell.

Work on Philips's letters is surprisingly scant.[95] Thomas himself states that the letters 'of Orinda to Poliarchus provide the only documentation

[88] Ibid., 47.

[89] Humiliata, Mary, 'Standards of Taste Advocated for Feminine Letter Writing, 1640–1779.' *Huntington Library Quarterly* 13.3 (May, 1950): 261–277, 261.

[90] Ibid., 262.

[91] For more contemporary examples see: *The Treasure of the City of Ladies* (1536) by Christine de Pizane; *The Enemie of Idleness* (1568) by William Fulwood; *The Female Secretary* (1671), by Henry Care.

[92] Daybell, James, 'Letters' in *The Cambridge Companion to Early Modern Women's Writing*. Laura Lunger Knoppers ed. (New York: Cambridge University Press, 2009): 181–193, p. 181.

[93] Ibid., 184.

[94] Ibid., 187.

[95] Patrick Thomas's edition is the definitive edition thus far, with his appendices being particularly illuminating. Appendix 4 provides an in-depth tracing of Cotterell's relationship

we have of the struggle of a remarkably gifted and serious female artist to gain access to the literary establishment without incurring loss of status and reputation'.[96] This observation is met by Philip Souers with an equal gravitas as he perceived Philips's letters 'as not only examples of her best essay style' but also an insight to a 'psychoanalysis of her mind' at a time 'when reflection conquered indignation and sorrow',[97] and he intensively reads the letters as a biographical narrative of Philips's time spent in Ireland in particular. However, Elaine Hobby returns to the subject of Philips's authorship as she notes that 'Philips's letters are preoccupied largely with finding ways to justify writing as a female activity'.[98] Indeed, Philips's deft use of common epistolary gestures such as the humility and apologetic *topoi*, as well as lengthy *comprobatios*, are present throughout the letters. However, I argue that Philips surmounted her goal to justify herself by a range of other means as well; that in places she leaves behind the necessity for justification altogether as she focuses on specific ambitions. Other interventions come from Elizabeth Hageman who concentrates on Philips's concerns surrounding the pirated publication of her poems and the competition between herself and Edmund Waller (who also worked on a translation of Pompey) within the letter written to Dorothy Temple. Considering Ruth Perry's summation that in letters it is 'possible to tailor a self on paper to suit the expectations and desires of her audience', Hageman surmises that this notion of letters is 'especially well-suited to Philips'.[99] Other explorations from Troylander and Tenger focus on Philips's utilization of the letter form to enhance or control the reception of her work in the public sphere.[100] To do so, Troylander & Tenger

with Philips, and other interesting connections they had throughout the early war years and interregnum before they began their correspondence.

[96] Ibid., 163.

[97] Souers, 153/154. Souers is referring to the distance now between Philips and her closest female friend, Anne Lewis Owen-Lucasia. Philips had become distressed when Anne chose to marry Col. Trevor, a choice which resulted in her move to Ireland.

[98] Hobby, Elaine. 'Orinda and Female Intimacy' in *Early Modern Women writers 1600–1720*. Anita Pacheco ed. (London: Longman, 1998), pp. 73–88, 74.

[99] Hageman, Elizabeth, 'Making a Good Impression: Early Texts of Poems and Letters by Katherine Philips, the "Matchless Orinda"'. *South Central Review* 11.2, Creating Literary Series: The Brown University Women's Project and the Oxford University Press, "Women Writers in English, 1350–1850" Texts (Summer), 1994: 39–65, 53/59. See also, Perry, Ruth, *Women, Letters, and the Novel* (New York: AMS Press, 1980), 69.

[100] Paul Troylander & Zeynep Tenger, 'Katherine Philips and Coterie Critical Practices'. *Eighteenth-Century Studies*. 37. 3. *Critical Networks*. (Spring, 2004): 367–387, 370. See

examine Philips's capitalization on coterie critical practices such as, for example, the use of amendment criticism or vouching, and suggest that this careful utilization of such specific critical practices highlights the 'dizzying complexity of social, and political functions of critical discourse' and the 'critical activity filtering through or around' Philips at this time.[101]

This section argues for the presence of a distinctly duplicitous self within the letters as Philips endeavoured to navigate the boundaries between wifely duty and her ambition to control her emergence as an author, as well as remain connected to *literati* members. Asserting the letters are also highly performative, an arena within which Philips presented multiple and varied forms of identity—as wife, as author and as royalist supporter—this section posits that the genre of the letter allows for development of this complicated and marginalized self which other genres may not. However, ultimately, I argue, that the divided self we have come to understand throughout the previous chapters becomes whole through these letters, merging all the fractured and antagonistic pieces of her life together. However, while the letters appear to redeem her ruptured life and weave together each of the strands to produce a rich tapestry, that was the short life of Philips, the idea of the united self is ever complicated by the binary between duty (her identity as a wife) and ambition (her self-fashioned identity as a royalist woman writer).

Within her letters Philips was careful to portray herself as the good wife to her husband, Antenor (her sobriquet for James Philips),[102] while she carries on as an archipelagic member of the royalist *literati* and keeps correspondence with her royalist friends. However, this seemingly innocent display of wifely duty had an altogether more calculating side, which served not only her husband's interests but her own as well. In letter III, the conclusion in James Philips's case has obviously been reached and Orinda gushes with appreciation for Cotterell's efforts in clearing her

also: Beal, Peter, "Orinda to Silvander: A New Letter by Katherine Philips", *EMS* 4 (1993): 281–286; Beal, *In Praise of Scribes: Manuscripts and their Makers in Seventeenth-Century England* (Oxford & New York: Oxford University Press, 1998), includes a transcript of "Katherine Philips's Letter to Lady Fletcher" (Appendix V, 281); Salzman, Paul. *Reading Early Modern Women's Writing* (Oxford: Oxford University Press, 2006); Daybell, 'Letters'; Thompson, Elbert N.S., "Familiar Letters", *Literary Bypaths of the Renaissance*, 1924; rpt (Freeport, New York, 1968), 91–126.

[101] Ibid., 370.

[102] See letters IV, XIX, XXX, XXIII, XXXVI, XXIX, for example.

husband's name.[103] Almost dumbstruck she writes 'None certainly that can say so little, ever ow'd so much; and I can say it less, because I am so much oblig'd; for the fullness of my Soul stops all the Passages of Expression'.[104] Indeed, Cotterell's assistance and the positive outcome would have been cause for great relief. However, while she reverts to one aspect of the humility *topos*, she does not mention her husband's name but only writes 'I am now going to a *Person*, who must participate in the Obligation as he does the Benefit'[my emphasis]. Perhaps this secrecy is deployed due to the sensitivity of the case or of Cotterell's involvement with it. Either way, despite her joy at the outcome, it seems to render her husband as distant and outside of this relationship she has with Cotterell at this early stage of the correspondence. As if leaving nothing to chance, namely her reputation and the valuable connection with Cotterell, Philips goes on to speak for her husband and the tone here discloses a frustration on her part. Philips clearly states that should Antenor have 'not conceiv'd so becoming a sense of' Cotterell's 'Favours' and let slip his least 'Opportunity of expressing his Gratitude', then she would be deeply 'deceived', disappointed and perhaps even embarrassed. It seems, that having utilized her royalist connections to help her husband, Philips feared the tenuous connection may be ruptured and lost, and, for Philips, Cotterell was to play an extremely important role in her strategy to both ingratiate her family who sought reintegration with the court and royalist administration after the restoration and control her emergence as a royalist writer.

Philips's desire to smooth the way for her husband and by extension herself as an emergent author was further augmented by efforts to bond her husband and Cotterell together. In a series of letters Philips emits

[103] Cotterell had lobbied parliament on behalf of Philips's husband after the restoration in the case concerning the sentencing of John Gerard to death. See footnote below.

[104] Thomas, *The Letters*, 19. In a footnote to letter I (p. 14), Thomas writes 'Orinda's husband, Colonel James Philips, MP for Cardigan, was suspended by the House of Commons on 27 June 1661. A committee was appointed to investigate Colonel Hugh Butler's allegation that Philips had been a member of the High Court of Justice that sentenced the royalist, Colonel John Gerard, to death in 1654'. Additionally, 'Under section XLIV of the 1660 Act of Indemnity and Oblivion any member of the former High Court of Justice was banned from holding civil, military of ecclesiastical offices, or from sitting in Parliament after 1660. The committee reported in February, 1661/1662 and Philips was cleared by a vote of the House (*Journal of the House of Commons*, VIII, 282–283, 385; statues, V, 233)'. Appendix 4 in Thomas's edition is an extremely insightful here. See also letters II, VIII, XVII.

concerns regarding Antenor and elections in Cardigan,[105] and she concentrates intently on networking in these letters on a more political level. Letter XXVIII reveals skilful rhetoric which serves her networking purposes. In this letter Philips invokes the potent notion of 'Friendship' as she places pressure on Cotterell to engage and maintain connection. To do so, Philips deploys common '[s]enecan language of mutual beliefs, promising repayment of favours in kind and assuring the friendship' herself and her husband have to offer.[106] In this letter, Cotterell has already been submitted for the running of the election, given that her husband's election was declared void in April 1662, and Philips uses all her rhetorical skills to circumvent his possible annoyance at being 'sent to the House without his own Consent or Knowledge'.[107] Playing the good wife, she defends her husband's choice to keep secret his plot to submit Cotterell to the House and speaking on Antenor's behalf she reverts to the humility *topos* once more declaring 'tis all his Misfortunes have left him capable to give, of his Esteem and Gratitude' to Cotterell. She then swiftly moves to further assuage Cotterell's ego, deferentially insisting that her husband has 'a profound Respect and Veneration as for any Man living' as he does for Cotterell. However, to solidify the deal and dissolve any remaining resentment, Philips deploys the idea of a hopeful friendship between the three of them to justify what could have been viewed as quite a brazen act by the couple. She writes 'it was intended as a Testimony of the eternal Value and Friendship that ANTENOR and ORINDA must ever have for the noble POLIARCHUS' and she hopes 'he will not be angry' at them for this gesture. Thus, as she figuratively stands loyally by her husband here, she also politicizes friendship and its reciprocal benefits. However, while friendship is once more politicized, as it had been during the interregnum to galvanize royalists, in this case it is utilized to bring two men from 'opposite' sides together. To compound the union she hopes his election in Cardigan will 'be a new tie to' their 'Friendship, and that ANTENOR will by these means have sometimes the Honour of hearing from you'.

105 Letters XXIX, XXX, XXI, XXXII, XXXIV.

106 Daybell, 'Letters', 187. Philips was also drawing of course on her own well-established society of Friendship, its philosophies and ideals of which anyone connected to the coterie during the interregnum would have been acutely aware. It is safe to say that Cotterell would have known of the coterie given the connections he had.

107 Thomas directs us to letter VIII, footnote 7 here and writes that James Philips had nominated 'Sir Charles Cotterell to stand in the by-election, without first informing him', p. 82.

Philips utilized friendship as a most tactical tool here and this use is by no means restricted to her husband's political affairs, as I will discuss below. Setting up the connection between the two men, she then moves to include herself once more when she writes that should he 'contract that Intimacy with you', it would reflect her 'own Happiness', 'Satisfaction', and greatest 'Wishes in this World' of being in correspondence with the esteemed Cotterell. These words bond the three of them together both for the sake of friendship and politics, and bring realms of duty and ambition that bit closer together.

The years spent in Ireland saw Philips's sense of ambition take precedence over that of her duty as a wife. Now distanced from the patriarchal grip of England and Wales, Philips's sense of self could be more freely explored, especially that of her authorial self. As Philip Souers points out, the Irish letters 'are the record, not of Orinda's sorrow for her lost Lucasia, but of Orinda's triumphs among the brilliant gathering of English then living there'.[108] This period in Ireland, the circles she moved within[109] and meeting Lord Orrery, into whose hands 'by some accident'[110] her translated scene of Pompey fell, not only led to a generative environment within which Philips as an author could emerge with gathering degrees of confidence but also suited her political strategy to ingratiate herself and her husband with the newly restored court.[111] Lord Orrery, Roger Boyle, brother to Richard Boyle (Second Earl of Cork), was a hugely influential man whose political past had seen him on the winning side both during the interregnum (as a soldier fighting for Cromwell, as a member of Cromwell's council and as his peer) and after the restoration (as Lord President of Munster, Lord Chief Justice and member of the Privy councils of both England and Ireland). Indeed, Souers writes that 'next to Ormonde', he was 'the most important man in Ireland' and suggests that,

[108] Souers, *The Matchless Orinda*, 154. Souers goes on to say that Dublin had taken on 'the aspect of a miniature London'; so many English were there that 'the manners of the English metropolis were assumed', a new theatre had just been built by the masters of revels, John Ogilby, and a gathering of elegant society generated a small court around the Duke of Ormonde; Dublin at this point was second only to London, 155/156.

[109] The Boyle family, the Cork family, her royalist friends and members of her coterie John Jeffrey's and Sir Edward Dering.

[110] Philips, *The Letters*, letter XIV, 46–49.

[111] See letters XXI & XXIII for examples of Philips beginning to grow more confidently as a public author.

as a soldier, Orrery may well have been acquainted with James Philips and as a Cromwellian peer why should he not have known Katherine's relatives Oliver St John and Philip Skippon.[112] Through gaining patronage and support from Lord Orrery in Ireland and Cotterell in England Philips, then, had a foot in both political camps and could be assured of acceptance as an emerging writer and wife of a parliamentarian colonel looking to reintegrate with the court after 1660 with all the confidence and entitlement of a loyal royalist supporter. Under the 'protection of such a man as Orrery she could become bold'[113] and this protection and advocacy, coupled with the distance from England and Wales generated for Philips a sense of freedom, and initiated the development of another aspect of her character. In letter XIV Philips tells Cotterell that Lord Orrery has persuaded her to finish translating the scene: he has 'become a Petitioner to' her for what she considers 'such a Trifle' and that she 'obey'd him so far as to finish the act in which that Scene is'. Additionally, he had 'enjoin'd' her 'to go on to the extent that she writes he 'will not be refus'd'.[114] This petitioning and encouragement for Philips is quite fortuitous, yet immediately she weaves humility through the following sentences referring to her 'Unworthyness', and the 'Temptation from Vanity' and 'Pride' already provoked by Cotterell's kind words to present herself as the virtuous woman still acutely aware of her place. However, this return to the humility *topos* is curtailed as she returns directly to place demands on Cotterell. Philips writes that she will send Lord Orrery's verses in commendation to her 'on Condition that in Exchange' Cotterell will let her have his translation of *Le Temple de la Mort*, adding that this will 'infinitely Oblige her' as Orrery 'is in Love with the original'. Philips also mentions sending her translation of Pompey as a further bribe and along with it some 'Translations from VIRGIL by Mr. COWLEY'. This complex exchange system positions Philips as much less the humble wife and far more the deft, dominant and interactive coterie participant. Without doubt, the patronage from Orrery, the correspondence with the excellently connected Cotterell and the autonomy enjoyed by Philips in Ireland made for interesting terrain, which points to a loosening of gender restrictions concerning her work and her emergence into the public domain.

[112] Souers, 166, 167.
[113] Ibid., 171.
[114] Philips, letter XIV.

While Philips's work on *Pompey* was making an impact in Ireland, she further capitalized on Cotterell's connections to get her work circulated at the court in London. As Troylander and Tenger point out, 'the more far flung the audience, the greater need for sponsors of high social rank and reputation at the court and London'.[115] Hence, through Cotterell, Philips sent poems and a copy of Pompey to both the Duchess of York and the King himself. In letter IX Philips comments some verses which she requested Cotterell 'send the dutchess'.[116] Indeed, having seen Philips's 'elegy on the Queen of Bohemia', the Duchess 'was pleas'd to lay' upon Philips that she 'should let her see all' her 'trifles of this nature'. Clearly, through her occasional panegyrics, Philips had already made a name for herself in court circles, however, now with *Pompey* about to be published, Philips turned to that source of support once more. In letter XX Philips's tone of concern and sense of urgency are palpable as she urges Cotterell to render the translation to be 'a tolerable offering to be laid at the feet of that great person for whom I design'd it'.[117] She goes on to request 'I cannot doubt, but when you present it to her, you will say much more in my behalf than I have either courage or skill to say for myself', once more pushing the humility *topos* to its limits, she thus flatters him and simultaneously manoeuvres him to vouch for her. Moreover, her objective is clear here as she writes 'for the bounds of my ambition aspire no higher, than to be able to give her one moment's entertainment'. To be sure, Philips also courts the favour of the King when she writes:

> I have sent you [Cotterell] a packet of printed Pompey's to dispose of as you see fit. Be pleas'd to get one bound and present it to the Dutchess; and if you think the King would allow such a Trifle a Place in his Closet, let him have another.[118]

All of these requests which Cotterell must carry out not only show his connection to the court as vital to Philips's strategy to manage the dissemination of her work but also prove how driven she is in setting herself up as an author in London before she even arrives there.[119] This drive to

[115] Troylander and Tenger, 'Coterie Practices', 372.

[116] Philips, letter IX, 32.

[117] Philips, letter XX, 62. Thomas's footnote here reads 'Anne, Duchess of York. See letter ix, Note.1'.

[118] Philips, letter XXVI, 77. See also letter XXX.

[119] See also letters XXXII, XLII & XLV regarding Philips's authorial concerns in general.

get Pompey out and have it endorsed by the esteemed nobles of Ireland (Orrery) and in England (Cotterell), as well as royalty including the Duchess of York and the King, appears to be part of the plan when once accomplished would not only provide protection from ridicule as a female writer but also act as insurance at a time when loyalty to one side or the other was being retrospectively examined. Hence, by harnessing preeminent figures from both 'camps', Philips accomplished much more than assurance of patronage and support—she blurred cultural and political boundaries by bridging the parliamentarian and royalist divide.

The successful emergence and the reception of Philips's translation of *Pompey* was of crucial importance to her building a respectable authorial profile and was managed not only through deliberate presentations to specific members of the royal family but also by exploiting critical coterie practices, such as 'amendment criticism', for example.[120] This would ensure, on the one hand, that her work was presentable, but on the other hand, her authorial stance would be bolstered and ultimately made the responsibility of the entire coterie. For Philips, definitive responsibility lies with Cotterell, as Troylander and Tenger have pointed out, 'to ensure that her public reputation not be embarrassed and to control and maintain the work's proper reception'.[121] In letter XXII, Philips defends her authorial right to have chosen to write the dedicatory letter in Pompey to the Duchess in prose rather than rhyme.[122] She defends this choice by pointing out that 'having so lately written to her in Verse' she chose to 'write in Prose now'. However, within the same breath Philips directs the responsibility for this choice first to her friends and then to Cotterell. She writes:

> I strictly enjoyn'd myself to write in Prose now, and that too by the Advice of *all my Friends* here; who, I hope were not mistaken *in their Opinions*, and that the matter of my Application to her Highness will not be misunderstood, nor taken amiss. However, I have so great a Deference *for your Judgement*, that *had you* sent me word utterly disapprov'd my accosting her in Prose, I would have attempted something or other in Verse to have sent you by this Post; but *your not having wholly condemn'd* my having made my address in Prose, has prevented me.[123] [my emphasis]

[120] Troylander & Tenger, 'Coterie Practices', 372.

[121] Ibid., 374.

[122] See also letters XXIX, XXVII.

[123] Philips, letter XXII, 66.

Here Philips lays responsibility on both her friends in Ireland and Cotterell. She indicates that it is by her friends' opinion that she wrote in prose and that had Cotterell written to her promptly with critical evaluation she would have followed it, but having no word from him renders the prose piece his responsibility should it offend the Duchess. At this point *Pompey* is about to be released and Philips returns to the job of encouraging Cotterell to vouch for her. She implores him to 'please be its Champion, and persuade her royal Highness to favour it with her protection', thus Philips not only seeks patronage but also seeks defence from censures and critics. In other instances, the coterie circulation of poems, prologues and epilogues also represent forms of vouching which protect her reputation.[124] This vouching is not only part of coterie critical practices, as Troylander and Tenger have convincingly argued, but it is a tactic by which Philips may ensure her work is supported as she emerges as a publicly renowned author for the first time. Paul Salzman points out that at this time Philips was attempting to navigate her way from being a well-known coterie writer towards establishing a reputable public profile as a published writer. Thus, Philips, 'in a sense, had two literary careers: the first saw her controlling her Society…the second followed the sudden, much more public fame achieved by the performance of Pompey in Dublin'.[125] In her letters, it is the second career that Philips so tenaciously seeks. Hence, the letters stand as a unique forum from within which Philips can capitalize on key members of the coterie and gain access to the court itself, and, through these avenues, emerge with her reputation intact.

While Philips lived a nomadic life during the wars, interregnum and even more so after the restoration, she was ironically faced with a period of 'exile' and isolation upon her return to Cardigan in August of 1663. For Philips, this short spell of approximately nine months was a troubled time beset with frustration, loneliness and only exacerbated by her deep desire to get to London to be among her royalist friends and the literary scene and to defend herself against critics concerning the pirated edition of her poetry published there. While Philips was still in Ireland she already had designs on getting to London, and had urged Cotterell to set a plan in

[124] NLW MS 218073 shows the prologue written by the Earl of Roscommon and the epilogue written by Sir Edward Dering; 1r & 41r, respectively.

[125] Salzman, Paul, *Reading Early Modern Women's Writing*. (Oxford: Oxford University Press, 2006), 182.

motion,[126] such was the sense of physical distance which had always been an issue for Philips.[127] Now, in Cardigan, this sense of separation from her native place was unbearably heightened. In November of 1663, Philips writes that she has 'grown so dull, so heavy' and 'good for nothing', a condition brought on by 'Absence from all Coversation that can refine' her wit. The 'Country Life' that was, during the early war years and interregnum, such a solace and inspiration has now become the instrument 'able to blunt' her writerly abilities.[128] Philips writes, 'I find the Weights of my Misfortune sink me down so low that unless I am quickly restor'd to the refreshing Charms of your Company, I shall be past Recovery'. Moreover, she is concerned that her 'Absence' may have 'robb'd'[129] her of the esteem of her new friend, Lady Cork, and writes 'the Loss of a Friendship is to me the greatest of all Losses'.[130] To be sure, in letter XLIII the sense of cultural 'exile' manifest most severely as the distance and isolation begins to affect Philips's self-confidence. She worries about Cotterell's possible 'Indifference and Coldness', and Lady Cork's growing 'cool'. She declares she is 'uneasie' and the letter is further interspersed with negative adjectives such as 'Melancholy' and 'Fear'. The tone of despondency is palpable and one cannot help but get the sense that Philips is beginning to psychologically unravel. Hence, location for Philips had now become far less than positive and during this time in particular she is acutely aware of her sense of self as a displaced writer. In contrast to her work during the 1650s, her peripheral position was no longer comforted by writing and correspondence, and her getting to London had become absolutely paramount to the maintenance of her sense of self as a royalist woman writer as well as the continuance of her aristocratic friendships.

However, to relieve herself of this 'exile', she constructs a plot to 'countenance our Journey to a Place, which tho' it be my native one, is not so dear to me on that account, as because it will give me an Opportunity to converse with some few worthy Friends'.[131] Thus, Philips was at all times focusing on London as the seat of culture and the place in which, now after the restoration, she can finally step into the public sphere as a royalist

[126] See letter XVI for example.

[127] See letters III, VI, XII, XXIX in which Philips hints at fears about returning to Cardigan, XLI (unhappy), XLIII (distance is unbearable).

[128] Philips, letter, XLI, 117/118.

[129] Philips, letter, XLIV, 126.

[130] Philips, letter, XLIII, 123.

[131] Philips, letter XXXVI, 102.

woman writer. To accomplish this, she looks to all of her friends, both new and old and her networking now stands to be tested as she relied upon the power of friendship one last time to enable her coming home both in the literal and authorial senses. In letter XXX she writes:

> If Friends so dear to me as my Lady CORK, ROSANIA and POLIARCHUS, are pleas'd to think it worth their while to be troubled with my dull Company. I will flatter myself that when they next meet, they will easily contrive some way to bring me among them, that may not be prejudicial to ANTENOR'S affairs.[132]

Here, Philips sets out the plot and the key element which must be seen as the driving force behind it—Antenor's political affairs. Thus, she capitalizes on friendship and her wifely ambition to get where she so desires to be as an author.

Other letters further outline the development of Philips's plan. In letter XXXIX she writes that the Cork family, John Jeffreys and Lucasia are all in London. Philips desires Cotterell 'to wait on Lady Cork', and reminds him to refresh her memory concerning the plan. She writes 'whatever you three resolve on shall be at once my prescription and Happiness'.[133] Once again shifting possible blame from herself to her friends she protects herself should the plot be revealed. Letter XLIV mentions the plan to get to London. Philips adds to the plan, requesting that Cotterell ask Lady Cork (Elizabeth Boyle) to write on the subject to further persuade Antenor of the necessity of getting to London. Philips's tone here is still quite flat yet hope creeps in and she feels less isolated. Letter XLVI reveals good news as Antenor has taken the advice of Cotterell and 'hastening' her 'to London', once more placing responsibility on Cotterell. Philips is careful to point out that it is Cotterell's attempts and the good fortune that they (coincidentally) match Antenor's needs which allow her to undertake the trip. Reassuming the role of the good wife here, she writes:

> All your persuasions would have been in vain, and could never have prevail'd me to have undertaken that Attempt, were not the hopes I have of serving Antenor one of the chief Motives that induce me to it.[134]

[132] Philips, letter XXX, 89.
[133] Philips, letter XXXIX, 108.
[134] Philips letter, XLVI, 133.

Thus, the explicit utilization of her duty as a good wife is placed at the centre of her implicit ambition to get to London. Philips cautiously engineers this plot and places her duty to her husband as the reason she must get to London. However, the reality is that she seeks to manage her emergence as an author while there, and this cover story is but a further tactic to provide protection of her reputation should anyone accuse her of being distastefully ambitious. Hence, these manipulations of contemporary hierarchical gender roles not only serve Philips's strategy to remove herself from the isolated life in Cardigan during this time but also position her favourably in terms of managing her burgeoning career as a royalist woman writer.

Ironically, the patriarchal force that brought Philips to Ireland, namely that of setting her father's affairs in order, was the very force which inaugurated a period of great personal and authorial growth and autonomy.[135] As Marie Louise Coolahan writes, 'her social networks were strategically set up and maintained in order to provide her with important literary and social contacts in the London court, in Wales and at the Dublin court in the early 1660s'.[136] Philips carefully constructed these networks during the interregnum through her coterie and expanded them after the restoration through her letters, and, undoubtedly her travels to Ireland enhanced her position as a royalist woman writer as she formed new acquaintances, as well as gained support and patronage. The letters provide us with evidence of her capitalizing on these networks to serve her royalist self, her authorial self and eventually the self in 'exile' during the last nine months of her life. The distance afforded to her by her sojourn to Ireland enabled her to find a strong authorial voice and enough confidence to shape and carefully manage her emergence as a public author. Her performance of the good wife,[137] one metaphor for seventeenth-century society and

[135] During the 1641 rebellion while Charles I had been in the midst of troubles with the Scots and the English, Parliament forced him to sign a bill which handed Ireland over to a company of adventurers. The Bill took away the rights of the King to pardon the Irish before the adventurers were satisfied with money raised for arms. All good puritans in London, who could afford it, gave money to support the adventurers army. Fowler, Philips's father bid 200 pounds for 1000 acres in Ulster. The claim remained in the family and after the restoration Philips went to Ireland to sustain her father's rights.

[136] Coolahan, Marie-Louise., "We Live by Chance, and Slip into Events': Occassionality and the Manuscript verse of Katherine Philips.' *Eighteenth Century Ireland* 18 (2003): 9–23, 9.

[137] On this concept Margaret Ezell writes: 'The character of the good Wife did not originate in the seventeenth century, but nevertheless was popular during it. The character indi-

traditional hierarchy, is thus re-inscribed by the tenacious Philips in her letters. While Philips undeniably sets herself up as the centre to a flourishing coterie of displaced royalists during the interregnum—thereby complicating the core/periphery binary—her letters allowed her to once again necessarily relocate and recollect pieces of her displaced and fragmented self in relation to the restored court.

For Cavendish and Philips, the disruptive environment of the royalist diaspora paradoxically became a place of liberated potentiality. Writing about the potential of reading literature of the civil wars through the lens of exile, Philip Major states that the circumstance of exile 'cannot only be seen as a passive condition but also, and especially in literary terms, a generative one'.[138] Residency beyond the borders of England and Wales, and on opposite sides of the English Channel, undeniably granted these women a fertile space from which they could experiment with identity and cultivate their aspirations as royalist women writers. For Cavendish, the experience of multiple exiles and border crossing was a condition which shaped her authorial self and mind. While on the one hand, she compensated for the exterior disruptions in her life by creating interior imagined alternative worlds, worlds in which Catherine Gallagher notes allow 'female subjectivity to become absolute',[139] on the other hand, she nevertheless experienced a fragmentation of the self, due to border crossing. As we have seen, the discursive identity which emerges within the subject of diaspora leads to a development of a double consciousness which inevitably bleeds into literary works. Thus, the psychological interiority, or 'exile of the mind', to use Battigelli's phrase, is not totalizing in the diasporic environment, and focus on the interior sense of Cavendish's experience overlooks the disruption of border crossing and the double consciousness that ensues due to external forces. Within the diasporic environment the

cates conventional assumptions about the ideal marriage for seventeenth-century authors and readers, whether or not their own marriages bore any resemblance to it or not… the character of the Good Wife represents a conservative force, whose appeal is to tradition, not innovation'. Ezell, *The Patriarch's Wife*, 38.

[138] Major, *Literatures*, 5.

[139] Gallagher, Catherine, 'Embracing the Absolute: Margaret Cavendish and the Politics of the Female Subject in Seventeenth-Century England' *in Early Modern Women Writers 1600–1720.* Anita Pacheco ed. (New York: Addison Wesley Longman, 1998): 133–145, 138. Anna Battigelli also relies heavily on isolation and interiority of Cavendish's mind as a determinant of her exilic experience. Battigelli, *Margaret Cavendish and Exiles of the Mind.*

self as a site of 'true sovereignty' is exploded and becomes a composite of past and present, a commingling of the fractured pieces of here and there, inside and outside resulting in the dissolution of traditional binaries which hold the subject in place. Cavendish's multiple subjectivities are a result of exterior pressures on the interior mind, a pressure which is mediated through *Assaulted and Pursued Chastity* and as we will see through her later post-restoration work *The Blazing World*.

A political and cultural exile, Philips meanwhile utilized her exterior world as she initiated an inter-connective transnational coterie to ameliorate her geographical and cultural isolation. Philips's network of royalist friends and her new patronage with Lord Orrery were invaluable to her and her husband as they sought to reintegrate with the restored royalist court. Most importantly, Philips's travel to Ireland also liberated her from the oppression of her patria and allowed her a space to grow in confidence as a writer. As John Kerrigan writes, Philips 'became a Welsh poet through having an archipelagic sense of her situation'.[140] Yet, if Philips found her writerly voice in Wales during the interregnum, she developed that voice in Ireland during the early years of the restoration, a development not only borne of her sense of situatedness in relation to other experienced locations such as London and Dublin, but also of a contrapuntal sense of being in one place but remembering another as is often experienced by exiles. Living in Cardigan, along with complicated allegiances to family and friends, Philips resided outside the geo-politico-cultural sphere she celebrated in her later restoration panegyric poetry and navigated her way back to in her letters, yet her expansive trans-territorial archipelagic coterie allowed her to virtually connect in ways which circumvented her geographical limitations and possibly her domestic tensions. If Cavendish no longer looked to London for identity and ideology as her family once did, Philips focused on little else and never gave up on London as the *locus* of culture and ideological importance and, particularly after the restoration, was engaged at all times with the idea of returning to the city. Unlike Cavendish, an external exile and aristocrat, part of the royalist community in exile who after the fall of the monarchy turned inwards to reconstitute identity, Philips spent much of her time on the geographical margins struggling to reintegrate fully socially, culturally and, after the restoration,

[140] Kerrigan, *Archipelagic English*, 213.

politically, through a balancing act of writing. While Cavendish's attitude seems to be one of acceptance, Philips's period of real marginality during the early restoration years in Cardigan paralysed her, a stark contrast to her freedom found while in Ireland. Thus, psychological differences emerge between the transnational Cavendish, who through Travellia's full and necessary integration leaves behind lamentations of the homeland and that sense of loss in contrast to Philips whose diasporic and displaced psyche continually looks back to that place from which they were dispelled and who is at all times negotiating her way back to the originary royalist powerbase of London.[141]

Reading these women's work side by side offers us opportunity to understand contrasting yet comparable strategies of exilic writing at various historical points and from multiple geo-political locations within the diasporic environment. Cavendish's politicized work speaks for the experience of de-territorialized royalists as a group and centred on navigating that transition. Struggling to articulate the painful experiences of displacement and exile within traditionally sanctioned genres and forms, she broke with generic norms and experimented with form. The blend of the picaresque and travel narrative, or imaginary voyage, produces a fractured allegory which articulates both the reality of the outcome of war—displacement and exile, disorientation and loss—juxtaposed with the potentiality opened up by the same experience to allow a reworking of a traumatic transition at a crucial point in Cavendish's own life. Through hybridized genre Cavendish found a way to combine chosen positive elements of her royalist self, the growth of her authorial self and her new-found transnational self and specificity of the allegorical details make it impossible to deny this prose fiction as a work which is semi-autobiographical. Both Cavendish and her protagonist are sent out of the country for safety; they both endure objectification and fetishization incumbent on women at the court during the period; both find an increasing sense of agency and empowerment the farther away from the nation state they are. While Cavendish did not learn foreign languages as Travellia did, she nevertheless understood the importance of language to ones' own identity and articulation of

[141] For discussions on the differences between diasporics and transnationals, see Toyolyan, Khachig, 'Diasporas and Disciplinarity Today', keynote speech from a two-day symposium entitled *Diaspora: Movement, Politics and Identity* held November 16–17, 2002, Dickinson College. Funded by the The Andrew Mellon Foundation & The Henry Luce Foundation, p. 4/5.

agency. As a subject of diaspora, this new self stands at the intersection of past state and host state attesting to the notion that freedom and autonomy come from the beyond the confines of nation state to produce a truly transnational consciousness.

While Cavendish navigated her experience of exile and experimentation with identity through generic reinvention during the interregnum, after the restoration Philips utilized the letter as a space from within which she sought construct and reconstitute herself and her husband's identity in relationship to the state and monarch, as well as negotiate her and her husband's contentious political reintegration to the re-instated centre of royalist power (London) when so much was at stake. While the letters may indeed have been written with the hope that Cotterell would be the only reader, Philips nevertheless cautiously deployed many tactics to ensure maintenance of her reputation should they be read by anyone else. During the last four years of Philips's life, she did indeed write some poetry and translated Cornielle's *Pompey*; however, it is the letters that grant a unique aperçus into a crucial time in her life, during which she not only managed the affairs of her husband and her emergence as writer but also highlighted just how central she was to the burgeoning trans-territorial Irish and English coteries. In this sense, Philips stood at the heart of a 'paranational community' of alliances shaped by location, dislocation and transnational relocation which sought connection both during the disorientating interregnum years and later to the newly restored court, and her letters testify to the busy exchange network which passed not just through the Dublin circle but traversed territorial boundaries to create cross-kingdom alliances, both cultural and political.[142]

While being drawn from disparate experiences of displacement and exile, there is a tangible sense of unity to be drawn from these women's work as they both exhibit diverse themes and metaphors common to literatures of exile. Cavendish's prose fiction discloses projections and composites of the re-modelled royalist self and the exilic self to produce a self-redefined and positively projected. Themes of exile present throughout the narrative include wandering and isolation, or what Claudio Guillen terms 'odysseys of the soul'.[143] Cavendish represents her de-territorialized culture as mov-

[142] See also Gray, Catherine, 'Katherine Philips in Ireland.' *English Literary Renaissance* (2009): 557–585.

[143] Guillen, Claudio, 'On the Literature of Exile and Counter-Exile.' *Books Abroad* 50.2 (Spring, 1976): 271–280, 273.

ing across contrary lands through a plethora of fantasy locales, and imaginatively created new communities that stand for the host countries into which royalists were dispersed, while her nomadic heroine initially represents the displaced and disorientated royalist diasporic subject who eventually integrates fully into the host country. Meanwhile, during her archipelagic travels between the years of 1660 and 1664, faced with her own odyssey of the soul after the restoration, Philips's letters exhibit exilic themes of friendship and solidarity and union and stand as a vital means to not only assert her burgeoning sense of her identity as a writer but, most importantly, connect her to royalist friends, her unisex coterie of esteemed royalist members and by extension that most important *locus*, London.

This chapter has shown that Cavendish's and Philips's divergent experiences of 'exile' can be fruitfully compared to explore and expose complications and complexities of taxonomical methods which produce unrealistic dichotomous representations of royalism and exile and which reflect the more fluid idea of 'royalisms' as it is suggested in this book. Royalism, like identity in the diasporic environment, is composed of variable sources contingent on location, status, affiliations, marriage and familial networks. The diverse lives of these women, the cultures they grew up within as well as their extended socio-political networks does not render them incomparable—on the contrary, they have much to tell us about the complexities of royalist support and allegiance, as well as the ways in which identification with royalism is negotiated and/or appropriated by these women through writing. Since we understand royalism as most certainly a concept within which it can be seen that personal and familial relationships and loyalties cut across factions, questions then emerge as to what kinds of cultural and ideological royalisms are projected through these texts and to what extent the personal has an inflective role in the shaping of cultural royalism. Further, as case studies, the differences between Cavendish's and Philips's lives illuminate the potential pitfalls of attempting to neatly catagorize royalism, royalist identity and exile during these years and say much more about royalism as a variegated concept, as well as encourage us to read their diverse lives and work carefully not just within their specific localized and national contexts but across broader transnational contexts of the royalist diasporic environment. Moreover, this chapter has shown that the diasporic environment, despite being fraught with uncertainty and upheaval, was one which was 'conducive to a positive renegotiation of gender relations'.[144]

[144] Clifford, 314.

Cavendish and Philips's gendered identities were transformed by the events of the civil wars, interregnum and, for Philips, the early years of the restoration. We have seen that dislocation *from* and movement *to* certain locations, extended periods spent within marginal yet inspiring environments and interaction with para-national communities of other royalist intellectuals, *literati*, or French *erudits* allowed opportunity for these women writers to develop their sense of selves as royalist women writers as they gravitated beyond static and restrictive expectations incumbent on women within the homeland. The conditions of the interregnum made life for both women difficult. Cavendish, having visited home in the early 1650s, had no desire to return having been treated like an alien in her native land and Philips, who had many royalist friends, endured periods of isolation ameliorated by connection to her coterie and society of friendship discussed in Chap. 3. While we know both women intersected with royalist para-national communities across the British Isles and the continent, no evidence has yet been found which suggests these two women may have met. The lack of evidence happily leaves room for speculation and it is conceivable that given the overlap between the years 1651–1653—during which Cavendish visited Henry Lawes' house and Philips contributed to the Cartwright Volume (1651)—that the women may, at the very least, heard of each other through conversation circulating among these circles. While Cavendish and Philips may not have intersected in person, through writing they nevertheless intersected with and responded to the royalist cultural cause which sought to preserve ideals and mores concomitant with monarchy. Moreover, as they found ways to navigate their own forms of personal, cultural and political marginalization and exile through writing, they surmounted their subordinate position as non-subjects in their homeland and re-inscribed their own subjective position by reconstituting the very binaries that intended to hold women in their 'peculiar offices' during the mid-seventeenth century.

## Works Cited

### Manuscript Sources

National Library of Wales. MS. 218073.

## Primary Books and Poems

[Cavendish, Margaret], *Assaulted and Pursued Chastity* in Lilley, *Margaret Cavendish: The Blazing World and Other Writings*, Kate Lilley, ed. (London: Penguin Group, 2004).

———. *The Description of a New World, Called The Blazing World written by the thrice noble, illustrious and excellent Princesse, The Duchess of Newcastle* (London: A Maxwell, 1666).

———. *Sociable Letters* (London, 1664).

———. 'A True Relation of My Birth, Breeding and Life' in *The Life of William Cavendish, Duke of Newcastle: To which is added the True Relation of My Birth, Breeding and Life*. Charles Harding Firth, ed. (New York: Scribner and Welford, 1886).

[Philips, Katherine], 'The Letters' in *The Collected Works of Katherine Philips*. Vol. II. Patrick Thomas, ed. (Stump Cross: Stump Cross Books, 1990).

Prynne, William, *The Third Part of the Soveraigne Power of Parliaments and Kingdomes* (1643).

## Secondary Sources

Ankers, Neil, 'Paradigms and Politics: Hobbes and Cavendish Contrasted' in *A Princely Brave Woman: Essays on Margaret Cavendish, Duchess of Newcastle*. Stephen Clucas, ed. (Aldershot, Hampshire: Ashgate, 2003), pp. 242–253.

Bate, Jonathon, 'Shakespeare's Islands' in Shakespeare and the Mediterranean, The Selected Proceedings of the International Shakespeare Association, World Congress, Valencia, 2001. Tom Clayton et al. eds. (Newark: University of Delaware Press, 2004).

Battigelli, Anna, *Margaret Cavendish and Exiles of the Mind* (Kentucky: Kentucky University Press, 1998).

Beal, Peter, 'Orinda to Silvander: A New Letter by Katherine Philips', *EMS* 4 (1993): 281–86.

———. *In Praise of Scribes: Manuscripts and Their Makers in Seventeenth-Century England* (Oxford & New York: Oxford University Press, 1998).

Beilin, "Redeeming Eve": Women Writers of the English Renaissance (Princeton, NJ, Guildford: Princeton University Press, 1987).

Benstock, Shari, 'Expatriate Modernism: Writing on the Cultural Rim' in *Women's Writing in Exile*. Mary Lyn Broe and Angela Ingram eds. (Chapel Hill & London: University of North Carolina Press, 1989) pp. 19–40.

Bowerbank, Sylvia and Sara Mendelson, *Paper Bodies: A Margaret Cavendish Reader* (Calgary: Broadview Press, 1999).

Brah, Avtar, *Cartographies of Diaspora: Contesting Identities* (London & New York: Routledge, 1996).

Bush, Douglas, *English Literature in the Earlier Seventeenth Century*, rev, edn. (Oxford: Oxford University Press, 1962).

Chalmers, Hero, *Royalist Women Writers 1650–1689* (Oxford & New York: Oxford University Press, 2004).

Clifford, James, 'Diasporas' in *Migration, Diasporas and Transnationalism*. Cohen & Vertovec, eds. (Cheltenham, Northampton & MA: Edward Elgar Publishing, 1999).

Coolahan, Marie-Louise, '"We Live by Chance, and Slip into Events": Occassionality and the Manuscript verse of Katherine Philips.' *Eighteenth Century Ireland* 18 (2003): 9–23.

D'Addario, Christopher, *Exile and Journey in Seventeenth Century Literature* (Cambridge: Cambridge University Press, 2007).

Daybell, James, 'Letters' in *The Cambridge Companion to Early Modern Women's Writing*. Laura Lunger Knoppers, ed. (New York: Cambridge University Press, 2009): 181–193.

De Brifwisseling van Constantijn Huygens (1608–1687), ed J.A. Worp, 6 vols. (The Hague: Martinus Nijhoff, 1911–1917): 186–187.

de Groot, Jerome, *Royalist Identities* (Hampshire & New York: Palgrave Macmillan, 2004).

Ezell, Margaret, *The Patriarch's Wife* (Chapel Hill & London: University of North Carolina Press, 1987).

Fitzmaurice, James, 'Fancy and the Family: Self Characterisations of Margaret Cavendish.' *The Huntington Library Quarterly* 53.3 (Summer 1990): 198–209.

Gallagher, Catherine, 'Embracing the Absolute: Margaret Cavendish and the Politics of the Female Subject in Seventeenth-Century England' in *Early Modern Women Writers 1600–1720*. Anita Pacheco, ed. (New York: Addison Wesley Longman, 1998): 133–145.

Goldsmsith, Elizabeth C., *Writing the Female Voice: Essays on Epistolary Literature*. London: Printer Publishers, 1989).

Goreau, Angeline, *The Whole Duty of a Woman: Female Writers in Seventeenth-Century England* (Garden City, New York: Doubleday & Company Inc., 1985).

Gray, Catherine, 'Katherine Philips in Ireland' *English Literary Renaissance* (2009): 557–585.

Green, Mary Anne Everett, *Letters of Queen Henrietta Maria* (London, 1857).

Guillen, Claudio, 'On the Literature of Exile and Counter-Exile.' *Books Abroad* 50.2 (Spring, 1976): 271–280.

Hageman, Elizabeth, 'Making a Good Impression: Early Texts of Poems and Letters by Katherine Philips, the "Matchless Orinda".' *South Central Review* 11.2, Creating Literary Series: The Brown University Women's Project and the Oxford University Press, "Women Writers in English, 1350–1850" Texts (Summer, 1994): 39–65.

Hall, Stuart, 'Cultural Identity and Diaspora' in *Colonial Discourse and Post-colonial Theory: A Reader*, Patrick Williams and Laura Chrisman eds. (Columbia University Press, 1994).
Harvey, Elizabeth D., *Body Narratives: Writing the Nation and Fashioning the Subject in Early Modern England* (Basingstoke & London: Macmillan Press, 2000).
Hobby, Elaine, 'A Discourse so Unsavoury' in *Women, Writing History 1640–1740.* Isobel Grundy and Susan Wiseman, eds. (Athens: University of Georgia Press, 1992).
———. *Virtue of Necessity: English Women's Writing 1649–1688* (London: Virago, 1988).
———. 'Orinda and Female Intimacy' in *Early Modern Women writers 1600–1720.* Anita Pacheco, ed. (London: Longman, 1998), pp. 73–88.
Humiliata, Mary, 'Standards of Taste Advocated for Feminine Letter Writing, 1640–1779.' *Huntington Library Quarterly* 13.3 (May, 1950): 261–277.
Iyengar, Sujata, 'Royalist, Romanticist, Racialist: Rank and Gender, and Race in the Science Fiction of Margaret Cavendish.' *ELH* 69.3 (Fall, 2002): 649–672.
Jones, Kathleen, *A Glorious Fame: the Life of Margaret Cavendish, Duchess of Newcastle, 1623–1673* (London: Bloomsbury, 1988).
Kerrigan, John, *Archipelagic English: Literature, History and Politics 1603–1707* (Oxford & New York: Oxford University Press, 2008).
Lilley, Kate, 'Blazing Worlds: Seventeenth Century Women's Utopian Writing' in *Women, Texts and Histories 1575–1760.* Clare Brant and Diane Purkiss, eds. (London: Routledge, 1992).
———. *Margaret Cavendish: The Blazing World and Other Writings.* 3rd ed. (London: Penguin Group, 2004).
Major, Philip, *Literatures of Exile in the English Revolution and its Aftermath 1640–1660* (Surrey: Ashgate, 2010).
———. *Writings of Exile in the English Revolution and Restoration* (Surrey & Burlington, VT: Ashgate, 2013).
McDowd, Michelle, M., *Genre and Women's Life Writing in Early Modern England* (Hampshire & Burlington: Ashgate, 2007).
McGrath, Lynette, *Subjectivity and Women's Poetry in Early Modern England* (Aldershot & Burlington: Ashgate, 2002).
McLeod, John, *Beginning Postcolonialism* (Manchester: Manchester University Press, 2000).
McManus, Clare, *Women and Culture at the Courts of the Stuart Queens.* Clare McManus, ed. (Basingstoke & New York: Palgrave Macmillan, 2003).
Mendelson, Sara, *The Mental World of Stuart Women: Three Studies* (Brighton: Harvester, 1987).
Mihoko, Suzuki, *Subordinate Subjects: Gender, the Political Nation, and Literary Form in England, 1588–1688* (Hampshire & Burlington: Ashgate, 2003).

Myers, Mitzi, 'Fictions of the Self.' *Women's Review of Books* 8.4 (1991): 20–22.

Norbrook, David, 'Women, the Republic of Letters, and the Public Sphere in the Mid-Seventeenth Century.' *Criticism* 46.2 (Detroit, Spring 2013): 223–241. http://lionchadwyck.co.uk

Pacheco, Anita, *Early Modern Women Writers 1600–1720.* Anita Pacheco, ed. (London & New York: Routledge, 1998).

Perry, Ruth, *Women, Letters, and the Novel* (New York: AMS Press, 1980).

van Peta, Beek. *The First Female University Student: Anna Maria van Schurman 9. 163 (1636).* (Utrecht: Igitur Utrect Publishing and Archiving Services, 2010).

Poynting, Sarah, 'In the Name of All the Sisters': Hentrietta Maria's Notorious Whores' in *Women and Culture at the Courts of the Stuart Queens.* Clare McManus, ed. (Basingstoke & New York: Palgrave Macmillan, 2003), pp. 163–185.

Price, Bronwin, 'Feminine Modes of Knowing and Scientific Enquiry: Margaret Cavendish's Poetry as case study in *Women and Literature in Britain 1500–1700.* Helen Wilcox, ed. (Cambridge: Cambridge University Press, 1996), pp. 117–139.

Purkiss, Diane, *Literature, Gender and Politics during the English Civil War* (Cambridge: Cambridge University Press, 2005).

Raber, Karen, *Dramatic Difference: Gender, Class, and Genre in the Early Modern Closet Drama* (Newark: University of Delaware Press; London: Associated University Presses, 2001).

Rees, Emma, *Margaret Cavendish: Gender, Genre and Exile* (Manchester: Manchester University Press, 2003)

Salzman, Paul, *English Prose Fiction 1558–1700* (Oxford: Clarendon Press, 1985).

———. *Reading Early Modern Women's Writing* (Oxford: Oxford University Press, 2006).

Seidel, Michael, *Exile and the Narrative Imagination* (New Haven & London: Yale University Press, 1986).

Smith, Charles Kay, 'French Philosophy and English Politics in Interregnum Poetry' in *The Stuart Court in Europe.* Malcom Smuts, ed. (New York & Melbourne: Cambridge University Press, 1996).

Smith, Geoffrey, *The Cavaliers in Exile 1640–1660* (Basingstoke & New York: Palgrave Macmillan, 2003).

Seyhan, Azade, *Writing Outside Nation* (Princeton, NJ & Oxford: Princeton University Press, 2001).

Souers, Philip Webster, *The Matchless Orinda* (Cambridge: Harvard University Press, 1931).

Summit, Jennifer, *Lost Property: The Woman Writer and English Literary History 1380–1589* (Chicago & London: University of Chicago Press, 2000).

Thomas, Patrick. *The Collected Works of Katherine Philips, The Matchless Orinda. Vol. II. The Letters* (Essex: Stump Cross Books, 1992).

Thompson, Elbert N.S., 'Familiar Letters.' *Literary Bypaths of the Renaissance* 1924; rpt (Freeport, New York, 1968): 91–126.

Tyson, Lois, *Critical Theory Today* (New York & London: Routledge, 2006).

Troylander, Paul and Zeynep Tenger, 'Katherine Philips and Coterie Critical Practices.' *Eighteenth-Century Studies* 37.3. *Critical Networks.* (Spring, 2004): 367–387.

Trubowitz, Rachel, 'The Reenchanment of Utopia and the Female Monarchical Self: Margaret Cavendish's Blazing World.' *Tulsa Studies in Women's Literature* 11.2 (Autumn, 1992): 229–245.

Wilcox, Helen, *Women and Literature in Britain 1500–1700* (Cambridge: Cambridge University Press, 1996).

Whitaker, Katie, *Mad Madge: Margaret Cavendish, Duchess of Newcastle, Royalist, Writer and Romantic* (London: Chatto and Windus, 2002).

CHAPTER 5

# The Homecoming: Conclusions

Hallo and consecrate any wilderness into a temple.[1]

Edward Hyde's (1747) description of the necessity of coming to terms with exile typifies the royalist experience during the civil wars and interregnum. In this quote, Hyde makes a virtue out of exile, transforming marginality into centrality as he relocates the centre of power. This imaginative re-scripting of the disorientating present has been the subject of this book. I have examined how cultural manifestations on the margins represent a vital perspective of six royalist women and their contribution to English literary and cultural history at a pivotal moment in British history. While preceding chapters in this book have shown how royalists circumvented parliamentarian infringements into their social and cultural lives, this concluding chapter will explore the relationship between the exile and homecoming. Having shown in previous chapters how these royalist women turned to their imaginations as they endeavoured to recreate 'Englands of the mind', in response to a

[1] Edward Hyde, 'Contemplations and Reflections upon the psalms of David' printed in *A Compleat Collection of Tracts, by the eminent statesman the Right Honourable Edward, Earl of Clarendon* (1747), p. 349–768, 530/1 (psalm 63). Hyde was made embassy to Madrid in 1649. Having begun Contemplations back in England, her resumed work on psalms IX–LXVII in Madrid. See David L. Smith, Constitutional Royalism, 275.



S. Cronin, *Women, Royalisms and Exiles 1640–1669*,
https://doi.org/10.1007/978-3-030-89609-6_5

homeland disturbed by war and enforced dispersion, this chapter focuses on the return of royalist exiles and the literary strategies used to overcome yet more psychological, geographical and political disjunctions after the restoration of the monarchy in 1660. For many returning exiles, it is a relationship doomed to disappointment. As Michael Seidel (1986) notes, '[I]t is common enough even in cases of actual exilic return that the mental energy expended on the image of home in absence proves incommensurate with the reality of home as presence'.[2] Hence, for returning exiles there is a rupture between the idealized home and the reality of homecoming. Considering the restoration, the reception of Charles II and the religious and political climate which left many royalists bitter for revenge on their old enemies, I conclude by reflecting on the moment of return as it is presented in Margaret Cavendish's utopian fiction *The Blazing World* (1666). I argue Cavendish's own experience of return was fraught with expectation and disappointment, and that her deeply fragmented imagination not only gives us a sense of the fractures still remaining in the royalist consciousness in the mid-1660s but that her narrative represents a broader unresolved cultural moment in royalist history—that for royalists the legacy of civil war and exile lingers on.

## Restoration and Reception of Charles II

The events which led to the restoration of Charles II began with the death of Oliver Cromwell in September 1658 and culminated on 1 May 1660 when a royalist emissary came before the parliament with the Declaration of Breda.[3] Drafted by Hyde, the document's main clauses focused on clemency and the willingness of Charles II to submit to parliament. That same day the parliament voted that Charles I's death was tyrannical and illegal and that Charles II was the rightful heir to the throne. Less than a month later, Charles entered England to considerable public rejoicing. Samuel Pepys (1660) recalls the royal arrival:

[2] Seidel, *Exile and the Narrative Imagination*, 12.

[3] The Declaration of Breda, an agreement of compromise, contained within it something for every faction in England—it promised lands returned to royalists and held out the continuation of religious tolerance of the 1650s, as well as promising pardon for all parliamentarians, except those regicides to be named by parliament.

> all got on shore when the King did, who was received by General Monk with all imaginable love and respect at his entrance upon the land of Dover. Infinite the crowd of people and the horsemen, citizens, and noblemen of all sorts.[4]

Pepys goes on to say that Charles was met by the mayor of the town. General Monck was also present and they spoke for a while under a canopy before setting off for Canterbury.[5] En route to London the party encountered bonfires at Deal, in celebration of the King's birthday and guns were fired as they passed.[6] All over England many other tokens of pre-war culture were resurrected to rejoice in the King's return: London was in festival for three days; Norwich for a week; Melton Mowbray kept bonfires lit for seventy-two hours and Oxford seemed 'perfectly mad'.[7] Thus, royalist culture was in the process of being, like the king, reinstated and reborn. As Ron Hutton (1985) notes:

> Maypoles, prohibited by the Long Parliament, featured prominently in the festivities, a reminder that the reforms of the 1640s had been an attack upon traditional culture of many commoners…[8]

Other forms of celebrations included toasts, oaths and bonfires, all representing a break with the parliamentarian imperatives. As Jose Nicholas (1984) points out, 'bonfires were lit to "exorcise" the old puritan rule' resulting in the 'resurgence of ancient English superstitions—bon-(good)-fires and theatrical burning at the stake—was a sign of the Restoration'.[9] Further to this, theatres were reopened after an eighteen-year ban, William Davenant and Thomas Killigrew receiving the first licences for theatres at Covent Garden and Drury Lane respectively. The reception rooms at Whitehall thronged with high society, royal processions made their way through the streets and once again Hyde Park was filled with royalty and gentry. Diarist and family friend of the Cavendishes, John Evelyn recalls:

[4] Pepys, Samuel, *The Diary of Samuel Pepys*, Friday 26 May 1660. http://www.pepysdiary.com/diary/1660/05/25/ [Accessed on 7/7/2015].

[5] Ibid.

[6] Pepys, *Diary*, 29 May 1660.

[7] Hutton, Ron, *The Restoration: A Political and Religious History of England and Wales 1658–1677* (London: Clarendon Press, 1985), 126.

[8] Ibid., 126.

[9] Nicholas, *Ideas of the Restoration in English Literature*, 4.

> This day, his Majesty, Charles II came to London, after a sad and long exile and calamitous suffering both of the King and Church, being seventeen years. This was also his birthday, and with a triumph of above 20,000 horse and foot, brandishing their swords, and shouting with inexpressible joy; the ways strewn with flowers, the bells ringing, the streets hung with tapestry, fountains running with wine; the Mayor, Aldermen, and all the companies, in their liveries, chains of gold, and banners; Lords and Nobles, clad in cloth of silver, gold, and velvet; the windows and balconies, all set with ladies; trumpets, music, and myriads of people flocking...[10]

Along with civic gaiety, writers jubilantly resumed the panegyric. Katherine Philips recorded the arrival of Charles II and royalist exiles in her poem 'Arion on a Dolphin, To his Majesty at his passage into England', in which Charles is portrayed as the rightful heir to 'that Throne/Which birth and Merit make' his own, 'Defender of the Faith', as well as the envied figure of the superpowers of Europe who all 'shall tremble' at his 'Frown'. Conscious of the exilic condition and the return of royalists from abroad, Philips noted 'As peace and Freedom with him went,/ With him they came from Banishment',[11] thus emerges a picture of a tribe of people led by their religious and rightful leader on their outward journey towards freedom is set against that of their triumphant return journey towards their homeland. Philips was not the only writer to comment on the return of the royal tribe from the wilderness. Abraham Cowley, for example, lamented the predicament of the royal 'race' and the 'years of trouble and distresses' they faced as 'They'd wandered in the fatall Wilderness' until the return and restoration of Charles reinstated them 'To their own *Promised Land*', thus aligning royalist exile and suffering with that of the Jewish condition.[12] This conflation of the royalist and the Jewish tribe is further emphasized by Cowley as he appropriates the myth of Charles I as a martyr to present Charles II as Christ figure. In Cowley's ode the image of Charles II wearing the 'Martyr's Crown' as he governs both the royal realms of 'Earth and Heaven' not only reaffirms the divine right of Kings to justify the restoration of the monarchy and Charles II's position as head

[10] Evelyn, John. *Diary*. 29 May 1660, 333. http://www.gutenberg.org/files/41218/41218-h/41218-h.htm. [Accessed on 9/7/2015].

[11] Philips, "Arion on a Dolphin, to his Majesty at his passage into England", *Poems*, 3.

[12] Cowley, Abraham, "Ode Upon the Blessed Restoration and returne of his sacred majestie, Charles the Second" (London: Herringman, 31st May 1660), 8. http://eebo.chadwyck.com.elib.tcd.ie. [Accessed on 10/7/2015].

of state and head of the church, but also reawakens the memory of Charles I to produce a genealogy that cannot be questioned. Further to this, Cowley aligned Charles's return with the image of rebirth when he wrote:

> No *Star* amomgst ye all did, I believe,
> Such vigorous asstistance give,
> As that which thrity years ago,
> At * *Charls* his *Birth*, did, in despight.[13]
> Of the proud *Sun's* Meridian Light...
> Auspicious *Star* again arise.
> And take thy *Noon-tide station* in the skies...
> For Loe! thy *Charls* again in Born.[14]

Thus, both female and male writers drew on themes of religion, exile, martyrdom and rebirth to figuratively exalt as well as justify Charles II's restoration, all of which echoed parliament's decision to call Charles II back on the basis of his right to rule as heir to the throne.

## Settling and Unsettling the Restoration

However, the overflowing of joy at the King's return was short-lived and by June, royalists were already accusing the King of 'granting favours to enemies'.[15] This was to be the beginning of resentment and yet more faction among royalist supporters. As discussed earlier, the provenance of royalism itself was based on the fracture of English identity, and even the loose grouping which we have termed 'the King's followers' was deeply fractured during the war years and interregnum.[16] On the multifarious royalist plots and schemes of insurgency in England in the mid-1650s, Hyde wrote that 'everybody chose their own knot with whom they would converse, and would not communicate with anybody else'.[17] Thus, royalists were not only deeply suspicious of opposition groups but also deeply fractured group suspicious of each other during the interregnum. Later still, exiles are determined by some scholars to be split into three groups,

[13] A note in the text reads: 'The Star that appeared at Noon, the day of the King's birth...'

[14] Cowley, "Ode", 1–2.

[15] Hutton, *The Restoration*, 137.

[16] See Smith, David, L., *Constitutional Royalism: Search for Settlement 1640–1649* (New York: Cambridge University Press, 1994), 274.

[17] Clarendon, *History*. Vol. 5, 386–9.

each believing in different religious and political principles, as well as various tactics to restore the monarchy in England; however, even these groupings were fluid with individuals moving between them.[18] With the restoration of Charles II came the need for military, political and religious settlements. Along with this, Charles endeavoured to reward those he thought most deserving. Causes of friction may have been initiated by Charles II's favouring of those exiles who had left England after the battle of Worchester in 1651 and who had returned just prior to the declaration of Breda or with him as part of his entourage from the continent. Geoffrey Smith (2003) points out that of the original group of 225 'long term exiles', at least 170 of them survived to welcome the restoration and return to England to receive rewards and that 48 of those played a significant part in the political life of the nation sitting in one or more parliaments for Charles II and James II.[19] Indeed, despite that Charles and his ministers could not satisfy the overwhelming amount of 'requests from petitioners', Smith (2003) states that the rewards were in fact 'extensive in both range and value';[20] they were 'granted in the form of places at court, government departments, commissions in the armed forces, titles, pensions, seats in Parliament, university fellowships, and monopolies and grants of one kind or another'.[21] Many families at various levels that had served in the royal household in exile were rewarded.[22] Royal servants were also rewarded, as were courtiers such as William Davenant and Thomas Killigrew who restored the theatre to London. Along with positions in the royal household, navy and army, many were rewarded with titles, offices and grants of land in Ireland conferred to both Irish and English returned exiles.[23] Hence, it would seem that for Charles II the long hard years in exile were considered a great loyalty to the crown which deserved to be rewarded handsomely, yet, this caused ill-feeling between those who had stayed behind and remained loyal and those who went into exile,

[18] Smith, *Constitutional Royalism*, 274.

[19] Smith, *Cavaliers in Exile*, 185. Smith provides his sources and rationale for these figures both in Chap. 4 of his monograph and on page 180 of Chap. 13. Smith names some of these politically significant figures as Sir Henry Bennet, Sir Stephen Fox, and courtiers Ned Progers, Sir Charles Cotterell, Sir John Denham.

[20] Ibid., 179.

[21] Ibid., 179.

[22] Ibid., 181. Smith notes the Proger and Chiffinch families.

[23] Ibid., 188.

returning during the late 1650s and the early months of 1660.[24] Moreover, these rewards were granted within the complex and heated climate of political and religious wrangling that took place in parliament during the early months of the restoration and, as such, they can only have added to the fractious environment.

Royalists sought not only reward but also vengeance on their enemies. However, initially the Convention Parliament (July 1660–Dec 1660) resisted demands of Cavaliers, passed Acts confirming judicial decisions made in the 1650s and continued with other acts in progress. It approved the Act of Indemnity which pardoned all except those who were directly involved with the regicide and it worked out land settlements of estates. All of this was done in a conciliatory way. However, the bitterness of the 1640s and 1650s was ever-present and later debates which raged over the Indemnity revealed the level of hatred felt by many for those who had been very closely associated with the death of Charles I.[25] This hatred led to the Act of Attainder 'convicting the fugitive regicides and confiscating their property, along with that of their colleagues who had died before the restoration'.[26] The bodies of those dead, including Cromwell, were exhumed, hung and their heads impaled in Westminster Hall. These must have been tense times for Katherine Philips and her husband given that he was one of many who were pursued by The Commons accused of sitting on the high court of justice at the time of the regicide, so it is no surprise that Philips felt she needed to smooth the way for herself and her husband

[24] Smith provides an illuminating picture of the return of royalist exiles from the continent. He points out that the return of royalists had begun as early as 1650 and 'continued unevenly throughout the 1650s peaking at times when the cause seemed most hopeless, in 1649, after the second Civil War and the execution of Charles I, and again in 1651, after the battle of Worchester. This uneven flow became a major flood during the first half of 1660, with a further trickle of stragglers continuing fitfully for another three or four years' 175. Equally, as we have seen, many took to the continent at these key moments in history. However, those that returned before the restoration returned as 'defeated submissive Malignants and Delinquents'... '[t]he Cavaliers who returned from exile at the Restoration did so in triumph, their sufferings at last vindicated, and their loyalty ... about to be rewarded', 175/6. See also: preface to *CSPD* 1660–61. (Mary Anne Everett Green) for letters and petitions to the King regarding loyal rewards. In particular, see 'To the King's most excellent Majesty', viii/ix.

[25] Coward, Barry, *The Stuart Age: England 1603–1714*. 4th ed. (New York: Routledge, 2012), 295.

[26] Hutton, *The Restoration*, 134.

during these years. However, all of this did not placate royalists who had suffered the loss of land, livestock and family under the Cromwellian regime. They found it hard to live alongside those who had profited from their loss, a point which the Act of Indemnity ignored. Along with this, former enemies of the King continued in offices and enjoyed honours. In many counties, royalists took out their frustrations on 'prominent parliamentarians and Cromwellian collaborators under the guise of proceedings against suspected conspirators'.[27] However, nothing was done to help royalists who had sold lands under duress to pay composition fines and royalists' hopes of receiving rewards were not fulfilled. Thus, the Convention had 'inflamed rather than soothed old wounds'.[28]

With the end of the Convention Parliament in December 1660 and the first restoration settlement, Charles had regained his throne, his lands and assumed the role as arbiter between the republicans (associated with conspiracy) and the gentry (who desired settlement, vengeance and punishment for the rebels). However, the reduction of the army (proponents of revenge and plots), the failure of Venner's rising led by Fifth Monarchists (Jan 1661) and the royalist sway in the March elections undid Charles's position.[29] The rising, which led to proclamations forbidding unlawful meetings, gave ammunition to those who 'wished to persecute separatist groups and former republicans'.[30] The rising also generated fears of rebellion and the choice to retain some of the armies to ensure the safety of the administration. The result of elections was the establishment of the Cavalier parliament, the return of episcopacy and the set out were objectives that would undo most of the constitutional reforms of 1641–1654 and replace the first Restoration settlement. Some of the key features of the second settlement included the burning of the Solemn League and Covenant, and four other legal agreements from 1644–1654; the statute that excluded bishops from parliament was repealed; an act was passed declaring the militia to be vested in the King; a new standing army, in case of emergency, was kept and it was made illegal to call the King a Catholic. There was intense censorship of the press, spearheaded by John Berkenhead and Robert L'Estrange, in an aim to suppress all seditious

[27] Coward, *Stuart Age*, 295.
[28] Ibid., 295.
[29] Hutton, *The Restoration*, 150.
[30] Ibid., 151.

materials by those who opposed the restoration and those by religious sects. Attempts were made to resolve financial debts of the state but 'neither King, or country behaved responsibly in the matter of finances'.[31] Along with this, the Militia Act (1662), the Corporation Act and the Religious settlement allowed 'much of the machinery of law enforcement and coercion' to remain in royalist hands and 'could be used for partisan vengeance'.[32] The Militia Act meant that much of 'the States near-monopoly of weaponry was in that hands of the Lord Lieutenant and their deputies, the majority of the old Cavaliers'.[33] The aim of the Corporation Act was to cleanse municipal offices and control the electoral agenda.

In Wales, this purging, once more, caused much concern for Katherine Philips and her husband James who, as we have seen, served on a number of committees for the Cromwellian regime. Indeed, Philips's letters to Cotterell, in particular letter XXVIII, deals explicitly with these county elections and her efforts to demonstrate support for the new regime. Thus, with the Corporation act, royalists sought to replace all who served under the republic with nominees appointed by parliament who would be royalists and the removal of 'so many "disaffected" persons without resistance could be seen as a triumph for the Cavaliers'.[34] However, the act frayed royalist tempers due to the reluctance of some corporations to either restore royalists or accept the King's nominations for offices. Quarrels broke out and the gentry, in particular, resented that supporters of the republic retained power in towns.[35] While the debates about who controlled local towns were raging and amendments were made to the bill,[36] the even more complex question of religion and religious settlement caused friction not only between religious groups, the parliament and King but among the royalists themselves.

## Margaret Cavendish and the (Re)Making of Home

Thus, restoration England was a homeland with a much altered socio-political landscape. For many returning home, they faced a new England, one which would not be politically stable for many years to come. Margaret

[31] Hutton, *The Restoration*, 155/8.
[32] Miller, *After the Civil Wars*, 171.
[33] Ibid., 171.
[34] Ibid., 173.
[35] Hutton, *The Restoration*, 158/9.
[36] Ibid., 159/60.

Cavendish wrote of this return in the biography of her husband, William Cavendish. Having been away from family since 1643, and from England since entering into exile as maid to Queen Henrietta Maria, Margaret was out of England for a period of sixteen years. In *The Life* Margaret writes that just prior to the restoration William left Antwerp ahead of her in a frigate 'transported with the joy of returning to his native country that he regarded not the vessel'.[37] William was eager, like many other returning royalists, to secure both his own position and that of his son from his first marriage, Henry at court back in England. However, before departure the King told William he was not to be made Master of the Horse as he had hoped and while Hyde was confirmed in offices, Lord Jermyn was made Earl of St Albans, William received nothing.[38] The Cavendishes eventually settled their debts in Antwerp, and, having said goodbye to friends, Margaret then departed for Flushing with her party where a man-of-war awaited to take them home.[39]

On arrival Margaret bemoaned that her husband was in lodgings not 'unhandsome; but yet they were not fit for a person of his rank and quality'. Neither was she entirely happy with his 'condition', and she wrote that 'wherefore out of some passion I desired him to leave the town, and retire to the country'.[40] Soon after, the couple moved to Dorset House yet this was still not 'altogether to my satisfaction', complained Margaret.[41] Thus, within the early days of arriving home full of joy and expectation of a triumphant return, Margaret was disappointed in their lodgings and her expectations were dashed regarding her husband's rewards of loyalty. William received some reward on 21 September 1660 when he was sworn in as a gentleman of the bedchamber and then made Lord Lieutenant of Nottinghamshire on 1 October. However, eight months later, the Cavendishes had retired to the country. A letter by Newcastle's Chaplin, dated 29 May 1661, comments on the retirement as that of a 'satisfaction', '[i]ndeed, the greatest reward his majesty can possibly recompense your services withal, is thus bestow yourself upon yourself'.[42] Yet, this removal to the country once more left the Cavendishes on the periphery, distanced from events at court. Further, their arrival in Nottinghamshire

[37] Cavendish, *The Life*, 126.
[38] Whitaker, *Mad Madge*, 227.
[39] Cavendish, *The Life*, 130.
[40] Ibid., 130.
[41] Ibid., 130.
[42] Ellis, Clement, Ecclesiastical and Civil Register, 455 in *The Life*, 131.

was not very grand as the estates were in ruin and they had little money to restore them. Once at Welbeck Abbey an examination of the estate revealed what little of his lands remained for William. Margaret wrote:

> Some lands he found could be recovered no further than for his life, and some not at all: some had been in the rebels hands, which he could not recover, but by his Highness the Duke of York's favour, to whom his Majesty had given all the estates of those that were condemned and executed for murdering his Royal Father.[43]

Thus, only by a special dispensation could William regain his estates. However, lands that were sold by William or his sons had sold during the interregnum were not redeemable. Moreover, while recent parliamentary acts of indemnity and oblivion regained and restored crown and church lands, lands owned by royalists and other dissenters sold during the interregnum were left for negotiation and private litigation much to the frustration of loyalists. Margaret commented on this annoyance concerning the act of Oblivion when she wrote that it 'showed no favour to him' and 'proved great hindrance and obstruction to those his designs as it did no less to all the royal party'.[44] Along with this, both Welbeck and Bolsover Castle were devastated as both had been garrisons during the wars. Loans had to be taken out to cover the family's needs, and later still William had to sell and rent land to cover costs, pay debts and fulfil dowries of his daughters.[45] Once in the country, and taken up with the restoration and management of the estates, William and Margaret rarely visited London, and William was represented at court by his son, Henry. Despite receiving his Dukedom in 1665, their desire for social pre-eminence went largely unfulfilled, the title proving 'powerless to advance the couples' social ambitions'.[46]

Cumulatively, the removal to the country, the losses endured and the manner in which William was treated upon initial arrival home left Margaret bitter. Despite his Dukedom, for them coming home had not been as grand or as rewarded as expected. Margaret believed William

[43] Cavendish, *The Life*, 132, footnote: 'The grant restoring these lands is amongst the Egerton MS. In the British Libarary Museum (No. 2551). The King grants to Newcastle three manors sold under the Commonwealth and bought by regicides'.

[44] Cavendish, *The Life*, 133.

[45] Whitaker, *Mad Madge*, 237.

[46] Mendelson, *The Mental World of Stuart Women*, 50.

deserved a leading role in political life, and return to their estates was demoralizing due to complicated land issues and the damage that had been done there. To counter this annoyance, Margaret justified retirement to the country in *Orations* (1662) in '[a]n Oration against those that lay Aspersion upon the Retirement of Nobelmen' which clearly berates those who 'pull out the right and truth, to place falsehood' regarding reasons for retirement to the country by nobles. Initially, it outlines a defence for reasons why men retire from the city for 'there is nothing but trouble, expense, noise and often times malignant diseases'. Yet, further on Cavendish unleashes what can only be described as her own unbridled dissatisfaction at the lack of recognition and reward bestowed upon her husband when she wrote:

> Some noblemen had not only been so loyal as never to adhere to the rebels, but had … ventured their lives, lost their estates and had endured great misery in a long banishment, and after an agreement of peace, and the proof of their honesty and loyalty, should be neglected or affronted instead of reward and favour; if these forsaken and ruined … persons should retire from court and city into the country … should they be railed and exclaimed against?[47]

This defence of retirement to Nottinghamshire was followed up by Cavendish's creation of a new territory in *The Blazing World* in which she reordered and re-scripted a new home, government and church. As Maria Antonia Oliver-Rotger (2015) notes, in a process of 'constant transformation, not fully belonging to their places of origin, nor to their new culture, migrants returning recreate the world a new'.[48] The homeland, as a socially constructed concept, is forever being remade and thus is never the same when imagined by either exiles or returnees. For many royalists returning to England in the 1660s, this may have posed an irreconcilable problem of homecoming. As Rob Nixon (2005) states 'while the glorious anticipation helps make the years of banishment bearable … such assumptions become

[47] Cavendish, "Orations of Divers Sorts, Accomodated to Divers Places. Written by the thrice Noble, illustrious and excellent Princess, the Lady marchioness of Newcastle" (London, 1662) in *Margaret Cavendish: Political Writings*. Susan James ed. (Cambridge: Cambridge University Press, 2003), 165/66.

[48] Oliver-Rotger, Maria Antonia, Introduction in *Identity, Diaspora and Return in American Literature*. Maria Antonia Oliver-Rotger ed. (New York & London: Routledge, 2015), 16/7.

an encumbrance when people re-enter'.[49] Hence, for royalist exiles, the rupture between what was (the idealized home) and what is (the reality of a politically unstable homeland) leads to a dichotomous binary in which memory and expectation versus reality and disappointment.

In 1666, Cavendish's utopian fiction *The Description of A New World called The Blazing World* was published as an appendix to *Observations on Experimental Philosophy*. Much scholarship on *The Blazing World* has tended to read her work through the prism of contemporary scientific, philosophical and theological debates in which scholars argue Cavendish satirizes in the narrative.[50] Rachel Trubowitz (1992), for example, reads *The Blazing World* as a gendered riposte. Working out the contradictions in the text, that which advocates for women, community and friendship set against the model of patriarchal sovereignty, she argues that *The Blazing World* challenges the patriarchal order and that it de-puritanizes and feminizes the genre of utopian fiction, thus reclaiming 'the genre for the royalist side'.[51] Meanwhile, reading the *The Blazing World* through a prism of isolationism and interiority, Hero Chalmers (2004) argues the text stands as 'a model in which women's aspirations towards absolute power may be satiated without vouchsafing any actual female political agency over the

[49] Nixon, Rob, 'Refugees and Homecomings: Bessie Head and the end of Exile' in *Traveller's Tales: Narratives of Home and Displacement*. Robertson et al. eds. (London & New York: Routledge, 2005), 114–128, p. 115.

[50] For example, see Gallagher, Catherine, 'Embracing the Absolute: Margaret Cavendish and the Politics of the Female Subject in Seventeenth-Century England' in *Early Modern Women Writers 1600–1720*, Anita Pacheco ed. (London & New York: Routledge, 1998), 133–145; Holmesland, Oddvar, 'Margaret Cavendish's "The Blazing World": Natural Art and the Body Politic'; Iyengar, Sujata, 'Royalist, Romanticist, Racialist: Rank, Gender and Race in the Science Fiction of Margaret Cavendish.' *ELH* 63.3 (fall, 2003): 649–672. Hutton, Sarah, 'Science and Satire: The Lucianic Voice of Margaret Cavendish's Description of a New World called Blazing World' in *Authorial Conquests: Essays on Genre in the Writings of Margaret Cavendish*, Line Cottegnies and Nancy Wietz eds. (London: Associated Press, 2003), 161–178. See also: Seelig, Sharon Cadman, 'Margaret Cavendish: Shy Person to Blazing Empress' in *Autobiography and Gender in Early Modern Literature: Reading Women's Lives 1600–1800* (Cambridge: Cambridge University Press, 2006), 147; Whitaker, *Mad Madge*, 282; for readings of genre, see Rees, *Gender, Genre and Exile*. For three influential utopian works that preceded *The Blazing World*, see *The Law of Freedom in a Platform* (1652) by Gerard Winstanley, *Leviathan* (1651) by Thomas Hobbes and *Oceana* (1656) by James Harrington.

[51] Trubowitz, Rachel, 'The Reenchantment of Utopia and the Female Monarchical Self: Margaret Cavendish's Blazing World.' *Tulsa Studies in Women's Literature* 11.2 (Autumn, 1992): 229–245, p. 235/6.

public wold of Restoration England'.[52] Indeed, Catherine Gallagher, also reading the work from a gendered perspective, has written that Cavendish's desire in *The Blazing World* to be 'sovereign Monarch ... derives from a certain disability ... from her inability to be a full subject of the Monarch' as a woman and that Cavendish creates *The Blazing World* to counter this gendered restriction—an 'all or nothing political alternative for women'.[53] Oddvar Holmesland (1999) argues that the Cavendishes' exile 'would induce' the 'metaphoric equivalence' of a transition from the 'ideology of absolute monarchy' to that of the 'absolute self'.[54] He further notes that 'banished and deprived of their high standing in the real kingdom, Margaret is seen to fall back on the imaginary state governed by her sovereign self' and that 'her exile ... opens up an alternative world to her'.[55] Sujata Iyengar (2003) brings us back to contemporary influences arguing that the narrative resists confusion about the meaning of both race and colour and that *The Blazing World* allowed Cavendish to circumvent new philosophies and theories of sexual and racial inferiority prevalent during the restoration.[56] Sarah Hutton (2003) draws generic comparisons between Cavendish's fiction and that of Lucian of Samosata, and suggests that Cavendish most certainly had her 'finger on the pulse of the intellectual revolution of the seventeenth century' and that her publication of *The Blazing World* as an appendix to *Observations* suggests *The Blazing World* was intended as a 'fictional shop window for Margaret Cavendishs's own philosophy of nature'. Hutton further suggests that Cavendish takes Francis Bacon's view that fiction or fable has a role in the promoting of new ideas; however, like preceding scholars she is quick to point out that, unlike Bacon, Cavendish uses satire to critique contemporary natural philosophy, exposing what she sees as the futility of scientific speculation.[57]

While I agree with Gallagher, as I read *The Blazing World* as a complex rendering of female sovereignty in which exclusion from political subjecthood has allowed the female subject to become absolute within herself, I argue that this autonomy is, in fact, initiated by the experience of border crossing and sixteen years spent living outside the nation state, as discussed above. As demonstrated throughout this book, I fully agree with

[52] Chalmers, *RWW*, 129.
[53] Gallagher, 'Embracing', 137.
[54] Holmesland, 'Natural Art', 459.
[55] Ibid., 459/ 461.
[56] Iyengar, 'Royalist, Romanticist, Racialist', 651.
[57] Hutton, 'Science and Satire', 166–168.

Holmesland's theory that exile opens up new opportunities for Cavendish, however, I expand on this to argue that this presentation of multiple subjectivities within her post-restoration text is a direct result of not just exile but of homecoming also. Moreover, I argue that while female sovereignty is indeed central to the text, the re-scripting of home, the re-scripting of the trauma of the civil wars and the (re)-scripting of the self within the text reflect Cavendish's struggle to reconcile the disappointing experience of homecoming alongside that of being in exile for so many years. This section posits that *The Blazing World* is a text in which Cavendish explores the narrative of homecoming by setting up the binary of home versus abroad as two alternate worlds, or dimensions. Within this imaginative construction of a new world set against that of the old homeland, Cavendish reaches a zenith moment in her work by writing herself into the text as the alter ego to the heroine of this new world. It is these bifurcations that allow *The Blazing World* to be read as a text within which the geographical and psychological ruptures that accompany exile are worked out. However, the narrative of *The Blazing World* is not a story of homecoming at all, rather it is an anti-homecoming text that proves that the rupture of exile is insurmountable and that the legacy of war and displacement lingers on. Cavendish's text is permeated with pathos as the reader is faced with the notion that either psychologically, or imaginatively, Cavendish cannot fully return home—that for the exile homecoming complicates ideas of place and identity to the extent that both the returnee self and the self who could have been had she never left are figured as two narratives of self-alienation which require an alternative space in which to imaginatively dwell in the post-restoration world.

To overcome this disjunction between past and present, Cavendish devises a new habitat in which to imaginatively dwell. In *The Blazing World* Cavendish rationalizes the other space of her exile as existing adjacent to that of home. She imaginatively perceives that one may 'enter into another world' by 'the Poles of the other world, joining to the Poles of this'[58] thus presenting to her readers a textual representation of shifting poles of reality for Cavendish in the 1660s—home and abroad—conjoined yet apart. Here we are reminded of Ovid's Tristia wherein Ovid refers to

[58] Cavendish, Margaret, 'The Description of a New World Called the Blazing World' in *Margaret Cavendish: Blazing World and other Writings*. Kate Lilley ed. 2nd ed. (London: Penguin Books, 2004), 126. All citations are from this edition and the text will be cited in abbreviated form as *BW*.

the land of nomads (Scythia) and the land that lies under the Lycaonian North Pole. In *The Blazing World*, this alternative utopia is imagined as a 'large and spacious kingdom', with 'but one language', a place which 'lived in continued peace and happiness, not acquainted with other foreign wars, or homebred insurrections'.[59] Through this particular conflation, Cavendish ameliorates painful memories of war and feelings of linguistic isolation felt on the continent, to once more produce a more acceptable 'England of the mind'. Further to this, she sets out to reconstruct the body politic so disrupted and wounded throughout the years of war and the interregnum:

> That it is natural for one body to have but one head, so it is also natural for a politic body to have but one governor; and that a commonwealth, which has many governors was like a monster with many heads … a monarchy is a divine form of government, and agrees most with our religion.[60]

While Cavendish reconfirms her memories of the pre-eminence of the rule of the king as a divine right and, as such, draws on the cultural memory bank available to her, she also takes to reordering religion in this present imaginative land. As Cavendish reimagines and rescripts the contentious and highly topical subject of religious debate which rumbled on through the restoration years, the reader finds religion in *The Blazing World* 'defective' and as the Empress takes to converting 'them all … she resolved to build churches, and … instruct them on several points of her religion'.[61] Thus, not unlike the political and religious settlements which spanned many years after the restoration, Cavendish imaginatively concludes these contemporary debates by reaffirming monarchical status and carrying out religious conversion of the people in her idealistic imaginary realm.

Further articulation of Cavendish's struggle to assimilate into her homeland is evident by the insertion of herself as the Duchess into the narrative. As we have seen, the concept of home is inherently tied to the notion of identity. On the outward journey, previously explored in Chap. 4, identity is remade or hybridized. On the homeward journey, the new transformed self meets the old self who never left.[62] Thus, homecoming for exiles is not simply an act of physical return but is a sort of

[59] *BW*, 130.
[60] Ibid., 134.
[61] *BW*, 162.
[62] Polouektova, Ksenia, 'Between Home and Host Cultures: Twentieth Century East European Writers in Exile', (Central European University). Project co-organized by Pasts,

re-crossing, not only of the boundaries of nation state but also of the psychological boundaries which contain the self. In *The Blazing World*, Cavendish renders this complicated presence by importing herself into the narrative as herself (the Duchess of Newcastle) who becomes scribe for her imaginative self (the empress of *The Blazing World*). Thus, Cavendish plays with notions of identity once more, creating a dialectical other or doppelganger, to explore this plurality of being, thus proving her awareness of the psychic fragmentation caused by exile and return.

At this point in the narrative there are 'three worlds … the Blazing World where she [empress] was in, the world in which she came from, and the world where the Duchess lived'.[63] With each of these worlds already governed, both the Empress and the Duchess set out to 'reject and despise all the worlds without … and create' worlds of their own imaginative making. Looking to her own world, the Duchess draws inspiration from Pythagoras's doctrine, the opinion of Plato, Epicurus and Descartes, and Aristotle's principle; however, when 'the Duchess saw no patterns that would do her any good in the framing of her world; she resolved to make a world of her own invention'.[64] Here we begin to sense the pathos in the Duchess's story. Despite a contemporary world brimming with new and exciting scientific, philosophical and theological theories, the Duchess cannot escape the past. Her home is one 'very much disturbed with factions, divisions and wars'.[65] Indeed, when the empress and Duchess travel to the Duchess's 'native land', the Empress notes that their 'greatest glory was in plunder and slaughter', and was surprised that they did 'value dirt more than men's lives'.[66] Thus, while place is irrevocably changed by socio-historical and political narratives and the self continues to be remade by border crossing and re-crossing, the author occupies a unique vantage point poised at the cross roads of possibility. Santiago Vaquera Vasquez (2015) relates the concept of storytelling by exiles and migrants as 'border thinking'—a process that can 'lay bare the discourses which impose hegemonic control and open a space for critical awareness and understanding'.[67]

Inc. and Collegium Budapest, an Institute of Advanced Study. Sponsored by the Fritz Thyssen Foundation, Cologne, 2006–2007, 1.

[63] *BW*, 184.

[64] Ibid., 188.

[65] Ibid., 189.

[66] *BW*, 190.

[67] Vasquez, Santiago Vaquera, 'The Inextinguishable longings of Elsewheres: the Impossibility of Return in Junot Diaz' in *Identity, Diaspora and Return in American*

However, for Cavendish, her effort to reconstitute her broken life through an imaginative reconstruction of place and subjectivity seems impossible to contain and maintain as even the fictional Duchess desires to return home, poignantly reminding us that migrants continually suspect reality understanding its illusionary nature.[68]

With no place to assimilate into after the restoration, the only option available to Cavendish is to 'assimilate into the very splintering'[69] and through *The Blazing World* she is constantly theorizing her liminal in-between state as the narrative manifests her sense of alienation upon returning home. To escape this psychological isolation, she creates herself as script in this tripartite fictional world, thus while, on the one hand, Cavendish is dealing with the strangeness of homecoming, on the other hand she is simultaneously dealing with the 'idea of strangeness within the self'.[70] Struggling with this reconciliation Cavendish not only devises a series of 'necessary elsewheres'[71] but also utilizes the device of meeting herself to articulate the spilt between home and abroad, as well as past and present.

As Edward Said (2012) states, the refusal of the state of affairs in the homeland is the intellectual mission of the exile.[72] *The Blazing World* is, in its reordering of the state of affairs at home, a cathartic form by which internalized feelings of isolation and disappointment may be expressed by this royalist returnee. The power of imagination is harnessed once more to enable the exile to overcome the disjunctions of returning home. As she stands at 'the cross roads of dispossession',[73] Cavendish compensates for that loss by reconfiguring herself through the prism of a new world set against that of the old. Utopian in tradition and ambition the narrative may be, yet the trauma of war and exile, and the sense of alienation upon the return, is palpable within the text. Thus, while Cavendish may indeed be sovereign in her own mind, the legacy of war and exile nevertheless

*Literature*. Maria Antonia Oliver-Rotger ed. (New York & London: Routledge, 2015), 170–188, p. 171.

[68] Rushdie, *Imaginary Homelands*, 124/5.

[69] Polouektova, 1.

[70] Sarup, Madan, 'Home and Identity' in *Traveler's Tales: Narratives of home and Displacement*. Robertson et al. eds. (London & New York: Routledge, 2005), 93–104, 99.

[71] Seidel, *Exile and the Narrative Imagination*, 15.

[72] Said, *Reflections on Exile, and Other Essays* (London: Granta, 2012), 148.

[73] Nixon, 'Refugees and Homecomings', 119.

permeates even the most idyllic of imaginary realms created by this most ambitious of writers—this self-proclaimed 'happy creatoress'.[74]

## Conclusions

Beginning in the early 1640s, this book explored the royalist cultural response to war, enforced dispersion, diaspora and exile through a rich variety of media, and across multiple geographies of the archipelago of the British Isles and as far as The Hague and Antwerp on the continent as it documented unexplored links between women's cultural forms, types of exile and political allegiance between 1640 and 1669. Reading the royalist experience of war and dispersion through the theoretical lens of diaspora theory has provided a narrative against which we might more fully understand these women and others like them from all strata of society who supported royalism, as well as providing a novel way to understand royalist women's cultural production during the period in question. The chronology of this book has allowed for the tracing of a unique theoretical arc and demonstrated the cultural means by which these women sought to re-establish order, re-orientate themselves within the shattered royalist community and eventually transcend the experience of diaspora. We have seen the ways in which isolation is overcome in the diasporic environment, how gender became less inhibited and how cultural heritage and allegiance was maintained. This book has shown that royalists, dispersed throughout England, Ireland, Wales and to the continent, most certainly did exhibit the characteristics of the prototypical or classical victim diaspora, outlined by Cohen and Vertovec, as they retained a collective memory, a vision or mythological status concerning their homeland, which included its location, history and its achievements. Indeed, the royalist diasporic community has been shown here to be a repository within which royalist cultural identity could be protected and projected, and was fervently maintained across multiple and expansive geographies.

This book has argued that the work of the women here constitutes a tradition of women's cultural responses to the event of the royalist diaspora. In Chap. 2, we have seen how Katherine Philips's and Margaret Cavendish's poetry mirrors Hyde's quotation above as they set out to 'hallow' the war-torn wilderness of the English countryside into sites of order. Poetry was seen to idealize England and offer alternative yet

[74] Cavendish, 'To the Reader', *BW*, 124.

recognizable imaginative *loci* of communal refuge and solidarity for dispersed royalists. Moreover, as they advocated a relocation of royalist power to the valleys of Wales through the trope of retreat or through symbolic enclosures which invoked the vestiges of the disbanded court, they each strongly opposed socio-political marginalization and flagged allegiance to the royalist cause. Also striving to remain connected, as well as project their royalist heritage, lineage and identity, in Chap. 3, the Cavendish sisters in Nottingham and Queen Elizabeth of Bohemia and Mary of Orange at The Hague utilized a wide variety of literary genres and performative media by which they too could confirm allegiance, reach out to family and the scattered royalist diaspora, respectively. For the Cavendish sisters, manuscript culture enabled the continuance of the aristocratic traditions of compilation and circulation, serving to commemorate their own royalist family and connections under traumatic and oppressive conditions. Moreover, in the absence of any real gathering and under house arrest, they drew on the potent trope of the royalist family to virtually unite members near and far, past and present. Meanwhile, members of the Stuart family at The Hague generated a royalist counter-public of defiant political resistance through employing exiled royalists throughout the royal households, by staging and participation in, distinctly royalist entertainments as well as direct involvement in the turbulent political milieu there. While royal entertainments celebrated and maintained the memory of their homeland and a shared cultural history to generate an alternate diasporic community within their host countries, in west Wales Philips utilized her coterie as a virtual society through which separated royalist friends could connect and royalist values of friendship, unity and political solidarity could be expressed. Each of these spaces of reunion created diasporic counter-publics which attest to both personal and culturally driven ambitions to maintain royalist identity and to unite with the wider network of royalist cultural rebellion which aimed to keep alive those cultural traditions concomitant with the monarchy. Importantly, this book has proved that the royalist diaspora as a group aimed to stay unified in the face of adversity and that endeavours of solidarity and connection could be found in many forms. For instance, the compilation and circulation of manuscripts now took on new meaning, becoming a subversive and coded tool of resistance and communication. Meanwhile, coterie practices could also enable clandestine communications and offer a virtual counter-public alternative to objectionable political regimes, and royal entertainments could unite and buoy royalists through poignant themes of restored kingship, family and reunification while wider pamphlet circulation crucially reached across nation states and borders to galvanize royalist support.

This comparative study has found both commonalities and divergences throughout the cultural media examined. The term 'royalisms' has been deployed here as a malleable tool which reflects complicated, varied and particular cultural responses to diaspora, as well as representations of personal and political royalist identity and allegiance during the years in question. Additionally, it has been stressed that these sometimes diverse 'royalisms' nevertheless allow us to trace a palpable sense of unity across the diasporic group. We have seen how common literary trends such as the trope of retreat or royalist ideals of friendship, for example, were employed to unite subjects of this diaspora from various geographical locations across their homeland. We have also seen that on the continent theatrical genre and pre-war productions with similar themes of re-unification were capitalized on to remind royalists of their shared history. In both cases, we have seen how each royalist mode was shaped by place, local politics, social networks and personal experience. Moreover, as it has proven royalist cultural production across the British Isles and geo-expansive territories on the continent intersected through the use of shared tropes and themes, this book has revealed the existence of both a royalist rhetoric of exile, which articulates exilic experience, *and* a counter rhetoric of exile, which resists the negative aspects of that experience. Finally, we have seen how these comparable rhetorics further intersected with other contemporary poetics of retreat, order, desolation or confinement, for example, to reveal overarching and evolving sets of literary and cultural 'royalisms' as they were deployed by individuals across different locations and through a variety of media.

Expanding the notion of exile to include both internal (those who were diasporised *in situ*) and external exile (those who were dispersed to other countries) has allowed for the first trans-channel comparative study of these royalist women's response to enforced dispersion and a re-reading of their cultural manifestations side by side within the context of the group event of the royalist diaspora. While internal experiences are not commonly a consideration for theorists of diaspora, this book has shown that reflection on internal dispersion can in fact be a meaningful component of the phenomenon of diaspora and that investigation of divergent conditions in the homeland, as well as with those abroad, allows for a fruitful comparison of the cultural responses in each location. England was unrecognizable due to parliamentarian curtailments, along with the devastation of civil war, therefore the trauma of socio-political marginalization and deterritorialization imposed by the acts for banishment should be necessarily considered with equal gravity in the context of the wider diasporic group. We have seen that The Hague offered a safe haven to royalists as well as a *locus* of reunion and a celebration of royalism through entertainments staged there. Antwerp too was exciting *locus* of cultural engagement that became both a home and a site of inspiration. Dublin also proved to be a site of cultural evolution, second only to London. However, internal locations such as Nottingham and Cardigan, for example, also proved to be sites from which the King's supporters set out to culturally resist the opposition. Exploration and comparison of royalism across various locations throughout the British Isles and the continent allows for appreciation of not only these womens' work in relation to the geo-political core (London), but more importantly, in relation to each other as well. In this way, this book intersects with points of evolution to the field of diaspora theory itself, and suggests that the royalist diaspora, as a model, may be studied productively as a methodological tool to gain further insights into the variant and dynamic ways in which diaspora communities act. Indeed, this particular diasporic event grants an exclusive opportunity to study the effects of all phases of the diaspora, within an unusually short time frame, as well as developing theory regarding the dispersal. Additionally, by locating these women in these vibrant locales, this book automatically re-contextualizes, re-conceptualizes and re-theorizes their cultural contributions, and, as such, their very identities. As we have seen, by re-contextualizing these women and their work, they may be considered not only as English writers but also as transnational writers. Royalist women writers, such as Philips or Cavendish, for example, wrote of their displacement from multiple locations, while they lived in, and were influenced by, alternate countries and cultures. To ignore the status of the women studied herein as transnational or diasporic is to deny their worth as royalist writers in a general sense, and, more specifically, as writers *of* the royalist diasporic experience.

In addition to expanding our investigative range geographically, and by examining every phase of the royalist diaspora, from dispersal to homecoming, this book has provided a fresh way to understand the psychological conditions of the English civil wars, royalist dispersion and exile throughout the years in question. It has shown the ways in which the experience of diaspora offered new modalities of being for these royalist women—fissures of opportunity by which new identities could be explored, tried on or hybridized. In Antwerp, Margaret Cavendish wrote semi-autobiographical fictions concerned with integration in a bid to come to terms with the past trauma of war and exile. Katherine Philips, in Ireland, capitalized on the distance from her homeland and new *literati* connections there to control her emergence as a poet and translator. Both of these women found space outside their nation state for autonomous existence and were empowered by this to invoke a self-re-creation as early modern women, as writers and as royalists. In contrast, in The Hague, both Mary of Orange and Queen Elizabeth of Bohemia were inspired to consolidate and reassert their originary identity manifest through their profoundly royalist entertainments.

As it has offered up the first full-length study to theorize and categorize the royalist experience between 1640 and 1669 as one of diaspora, this book has complicated the usual frames of reference deployed to understand these women's lives and cultural contributions and has sought to make a unique contribution to the field of early modern women's writing. Situating these women historically, it has shown that, unlike their female predecessors who negotiated the terms of their gender from inside society, the royalist diaspora allowed these royalist women to negotiate their position as women writers from outside the usual societal parameters. Less restricted by patriarchal proscriptions and expectations these women could not only re-imagine their lost home as writers but also re-invent the self, thus initiating a new era for women writers. By merging socio-political and cultural constructions of gender, historical events and diaspora theory, this book has provided a distinctive way to understand the psychological conditions of the royalist dispersion, as well as offering a fresh way to read these women's cultural productions, thus aiming to grant an exciting alternative to the contemplation of works already known to scholars, which, opened up to a wider spectrum of socio-political thought, gain depth and meaning hitherto unconsidered.

While the study here examines a small portion of royalist women's work by exploring the areas of gender, community and identity in relation to the royalist diasporic experience, it is of course by no means exhaustive and there is much potential for further investigations into the effects of diaspora on English culture, identity and more specifically royalist identity during the period. Other areas of consideration might include but are not limited to a more specifically and sustained political and historical analysis, focused on the experience of dispossession from a royalist point of view; the emergence of new classes, variances and degrees of royalism in the post-restoration landscape; the experience of re-integration for royalists and the impact this had socially, culturally and politically; comparative analysis of the return of royalists versus those who never left; men's experience of the royalist diaspora and the impact of psychological, political and personal dispossession; more in-depth study of the diasporean/transnational nexus and its cultural manifestations within the early modern royalist context; comparing and contrasting those who evolved towards new identities in host countries versus those who were diasporised *in situ*; there is much to be explored in relation to trauma studies, for example examination of the impact of diaspora on the inner worlds of royalist supporters, notwithstanding the after-shock of diaspora and the complications of the return. Thus, while there is much work to be done and conversation to be had, this book aims to initiate that engagement with royalist cultural output between 1640 and 1669 as a product of diaspora. Hence, it is necessarily imperative that the diasporic experiences and the cultural contributions of the six women included here be brought in from the margins of the canon, be ushered in from the margins of our perceived understanding and be rescued from the margins of the consciousness of future scholars of the early modern period. For, if we are to continue to learn more about this relatively unknown narrative of royalist experience, and indeed the very concept of 'royalism' itself, then these women, and no doubt many others, have much to yield up to us—much information that contributes in a variety of significant ways to the literary, cultural and social history of Britain, Ireland and Europe. As Kate Chedgzoy (2006) states 'locatedness matters',[75] and this book has demonstrated not just how locatedness matters but how its very antithesis, dislocation, positively shaped cultural production, as well as the lives of these six royalist women as they set out to create various 'Englands of the mind' and once more imagine seeing both their 'Native Countrey' and their 'Native Friends'.

[75] Chedgzoy, Kate, 'The Cultural Geographies of Early Modern Women's Writing: Journeys Across Spaces and Times.' *Literature Compass* 3 (2006): 884–895.

## Works Cited

### Manuscripts

### Primary Books and Poems

[Cavendish, Margaret], 'A True Relation of My Birth, Breeding and Life' in *The Life of William Cavendish, Duke of Newcastle: To which is added the True Relation of My Birth, Breeding and Life*, Charles Harding Firth ed. (New York: Scribner and Welford, 1886).

______. 'Orations of Divers Sorts, Accommodated to Divers Places. Written by the thrice Noble, illustrious and excellent Princess, the Lady marchioness of Newcastle' (London, 1662) in *Margaret Cavendish, Duchess of Newcastle: Political Writings*. Susan James ed. (Cambridge: Cambridge University Press, 2003).

______. 'The Description of a New World Called the Blazing World' in *Margaret Cavendish: Blazing World and other Writings*. Kate Lilley ed. 2nd ed. (London: Penguin Books, 2004a).

______. *Sociable Letters*. James Fitzmaurice ed. (Peterborough, Ontario: Broadview, 2004b).

Cowley, Abraham, "Ode Upon the Blessed Restoration and returne of his sacred majestie, Charles the Second" (London: Herringman, 31 May 1660). http://eebo.chadwyck.com.elib.tcd.ie.

Evelyn, John, 1660. Diary. http://www.gutenberg.org/files/41218/41218-h/41218-h.htm.

[Philips, Katherine], *The Collected Works of Katherine Philips, the Matchless Orinda*. Patrick Thomas ed. (Stump Cross, Essex: Stump Cross Books, 1990)

[Hyde, Edward], 'Contemplations and Reflections upon the psalms of David' printed in *A Complete Collection of Tracts, by the eminent statesman the Right Honourable Edward, Earl of Clarendon* (1747), p. 349–768.

Pepys, Samuel, *The Diary of Samuel Pepys* (1660). http://www.pepysdiary.com/diary/1660/05/25/.

### Calendars and Papers

### Secondary Sources

Chalmers, Hero, *Royalist Women Writers 1650–1689* (Oxford & New York: Oxford University Press, 2004).

Chedgzoy, Kate, 'The Cultural Geographies of Early Modern Women's Writing: Journeys Across Spaces and Times.' *Literature Compass* 3 (2006): 884–895.

Coward, Barry, *The Stuart Age: England 1603–1714*. 4th ed. (New York: Routledge, 2012).

Gallagher, 'Embracing the Absolute: Margaret Cavendish and the Politics of the Female Subject in Seventeenth-Century England' in *Early Modern Women Writers 1600–1720*, Anita Pacheco ed. (London & New York: Routledge, 1998), p. 133–145.

Holmesland, Oddvar, 'Margaret Cavendish's "The Blazing World": Natural Art and the Body Politic.' *Studies in Philology* 46 (1999): 457–479.

Hutton, Ron, *The Restoration: A Political and Religious History of England and Wales 1658–1677* (London: Clarendon Press, 1985).

Hutton, Sarah, 'Science and Satire: The Lucianic Voice of Margaret Cavendish's Description of a New World called Blazing World' in *Authorial Conquests: Essays on Genre in the Writings of Margaret Cavendish*, Line Cottegnies and Nancy Wietz eds. (London: Associated Press, 2003), p. 61–178.

Iyengar, Sujata, 'Royalist, Romanticist, Racialist: Rank, Gender and Race in the Science Fiction of Margaret Cavendish.' *ELH* 63.3 (Fall, 2003): 649–672.

Jose, Nicholas, *Ideas of the Restoration in English Literature 1660–1671* (London & Basingstoke: Macmillan Press, 1984).

Mendelson, Sarah, *The Mental Worlds of Stuart Women: Three Studies* (Brighton: Harvester, 1987).

Miller, John, *After the Civil Wars: English Politics and Government in the Reign of Charles II* (London, New York: Longman, 2000).

Nixon, Rob, 'Refugees and Homecomings: Bessie Head and the end of Exile' in *Traveller's Tales: Narratives of Home and Displacement*. Robertson et al. eds. (London & New York: Routledge, 2005), p. 114–128.

Oliver-Rotger, Maria Antonia, 'Introduction' in *Identity, Diaspora and Return in American Literature*. Maria Antonia Oliver-Rotger ed. (New York & London: Routledge, 2015).

Polouektova, Ksenia, 'Between Home and Host Cultures: Twentieth Century East European Writers in Exile' (Central European University) 2006–2007.

Rees, Emma, *Margaret Cavendish: Gender, Genre and Exile* (Manchester: Manchester University Press, 2003).

Rushdie, Salman, *Imaginary Homelands* (London: Granta Books in assoc. with Penguin Books, 1992).

Said, Edward, *Reflections on Exile, and Other Essays* (London: Granta, 2012).

Sarup, Madan, 'Home and Identity' in *Traveler's Tales: Narratives of home and Displacement*. Robertson et al. eds. (London & New York: Routledge, 2005).

Seelig, Sharon Cadman, 'Margaret Cavendish: Shy Person to Blazing Empress' in *Autobiography and Gender in Early Modern Literature: Reading Women's Lives 1600–1800* (Cambridge: Cambridge University Press, 2006).

Seidel, Michael, *Exile and the Narrative Imagination* (New Haven & London: Yale University Press, 1986).

Smith, David L., *Constitutional Royalism: Search for Settlement 1640–1649* (New York: Cambridge University Press, 1994).

Smith, Geoffrey, *The Cavaliers in Exile 1640–1660* (Basingstoke & New York: Palgrave, 2003).

Trubowitz, Rachel, 'The Reenchantment of Utopia and the Female Monarchical Self: Margaret Cavendish's Blazing World.' *Tulsa Studies in Women's Literature* 11.2 (Autumn, 1992): 229–245.

Vasquez, Santiago Vaquera, 'The Inextinguishable longings of Elsewheres: the Impossibility of Return in Junot Diaz' in *Identity, Diaspora and Return in American Literature*. Maria Antonia Oliver-Rotger ed. (New York & London: Routledge, 2015), p. 170–188.

Whitaker, Katie, *Mad Madge: The Extraordinary Life of Margaret Cavendish, Duchess of Newcastle, the First Woman to Live by Her Pen* (New York: Basic Books, 2002).

# Index[1]



[1] Note: Page numbers followed by 'n' refer to notes.



S. Cronin, *Women, Royalisms and Exiles 1640–1669*,
https://doi.org/10.1007/978-3-030-89609-6

## P

## S



## T



## V

CPSIA information can be obtained
at www.ICGtesting.com
Printed in the USA
LVHW081048170422
716382LV00018BA/79